DARK PSYC
ANI
MANIPULATION

Explore the Secrets of the Mind, NLP and body Language. How to use Emotional Intelligence and Persuasion to Master Manipulation Techniques

By

Stephen Tower

Dark Psychology and Manipulation

© **Copyright 2020 by (Stephen Tower) - All rights reserved.**

This document is geared towards providing exact and reliable information in regards to the topic and issue covered. The publication is sold with the idea that the publisher is not required to render accounting, officially permitted, or otherwise, qualified services. If advice is necessary, legal or professional, a practiced individual in the profession should be ordered.

- From a Declaration of Principles which was accepted and approved equally by a Committee of the American Bar Association and a Committee of Publishers and Associations.

In no way is it legal to reproduce, duplicate, or transmit any part of this document in either electronic means or in printed format. Recording of this publication is strictly prohibited and any storage of this document is not allowed unless with written permission from the publisher. All rights reserved.

The information provided herein is stated to be truthful and consistent, in that any liability, in terms of inattention or otherwise, by any usage or abuse of any policies, processes, or directions contained within is the solitary and utter responsibility of the recipient reader. Under no circumstances will any legal responsibility or blame be held against the publisher for any reparation, damages, or monetary loss due to the information herein, either directly or indirectly.

Respective authors own all copyrights not held by the publisher.

The information herein is offered for informational purposes solely, and is universal as so. The presentation of the information is without contract or any type of guarantee assurance.

The trademarks that are used are without any consent, and the publication of the trademark is without permission or backing by the trademark owner. All trademarks and brands within this book are for clarifying purposes only and are the owned by the owners themselves, not affiliated with this document.

Dark Psychology and Manipulation

Table of contents:

Dark Psychology Secrets and Manipulation Techniques

Introduction **13**

PART ONE: DARK PSYCHOLOGY SECRETS **18**

Chapter 1: What Is Dark Psychology? **19**
- *1.1 Composition of Dark Psychology* *20*
- *1.2 Dark Psychology and Evolution* *22*

Chapter 2: Understanding Psychological Manipulation .. **26**
- *2.1 Components of Psychological Manipulation* *26*
- *2.2 Psychological Manipulation in Social Settings* *29*

Chapter 3: Understanding Manipulation Tactics and Schemes **35**
- *3.1 Manipulative Tactics to Watch Out For* *35*

Chapter 4: Different Manipulative Personalities **48**
- *4.1 Deceitful Personalities* *49*

Chapter 5: A Walkthrough to Body Language and How It Works with Manipulation **53**
- *5.1 How Body Language Functions* *53*
- *5.2 The Reason We Speak With Our Bodies and How We Do It* *55*
- *5.3 Body Language Signs of Manipulation* *56*
- *5.4 How to Recognize Emotional Manipulation and Tricksters* *58*
- *6.1 How Manipulators Act* *75*
- *6.2 The Growth Cycle* *77*
- *6.3 Individuals during Trial: The Contest for Credibility* *79*

Dark Psychology and Manipulation

   6.4 The Ruse in Mutual Transparency 81

   6.5 The Disguise of Malevolence 83

   6.6 Victims Have a Loss of Reputation 84

   6.7 How to Stay Below the Table: The Toolkit for Predator 88

Chapter 7: Identifying Manipulative Behaviors 90

   7.1 How Manipulators Affect Your Behavior 90

   7.2 If You Are Being Manipulated, What Can You Do? 93

Chapter 8: Dealing With Manipulation in a Relationship 95

   8.1 Signs That You Are Exploited In a Relationship 95

   8.2 Deal with Manipulation 103

PART TWO: MANIPULATION TECHNIQUES 110

Chapter 9: What Is Manipulation? 111

   9.1 Manipulation's Impact on Emotional Wellbeing 111

   9.2 Relationship Manipulation 113

   9.3 How to Treat Misleading People 115

Chapter 10: Covert Emotional Manipulation 118

   10.1 Concept of Covert Emotional Manipulation 118

   10.2 Manipulators in Different Situations 120

   10.3 Methods 122

Chapter 11: Manipulation Techniques 129

   11.1 Blackmail 129

   11.2 Putting Down the Other Person 131

   11.3 Lying 132

   11.4 Creating a Hallucination 134

Chapter 12: Emotional Influence 136

   12.1 What Is The Influence Of Emotions? 136

Dark Psychology and Manipulation

Chapter 13: How You Can Use Mind Control? 140
13.1 Each Type of Mind Control Does Not Go Unnoticed 141
13.2 Undetected Tactics of Mind Control 142
13.3 Mind Control through Pictures 146
13.4 Mind Control through Sound 147

Chapter 14: Persuasion Techniques 151
14.1 What Is Persuasion? 151
14.2 Different Ways to Persuade Someone 158

Chapter 15: Understanding Deception 166
15.1 Forms of Deception 166
15.2 Reasons for Deceit 168
15.3 Monitoring Deception 170

Chapter 16: Seduction Techniques 176
16.1 Seduction Tool Kit 176

Chapter 17: How to Take Full Control of Your Relationship 185
17.1 Tips on Gaining Upper Hand in the Relationship 185

Chapter 18: Signs of Being Manipulated 188
18.1 Dealing with a Toxic Person 188
18.2 Signs of Being Manipulated 189

Chapter 19: How to Win Friends with Persuasion? 198
19.1 Techniques to Win Friends 199
19.2 Protect Others' Pride and Win Big 203

Chapter 20: Watch the Behaviour of People 207
20.1 People Observation 207
20.2 Watching the Behavior 213

Dark Psychology and Manipulation

20.3 Conflicts between different types of behavior *218*

Chapter 21: How To Get Rid Of Manipulative People? .. 220
21.1 Techniques *220*

Conclusion 223

References 227

Dark Psychology and Body Language

Introduction: 233
Chapter 1: Delving into dark psychology 236
1.1 Intergroup vs. Intragroup predation *239*
1.2 Uncovering a human predator *240*
1.3 Their feelings aren't real *246*
1.4 They like sacrifices *247*
1.5 The basic principles of defending yourselves from human predators *248*

Chapter 2: A brief history of dark psychology 251
2.1 History of Dark Psychology Study *253*
2.2 Famous historical manipulators *259*

Chapter 3: Manipulation and persuasion basics 265
3.1 Psychological Manipulation *267*
3.2 Why human beings manipulate others *272*
3.3 Standard traits of a Manipulator *274*
3.4 How to Control People *278*
3.5 How you can prepare certain individuals (and be trained too) *281*

Dark Psychology and Manipulation

Chapter 4: Body language reading strategies and laws of manipulation 283

   4.1 Methods to help in the analysis of body language 284

   4.2 Certain body language searching indicators 291

   4.3 Manipulation Laws 296

Chapter 5: Understanding dark triad personalities 306

   5.1 Dark Triad: Narcissism 308

   5.2 Dark Triad: Machiavellianism 313

   5.3 Dark Triad: Psychopathy 318

   5.4 The Dark Triad practice 322

Chapter 6: Neuro-linguistic Programming 324

   6.1 What is NLP? 325

   6.2 History of NLP 326

   6.3 The Techniques of NLP 327

Chapter 7: Understanding the concept of brain washing 331

   7.1 Ten Steps of Brainwashing 335

   7.2 What makes people brainwashing susceptible? 344

   7.3 Shield yourselves from brainwashers 348

Chapter 8: The art of deception and persuasion 352

   8.1 The Principles of Persuasion 354

   8.2 Persuasion Ideas for Daily Use 360

   8.3 Types of Deception and How to Get stronger at them? 364

Chapter 9: The Truth of Hypnosis 372

   9.1 The Misconceptions about Hypnosis and Manipulation Burst 373

   9.2 How to Hypnotize Someone Without Them Knowing 376

   9.3 Keeping Yourself safe Against Hypnosis 382

9.4 What about Hypnotherapy? *384*

Chapter 10: How to defend yourself against dark psychology..**385**

10.1 Factors which make you more manipulative..................... *386*

Chapter 11: Tips to guard yourself against mind control 396

Chapter 12: Misconceptions and myths about dark psychology..**401**

Chapter 13: Some frequently asked questions about dark psychology... **413**

Conclusion: **431**

References: **433**

Dark Psychology Secrets and Manipulation Techniques

The Guide to Recognize Mind Control Techniques and Use the Secrets of Emotional Intelligence, Persuasion and Influence for Your Advantage

By

Stephen Tower

© **Copyright 2020 by (Stephen Tower) - All rights reserved.**

This document is geared towards providing exact and reliable information in regards to the topic and issue covered. The publication is sold with the idea that the publisher is not required to render accounting, officially permitted, or otherwise, qualified services. If advice is necessary, legal or professional, a practiced individual in the profession should be ordered.

From a Declaration of Principles which was accepted and approved equally by a Committee of the American Bar Association and a Committee of Publishers and Associations.

In no way is it legal to reproduce, duplicate, or transmit any part of this document in either electronic means or in printed format. Recording of this publication is strictly prohibited and any storage of this document is not allowed unless with written permission from the publisher.

All rights reserved. The information provided herein is stated to be truthful and consistent, in that any liability, in terms of inattention or otherwise, by any usage or abuse of any policies, processes, or directions contained within is the solitary and utter responsibility of the recipient reader. Under no circumstances will any legal responsibility or blame be held

Dark Psychology and Manipulation

against the publisher for any reparation, damages, or monetary loss due to the information herein, either directly or indirectly.

Respective authors own all copyrights not held by the publisher.

The information herein is offered for informational purposes solely, and is universal as so. The presentation of the information is without contract or any type of guarantee assurance.

The trademarks that are used are without any consent, and the publication of the trademark is without permission or backing by the trademark owner. All trademarks and brands within this book are for clarifying purposes only and are the owned by the owners themselves, not affiliated with this document.

Introduction

Dark Psychology is manipulative art and science, as well as control of the mind. While Psychology is basically the study of human behavior and is central to our actions, interactions, and thoughts, the concept of Dark Psychology is the phenomena through which people use tactics of persuasion, motivation, coercion, and manipulation to get what they actually want.

Narcissism-Grandiosity, lack of empathy, and Selfishness.

Psychopathy – Sometimes attractive and polite and marked by impulsiveness, loss of empathy, selfishness, and guilt.

None of us like to be the object of manipulation, however very frequently it occurs. We might not be exposed to anyone directly in the Dark Triad but on a regular basis, we experience dark psychology strategies with average, ordinary people like you and me.

These strategies are mostly found in commercials, sales techniques, web ads, and even the behaviors of our manager. If you have children (especially teenagers) you would most likely witness such strategies when your kids play with behaviors to obtain what they want and try control for themselves. In fact, the people you trust and love often use dark persuasion and covert manipulation. Here are some of the tactics that an ordinary, everyday people use most often.

Dark Psychology and Manipulation

Machiavellianism – Use of manipulation to exploit and deceive people, and has no moral sense.

Love Flooding-Compliments, buttering someone or affection

Love Rejection-Withstand devotion and affection

Lying-Amplification, falsehoods, incomplete truths, fake tales

Withdrawal-Avoiding the person or treatment in silence

Restriction of choice – Giving certain options that distract you from the choice you don't want someone to make actually

Semantic manipulation – Using those words that are supposed to have a mutual or common definition, but later the manipulator tells you that he or she has a different definition of the conversation and understanding. Words are strong and they allow imports.

While some people who use dark tactics know exactly what they do and are willing to manipulate you to get what they want, others are using dark and inhumane tactics without being completely aware of it. All of these individuals learned techniques from their parents throughout their youth. Others learned the techniques by happenstance in their adulthood or teenage years. They unintentionally used a manipulative tactic and it worked. They did have what they wanted. And they keep using strategies to help them get their way.

Dark Psychology and Manipulation

People are trained in some cases to use those tactics. Typically your sales or marketing programs or sales are training programs that instruct unethical psychological, dark, and persuasion tactics. Many of these schemes use dark techniques to create a logo or sell a product solely for the purpose of getting serve themselves or their business, not the client. Many of the training programs persuade people that the use of such tactics is fine and is in the buyer's interest. Because, naturally, when they buy the product or service, their lives will get much better.

Who is using Dark Psychology and the tactics of manipulation? Here's a list of those people who seem to make the most of those tactics.

Reverse Psychology – Say one thing to a person or perform it with the aim of inspiring them to do the contrary that is actually what you want.

Narcissists – Really narcissistic people (meeting the clinical diagnosis) usually have an exaggerated sense of self-worth. They also need others to affirm their conviction that they are superior. They've dreamed of being adored and worshipped. To preserve them, they use techniques of dark ideology, coercion, and dishonest intimidation.

Dark Psychology and Manipulation

Sociopaths – People that are genuinely sociopathic (meeting the clinical diagnosis), are frequently intelligent, charming, yet impulsive. They use dark propagandas to build up a relationship that is superficial and further take advantage of people because of a lack of emotionality as well as the ability to feel remorse.

Attorneys – A few attorneys aim to win their case so intently that they resort to using dark manipulation strategies to have the result they want to get.

Selfish people – Whoever has a self-agenda before others can be this. First, they will use strategies to satisfy their own needs, even at the cost of someone else. They don't mind win-losing results.

Politicians – Some of the politicians use these dark psychological techniques and dark tactics of persuasion to persuade people that they are right, and to get votes even.

Salespeople – Almost all salespeople get so focused on getting a sale that they use these dark techniques to encourage and persuade somebody to buy their stuff.

Leaders-Few of the leaders uses dark tactics from their subordinates to obtain greater effort, compliance, or higher performance.

Dark Psychology and Manipulation

Public Speakers – A few speakers also use these dark tactics to enhance the audience's emotional state of knowing it leads to more products being sold at the back of the scene.

PART ONE: DARK PSYCHOLOGY SECRETS

Dark Psychology involves the study of the human experience as it refers to individuals' psychological nature of preying on other individuals motivated by unlawful and/or deviant intentions that lack meaning and particular assumptions of instinctual motives and the concept of social science. All human civilization has that potential to harm other human beings and living things. Although this ability is restrained or sublimated by many, a few other activities on such urges.

Dark Psychology attempts to understand such thoughts, emotions, perceptions, and structures of subjective handling that give rise to predatory behaviors that are directly opposed to contemporary human behavioral understandings. Dark Psychology implies that unlawful, deviant, and violent characteristics are intentional and 99.99 percent of the time do have reasonable goal-oriented ambition. It is the remaining parts.01 percent, Dark Psychology from Adlerian theory and Teleology. There is an area within the human mind that Dark Psychology postulates enable some individuals to carry atrocious acts without intent.

Chapter 1: What Is Dark Psychology?

Dark Psychology asserts that all mankind has a reserve of malevolent purpose against others varying from minimally obtrusive and transient thinking to absolute psychopathic deviant actions lacking some coherent reason. It is named the Dark Continuum. Mitigating factors that act as accelerators and/or attractants to encounter the Dark Singularity, and where horrific actions of a person fall upon the Dark Continuum, is what Dark Psychology calls Dark element. Dark Psychology is a notion that I have been grappling with for 15 years. It was only recently that I finally formulated the meaning, psychology, and philosophy of this human experience aspect.

1.1 Composition of Dark Psychology

Dark Psychology includes everything that helps make us who we are related to our evil side. This proverbial cancer is present in all societies, all faiths, and all of human existence. From the time we are born to the moment of death, within us there is an aspect wandering that some have named immoral and others have categorized as unlawful, deviant, and psychopathic. Dark Psychology brings a third philosophical concept which gives a different view to these behaviors as compared to religious dogmas and ideas of modern social science.

There are individuals who commit these same actions in Dark Psychology and do so for power, money, romantic love, vengeance, or any other recognized intent. Without a target, they commit those horrendous acts. In simple words, its ends don't justify its means. There are individuals who for the sake of doing so defy and wound others. That potential lies within each of us. The area which I explore is a possibility to harm someone without cause, justification, or intent. Dark Psychology implies that this dark potentiality is extremely complicated and even harder to describe.

Dark Psychology implies that we all have the ability for predator behaviors, and this capability has the full right to our thoughts, feelings, and experiences. We all have this capability as you will learn throughout this book, but only some of us act upon them.

Dark Psychology and Manipulation

At one time or another, we all had feelings and thoughts about intending to behave in a painful manner. We have all had thoughts that we want to seriously damage others without kindness. If you're truthful with yourself, you'll have to agree that you've had ideas and feel like you want to do heinous deeds.

Because of the fact, we perceive ourselves to be some kind of virtuous species; one would want to assume that these feelings and thoughts would not emerge. Sadly, all of us have these ideas, and thankfully, never practice them. Dark Psychology suggests that there are individuals who have similar ideas, emotions, and experiences but operate upon them in a meticulously planned or impulsive fashion. The important distinction is that they respond upon them whereas others have merely short-lived thoughts and emotions to do so.

Dark Psychology claims that this type of predator is intentional and has a certain logical, purpose-oriented motive. Religious belief, philosophy, psychology, and other belief systems have been cogent in their ways to explain Dark Psychology. It is true that almost all human behavior, connected to evil actions, is purposeful and purpose-oriented, though Dark Psychology implies that there is a region where purposeful behavior and purpose-oriented motivation appear to become vague. There is a spectrum of maltreatment of Dark Psychology varying from opinions to pure deranged deviance, with no evident reasoning or purpose. This spectrum, Dark Continuum, allows the Dark Psychology philosophy to be conceived.

Dark Psychology identifies that aspect of the human psyche or basic human status that enables unethical behavior and can even help persuade it. Some of the features of this change in behavior are the absence of apparently reasonable motivation, its universality as well as its lack of clarity in many instances. This basic human condition is assumed by Dark Psychology to be different or an outgrowth of evolution. Let's dig at those very simple evolutionary tenets. First, consider that we evolved from many other animals and are the shining beacon of all animal life at present. Our frontal lobe enabled us to become the entity at the peak. Now let us presume that being alpha predators doesn't exempt us from our animal impulses and aggressive behavior absolutely.

1.2 Dark Psychology and Evolution

If you adhere to evolution, believing that this is valid, so you conclude that all actions refer to 3 main instincts. The three main human forces are sex, violence, and the innate desire to self-sustain. Evolution tends to follow the survival principles of the fittest organisms and their reproduction. We and other such forms of life act in a way as to produce offspring and stay alive. Aggressive behavior occurs to define our region, protect our land, and ultimately win the right to reproduce. It sounds

Dark Psychology and Manipulation

sensible but in the truest form, it no longer forms part of the human circumstance.

Our control of reasoning and understanding has made us both peak species and brutality pinnacle. If you've ever seen a video about wildlife, you are bound to weep and express sorry for the antelope torn to pieces by a lion's pride. Even though vicious and tragic, the brutality purpose fits in with the evolutionary self-preservation framework. The lions are killing for food which is essential for survival. Usually, male animals battle over the passage of territories or the right to control till death. All of these cruel and bloody acts demonstrate evolution.

When animals hunt for food, the weakest, the youngest, or the females in the group are often stalked and killed. While this reality feels psychotic, the reason behind their chosen prey is the reduction in their own probability of injury or death. That way, all living things act and behave. Each of their vicious, violent, and deadly actions contribute to evolutionary theory, natural selection, and the ability to survive and reproductive instinct. As you will learn after reading this book, when it comes to the rest of the creatures on this planet there are no implementations of Dark Psychology. We, human beings are the ones that embody what Dark Science is seeking to discover.

Once we stare at the human mind, explanations of natural selection, evolution, and animal instincts, and their mathematical tenets, seem to dissolve. Humans are the only

Dark Psychology and Manipulation

beasts on the face of the planet to feast on one another for the species' preservation without the purpose of reproduction. Human beings are the only species who prey for unexplained motives at each other. Dark Psychology identifies that aspects of the human psyche or basic human situation that enables unethical behavior and can even impel it. Dark Psychology implies that there must be something intrapsychic that impacts our conduct and is anti-evolutionary. We are the single life form to kill each other for purposes other than sustainability, food, land, or procreation.

Over the centuries, philosophers and priestly writers have tried to explain that concept. We are going to look through some of those common examples of human destructive conduct. Only we people have a total absence of an apparent moral motive to hurt others. Dark Psychology believes that there is an aspect of us as we are human, which motivates evil and violent behavior.

This place or dimension, as you will read, is universal within all of our creatures. Now, then, or in the future, there is no race of men roaming the face of the planet who don't hold this dark side. Dark Psychology claims that this aspect of the human experience ignores logic and purpose. It is a component of us all and no clear explanation exists.

Dark Psychology also implies that this dark side cannot be predicted. Unpredictable in interpretation who is acting on these hazardous impulses, and far more unexpected in the extents few will go entirely nullified with their sense of kindness. There are individuals who rape, assassinate, torture, and endanger without motive or intent. Dark Psychology describes these actions of conduct as a person seeking human prey without precisely articulated reasons for these acts. We are extremely harmful to ourselves as human beings and to any single living being. The explanations for this are many and Dark Psychology attempts to discover those dangerous components.

Chapter 2: Understanding Psychological Manipulation

A psychological manipulation is a form of social control adopted for learning about your enemy's mental weaknesses. It is generally adopted to understand which strategies are probable to be the most lethal methods against them. Psychological abuse by underhanded, misleading, or even coercive methods affects others' beliefs or behaviors. Such techniques are often seen as predatory, cruel, devious, and disappointing. It's often used in an effort to control others' behavior. It uses different types of psychological abuse, bullying or brainwashing, emotional manipulation, to coerce others into doing things they normally would not want to do. It is also regarded as an abuse of emotions.

2.1 Components of Psychological Manipulation

You need to know three items first, to exploit people effectively.

You have to understand the nature of the people very well. Then discover their weaknesses you need to exploit and reap the benefits of. Adoration, trying to care nature, simplicity, desire to help others, confidence ...... these are "weak points" to you, not "qualities," and you must use them to dominate and control him.

Dark Psychology and Manipulation

Next, you need to create a wide range of skills to regulate your victim. Always keep in mind, it's not brute force that you are using, it's devious manipulative ability. You need to be skilled enough to use him cruelly for your own benefits and still retain him under your rule.

Last but not least, you must be ruthless and cold. If the victim is struggling to do what you desire, that is nothing for you! It's just the greedy ambition that counts.

Basic tools for manipulation come from a genuinely good acting skill. You need to be fantastic at persuading others. Be an austere investigator of the existence of the cultures and consider their weaknesses. Develop a false connection to the victim. It'll help you gain his confidence and affection.

The method of supremacy and mind control starts after that. This is the most demanding part. You must feed him with lies, enmesh him in your world of deceit. Feed him half-truths (gas-lighting) when required.

Play on feelings. Consider every opportunity to satisfy others with their adoration, sense of duty, and the illness. Seduce others with glamour, flattery, shallow sympathy, etc. Never wait to be polite and offer an apology when you seek support from the victim.

But, the most potent tool possibly will be your function as a victim. The victims are wrongly suspected of being greedy and not supporting. The individuals who were conscious and reasonable fell in this pit very quickly. Use this with a combination of emotional manipulation for the empathy victims.

What if the victim attempts to break the chastity? How can you suppress that rebellion? Here's another aspect of the manipulator, deeper and more threatening to the victim. You have to blow out quite unexpectedly in rage and anger, whenever the victim will attempt to interrogate you or refute you. But note, there's no out-of-control anger. It is "controlled wrath." It shocks the victim into sheer panic and submission in the majority of cases. Don't prolong this very long. Give him a couple of moments of relaxation despite the frustration. The victim will be longing to see your delightful and tricky sweetness. After a few of these incidents, victims lose the ability to fight the manipulator.

You need to recognize another thing. Manipulators have neither awareness nor compassion for their victims. The victim utilizes his conscience and power as tools during confrontations. On the other side, you'll use misinformation, deceit, humiliation, managed rage, emotional manipulation, etc. that innocent victims have no knowledge about. So, to split the person into submission you have the dark attributes. You only have to relentlessly use those.

You would be able to destroy his free-spirit through this method. When a feeling of powerlessness and despair sweeps through him, you'll know you've succeeded. He is now practically your prisoner, to your whims and full rule. He will do whatever you wish.

Manipulators are not dangerous psychopaths. Don't use any of these skills to make fun or just hurt somebody. That is what the power freaks do, not smart manipulators. You need to be a cold, brutal, self-centered, canny individual to be a clever manipulator, not certainly a psychological abuser!

2.2 Psychological Manipulation in Social Settings

Manipulation is all about psychological understanding and leverage. And every day we are affected by psychological powers. The following are some good tactics you could use in psychology.

This may also be used for both good and bad. I am not in any way supporting bad manipulation techniques. Don't take advantage of these to benefit from people. Be responsible, and make good use of these strong methods.

• Stick out and offer people a simple, vibrant impression of yourself or of your interaction with them. People recall the clearest start and finish of anything (e.g. number series, grocery

Dark Psychology and Manipulation

list, etc.). However, the center is where items can appear to be overlooked. When you set up an interview date, make sure that you are either first or last to be questioned. If you are on a date, choose the start or the end of the day. And, while on the date, make sure the start and end of the date make a great impression.

• You choose an exercise that requires an adrenaline rush when you're on a date. It will help to promote the brain's excitement and make the other individual believe they really spend their experience with you. They will attribute to you the cause of their attraction to the emotional peak.

• Mirroring can be quite useful if you want to earn people's trust faster. Subtly mimic their body language while you are having a conversation. Cleverly replicating the body language of individuals subconsciously leads them to believe that you are in alignment that works really well for building confidence.

• If you feel a person doesn't like you, request them for a little favor, like taking their pad. Even if they are inclined to say no, borrowing a pad is such a tiny favor, that it is extremely difficult for anybody to deny it. He will ultimately come to the realization after embracing your request for a tiny favor that you're all right after all. As he frequently applied it, this is also called the Benjamin Franklin Effect.

• To figure out whether a person wants you, pick a term and, if he/she uses that word or similar words, nods, and smiles.

Dark Psychology and Manipulation

Observe him/her begin using the word a lot if he/she does like you.

• Would you like people to treat the terms sincerely? Say your daddy told you this each time you inform them something. Individuals tend to innately believe in the advice of parents.

• If you have a colleague who is struggling to open up, tell you what they feel like. Pose a question, and if they partly answer or it seems like they're covering something, just maintain eye contact and keep quiet for a few moments. They will be uncomfortable due to the quietness coupled with eye contact. They are going to talk to rip this conflict, even though that means giving you the data that they held back.

• Become the supreme Champion of 'Rock, Paper, and Scissors! To succeed at the 'Rock, Paper, Scissors' game, ask your competitor a simple question just before you start it. Your puzzled buddy will throw out 'scissors' almost all of the time.

• Did you ever wish the metro wasn't packed that much in the early hours? Look straight in front of you in busy areas, in the path you are going in. You'll be amazed to see the crowd offer you practically a spot. This tactic is quite easy to understand: we usually look at other people in the eyes in busy areas so we know which path somebody is going in. We're taking the opposite approach so we don't run into one another.

Dark Psychology and Manipulation

• If you really want people to comply with you, only nod when you're speaking and keep eye contact. The "nodding" activity causes the individual to start believing that what you are saying is completely true and hence they will most likely start nodding and comply with you. Plus, people prefer to nod back following methods of social behavior.

• If music is trapped in your mind and you'd want to forget it, start dreaming towards the conclusion of the album. Our mind starts to remember things that we have left undone. So if you think about the end of the irritating earworm, you can get this out of your mind.

• If you keep talking while giving over the box, your colleague will most certainly help you hold, let's say, a container of your things! Most individuals wouldn't even realize that you hand them stuff and will hold it. Some individuals, more observant and less adjacent to you may get super confused though.

• When you believe someone is studying you, just bend down and glance around. If someone is really watching you, as yawning is extremely contagious, they'll yawn too. Looking at the watch tends to work as well.

• If you want anyone to assist you, start your sentence with the terms need your help...' People despise feeling guilty and so they can't refuse to assist. Also, be confident to use the word

Dark Psychology and Manipulation

"because." Simply adding that one term lets people realize there's a decent reason to assist, making them more involved.

- Whatever your buddy has just told, just rephrase it and repeat. The individual who's talking to you can subconsciously get the impression that you're a better listener. Just don't take the rephrasing thing very far.

- Smiling women are all the more alluring. Quite attractive are those men who chuckle less and seem serious. Alluring equal charm and makes psychological techniques simpler to use on your victim.

- If you think someone doesn't like you, ask if you can borrow their pencil or pen. On one side, people don't tend to assist those they don't like, but on the other hand, it's such a tiny favor that your 'hater' will most likely be unable to say 'no.' He will eventually come to the realization that you aren't so bad.

- Never touch someone's hands while the hands are cold. If you know that you will be holding hands with anyone, please ensure your hands are warm. Warm hands encourage an atmosphere of friendliness while chilly handshaking triggers the opposite.

- Find Connection Point. Now, you 2 are members of a "group." Searching for similar-minded individuals is a human instinct, and as we see them as being like us, we immediately believe them more. This generates a mentality that is us vs. them.

Dark Psychology and Manipulation

Stepping against someone in marketing can be just as strong as standing up for anything.

• Let them speak on their own. This is famous advice about networking, but it works even if the other individual is aware of this effect, and that is why I absolutely adore it so much. Tests found that the brain regions correlated with incentive and compensation were more involved when participants communicated knowledge publicly — but even when they talked about themselves, even though no one was listening.

Chapter 3: Understanding Manipulation Tactics and Schemes

There is no doubt that relationships are tricky. Whether you're speaking regarding close friends, family bonds, or romantic interactions, the relationships throughout our existences can either enhance or make awful our journey on earth. It can feel like you're trapped when challenged by a manipulating individual. Manipulating individuals can be difficult to detect, and even tougher to cope with as they have the skill to make you feel like you are the issue.

3.1 Manipulative Tactics to Watch Out For

If you've found yourself in the vicinity of someone who is controlling you or you highly doubt that they might be, this is how you can tell them.

Dark Psychology and Manipulation

They try to deceive.

We all value truth and accountability, but tricksters either conceal the truth or try to show you just one version of the story. Consider, for example, the boss or worker who deliberately circulates unverified rumors and gossips for a tactical advantage.

Tactic: Don't trust everything you listen to. Instead, focus the judgments on well-known facts, and pose questions when specifics are not obvious.

When you are happy they reap the benefits of it.

Frequently, when we're in a particularly positive mood, we're inclined to say yes to anything or hop on prospects that look really great at the time (but we didn't really think through that). Manipulators know how to manipulate certain moods.

Tactic: Strive to make your optimistic feelings more conscious almost as well as your harmful feelings. When making choices, aim to find a balance.

They're playing on worry.

In an effort to scare you into action, a trickster will misrepresent facts and overemphasize particular points.

Tactic: Beware of remarks that imply that you lack the courage or try to instill a fear of falling out. Before taking any action ensure you have the full picture of the problem.

They are pushing for an advantage in the home court.

A deceptive person can demand that you meet and engage in a physical space where more power and influence can be exerted.

These men may try to negotiate in an environment where they feel control and familiarity like their workplace, house, or some other where you may feel less secure.

Tactic: An invitation to do so in a neutral environment if you need to talk. To help you get your bearings if you have to meet the individual on his or her property, ask for a drink, and engage in small talk at the arrival.

They use reciprocity to their advantage.

Manipulators understand it's harder to say no if they do you a favor — so they may try to impress you, cheese you up, or say yes to little favors... and afterward ask for massive ones.

Tactic: offering brings more delight than receiving of course.

But knowing your limitations is also important. And don't be scared to say no if need be.

They show pessimistic emotions.

In an attempt to control your feelings, a few people purposely raise their voice or use powerful body language to show they're angry.

Dark Psychology and Manipulation

Tactic: Practice the timeout. If someone's exhibiting deep feelings, pause for a moment to respond. In certain situations, you might also take a few minutes to move away.

They ask plenty of questions.

Talking about ourselves is simple. Manipulators realize this and take advantage of it by posing questions with a secret agenda — discovering secret vulnerabilities or knowledge that they can exploit for their gain.

Tactic: Of course, in anyone who intends to get to understand you effectively you should not suspect false motives. But watch out for those who inquire only questions — whereas refusing to disclose the same details about themselves.

They offer you an incredibly limited amount of time for action.

A person may try and force you within a very unreasonable amount of time to make a decision. By so doing, before you even have time to consider the implications, he or she tries to persuade you into making a decision.

Tactic: Don't give in to excessive demands. When your partner fails to give you more time, then you're better off heading for something you need in another place.

They try to talk fast.

Manipulators may often talk at a quicker speed, or use

Dark Psychology and Manipulation

different terminology and phrases to try to gain benefit.

Tactic: Don't be scared to ask people to describe their statement, or ask specific questions. You could also repeat their argument in your phrases, or request them to mention an example — letting you reclaim control of the narrative.

They're dealing with you using the silent treatment.

By intentionally failing to respond to your acceptable calls, texts, emails, or other queries, the manipulator presupposes power by having you wait and intends to put doubt and confusion in your mind. The silent treatment is a head game, where secrecy is used as a power.

Tactic: Give your partner a time limit after you have tried communication to a fair extent. In cases where solutions are not accessible, it might be appropriate to provide a frank conversation about his or her contact style.

Hardly cruel.

Help accelerate somebody's objectives to get them to provide you a favor. It's a bit measured, but it's straight out of Zig Ziglar: If you help plenty other people gain what they want, you'll get everything you want in life.

Tricky.

To get clients to purchase your item, use an alternative item. Attempting to get people to purchase a more costly version of the product? A third alternative is introduced — one that is the same price, but less powerful.

Based on the context, Might, be malicious.

Start concentrating on what your trading partner is obtaining, not losing. Looks reasonable, but if you hide that you are offering a crap deal to somebody, I hope you're doing something else to address your karma.

Perhaps a little manipulative...

Modify the environment to get individuals to perform less selfishly. Asking favors in a social situation rather than a corporate setting helps make people more willing to behave like a buddy than a competitor.

Hypocritical, the least.

Show a picture of the eyes to encourage people to act in an appropriate way. When we see the eyes, we think that we are being monitored, so we believe like everything we do is being observed and evaluated.

Definitely manipulative.

Imitate the body language of the people to make them admire you. Research suggests that if you replicate their body language, people are more prone to subconsciously relate with you. And this makes them more inclined to perform what you would like.

Being attracted to insecurities.

Use nouns rather than words to encourage people to alter their habits. When people hear nouns they think of their self-identity. They think of actions when they notice verbs.

Scheming and Fallacy.

Ask people for help because they're sick of asking them to comply." Similar to a couple of other suggestions on the list, they're more inclined to accept as people are stressed down. Car dealers are using this tactic — that is why it's so hard to just turn up and get a quote.

Deceptive.

Speak fast to get a rival to comply with you. Overpower people with your pace, and bring them down. Sometimes they'll agree since they can't digest what you're saying — and don't want to acknowledge it.

Terrorizing.

Instill fear in people to make them give you what you need. That is the essence of most marketing— make people scared of something, and then offer them the antidote. That doesn't make them any less evil. It is very successful though.

They assume it's the correct approach.

Anyone who is hell-bound to exploit another human, no matter what would hold their ground. They appear to be very outspoken about how the only thing that will function is their

Dark Psychology and Manipulation

strategy to a specific problem or issue and they need everybody to get on the same page.

Very Evil.

Confuse others to cooperate with your order. Individuals don't like to accept that they don't grasp anything, so they're in compliance. The example cited is to interpret the cost of something in pennies, instead of in dollars, since processing takes longer.

There are many explanations for this; specifically, they need to manipulate people to handle the situation and control what people see to stay in control.

If they're telling lies about something or attempting to cover up something, the best way is to be in power to make sure they're not discovered.

Manipulative people "really assume that their way of dealing with situations is the only way to do so because it implies their requirements are satisfied, and that's all that is crucial."

You may have an iconic manipulator on your shoulders if you feel like you're attempting to deal with someone who never provides you an inch even though you give them a mile.

Their relationship crosses lines.

Manipulators can do whatever they can to make you feel small and incapable of their affection and care.

Dark Psychology and Manipulation

They're going to cross boundaries that make you doubt your integrity and you're going to wind up thinking like your relationship's collapse is your own.

People that are dishonest, insecure, and have a weak sense of self continue to break personal limits on many occasions. If you inform them not to do anything, you can bet your are that the very next opportunity they get they will take it. However, it is not because they're terrible people. This is because, no matter what, they ought to be the person in control.

It's like having to manage a kid who isn't going to stop throwing hissy fits because they want sweets in the shop.

Blaming you for their issues.

Take into account how many times you stroll away from a

discussion with them feeling terrible about yourself or being guilty about making their scenario worse when you are

Dark Psychology and Manipulation

interacting with someone you believe might be trying to exploit you.

This is identified as "gaslighting," in which trickery is used to get people to question themselves and what they have done wrong.

You may feel a sense of regret or defensiveness if you're being gaslighted – like you've done something bad. In fact, this is what I call "the blame of the manipulator" because "they are not taking responsibility."

In case you are trying to deal with a trickster, both of these accusations will be accurate. Manipulators have the means to skirt blame and point fingers at others.

They'll accuse you and other individuals for everything from why they're not earning enough money with their work to the reason they couldn't get Saturday night's concert tickets.

When it comes to making sure that they don't bear any responsibility for their own lives, they are professional artists.

Manipulators are crossing lines to have their own way.

And if you don't have limits right away, then for a manipulative individual you might be a perfect candidate.

Unfortunately, manipulative people sometimes claim victimhood and prey on caring caregivers with weak (or no) limits.

Dark Psychology and Manipulation

Looks like you're speaking to a wall of bricks.

Deceptive people are tough and swift in their reasoning. It's a form of protection but it's still a weapon they use to take charge of the situation. If you turn to someone you believe you are being manipulated by and you try to have a conversation with them, they will shut down. Deceptive people tend to participate in the "playing stupid game":

By claiming that she or he doesn't realize what you need or what you won't want her to do, the deceiver / passive-aggressive convince you to take on her duty, and convinces you to break a sweat. They would also transform the topic on you to make you sound like a poor guy in the first place for even raising the issue. They're just going to sit there feeling arrogant and be blunt with you, doing something like, "yup, all right, good, nice, mmhmm. It's distracting, which makes you sound like you're not making them understand.

They're playing on your feelings.

Manipulators are clever and subtle, and they will operate a scenario or a task with a level of pride that can leave you feeling icky. They not only undermine individuals' right next to them but also tend to feel ashamed regarding your feelings. They have a sneaky way to make you feel terrible when you're feeling sad. If you're annoyed, a manipulative individual may attempt to make you feel guilty for your emotions.

Dark Psychology and Manipulation

They may use words such as "if you really adored me, you would never ask me" or "I couldn't accept that job. I wouldn't want to be so distant from my children. When you want to speak to them about their actions they make you feel bad and they leave you feeling less capable of everything you already have and partnerships that already looked like they were working well.

If they realize you're an anxious individual they're going to leverage that against you to get the advantage.

Their words and actions don't match.

The easiest way to know if someone tries to manipulate you, or is generally a deceptive person, is to watch their acts. If they're saying one thing and doing another, they're likely trying to hide stuff or not being true to their commitment. You can judge individuals by their acts to detect dishonest people so you can never be tricked by their expressions. Remember, every time there are non-identical things regarding what a person tells and does.

You will always see people working to raise their emotional intelligence — in themselves and others alike. They will sometimes use that power to exert manipulative impact.

And that's precisely why, if they do, you must refine your own emotional maturity — to safeguard yourself.

We can't always recognize why people do the stuff they do, but one thing is clear: if somebody lies to you regarding their whereabouts, what they did, or who they were with, something isn't right.

The hardest thing about being deceived is that you're left reeling from being exploited, and at the same time you're left having to reason with someone who doesn't stay true to their word.

(Manipulative and destructive people will only wreck your existence if you allow them to do so. Discover how to stand up by loving the inner beast.

Chapter 4: Different Manipulative Personalities

Manipulators have perfected the art of trickery. They may seem reasonable and genuine but often it's just a cover; it's a way of drawing you in and pulling you into a connection before they reveal their hidden colors.

Manipulators are not really invested in you but use you as a tool that helps them to acquire charge and therefore you are a reluctant member. As you'll acknowledge, they have many ways to do this. They often end up taking what you say or do and wiggle it around so that what you've said and done will hardly be recognizable to you. They'll try to mislead you, and perhaps even make you feel like you're crazy. They stretch the facts, and if it helps their end they may succumb to lying.

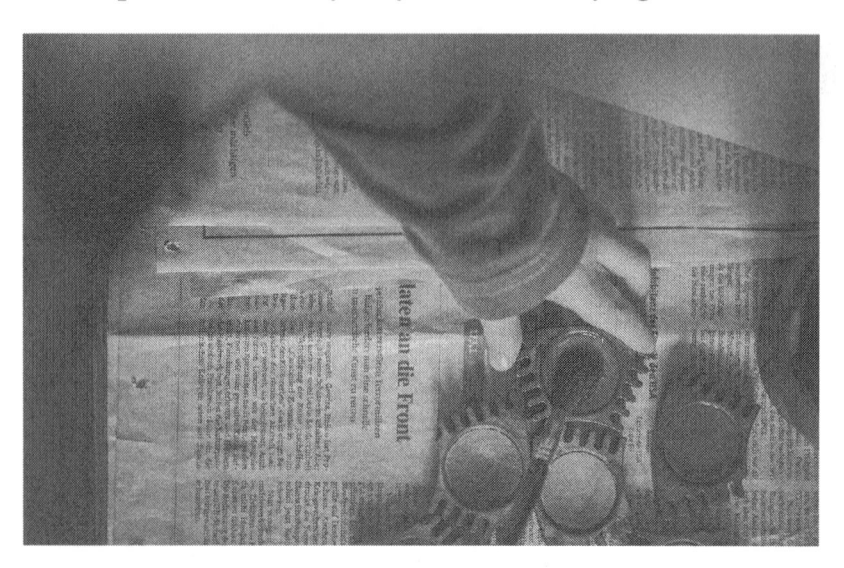

4.1 Deceitful Personalities

The victim role can be portrayed by dishonest men, making you appear to be the one who created a crisis they began but never accept accountability for. They can act as passive-aggressive or pleasant for one minute and standoff the next, keeping you speculating and prey on your fears and worries. Often, they do make you nervous. Also, they can be highly violent and brutal, resorting to character insults and criticism, savaged in their quest to get what they want. They are bullying and threatening, and will not let go till they wear you down.

Manipulators possess the following traits, so when one catches your eye, you'll know what to look out for. Knowing these underlying concepts of operation can help safeguard you from getting drawn into a deceitful relation. Staying vigilant, staying connected with what you know is true about yourself, and anticipating what is to come will allow you to prevent a dispute and preserve your own dignity.

1. Manipulative individuals often lack understanding of how they involve someone to construct those situations, or they genuinely feel that their method of coping with a problem is the right option as it ensures their desires are being fulfilled and it's all that counts. Inevitably, all the circumstances and partnerships are for them and it just doesn't matter what others say, hear, and want:

Dark Psychology and Manipulation

"Controllers, bullies, and men who are manipulators are not challenging themselves. They aren't asking themselves whether they are the problem. They always conclude others are the problem.

2. A manipulator shuns accountability for his own actions by accusing others of triggering it. It is not because dishonest men who do not recognize what responsibility is. They do; a dishonest person clearly finds nothing immoral with failing to accept accountability for their acts, even though they force you to take responsibility for yours. They can eventually seek to get you to assume accountability for fulfilling their needs, leaving no place to satisfy yours.

3. Manipulators do not understand borders. They are ruthless in pursuing whatever they want and have little consideration as to who gets caught along the way.

They're not worried about crowding into space — physically, mentally, socially, or religiously. They clearly have no understanding or just don't care about what private space and individuality mean. They can be compared to a parasite-this is mostly an appropriate relationship in the natural environment. However, in individual interaction feeding off others at their cost is depleting, draining, diminishing, and demeaning.

4. Manipulative people are prey to our sensibilities,

Dark Psychology and Manipulation

interpersonal sensitivity, and, in particular, conscience. They know they're going to have a decent chance to draw you into a friendship because you're loving, sensitive, compassionate, and of course, you want to support. For first, they will care for your goodwill and generosity, always thanking you for the amazing individual that you are. But over time, praise for these attributes will be lessened since you are being used to serve someone who doesn't truly care for you. They just really care what you can offer them.

5. Never spend your energy attempting to justify who you are to those who are dedicated to misunderstanding you. When someone doesn't see you, don't sit around wondering until they do. You don't have to make it your task to make them appreciate and understand you — they are not interested in you as an individual.

6. If you'd like a simple means of identifying manipulators from emphatic individuals, pay close attention to how they talk regarding others in relation to you. Frequently, they discuss you behind your back the same way they speak about someone else to you. They are masters of "triangulation"—creating situations and complexities that facilitate suspense, competition, and envy, and promoting and fostering disharmony.

7. Describe individuals by their acts and you'll never be deceived by their sayings. Always keep in mind that what an individual says and does are two very distinct aspects. Watch somebody

Dark Psychology and Manipulation

else carefully, without finding excuses for them – usually what you're seeing is what you get.

8. Investigate what you understand on a regular basis. We don't do this sufficiently. As life progresses, our perceptions and opinions may change, and we need to understand how these shifting ideas impact us. If we're not sure what we understand, it's all too easy to let somebody else who is sure that their views are right — not just for them but for you as well — to try to influence your thought process.

9. If an individual makes as much exertion to be a nice person as they do to pretend to be one, they might even be a good person in reality.

This is an important truth: Our initial contact and perspective of someone heavily color our growing connection with them. If we grasped from the outset that an individual is not who they appear to be, and is only hiding behind a facade of what appears to be culturally acceptable behavior, then maybe we would be more cautious about getting involved.

If it comes to manipulating human beings, there is no stronger tool than lies. Since, you know, people live through ideologies, and values can be twisted. The only thing that matters is the ability to exploit ideologies.

Chapter 5: A Walkthrough to Body Language and How It Works with Manipulation

Do you feel like you're being put under pressure or manipulated at work? Or are you asking more than average questions to yourself? Perhaps something seems rather off about a person who's bound to be on your corner but may not really have your best interests at heart. Those negative thoughts may be due to trickery. Fortunately, through their body language as well as other nonverbal clues, you will learn to recognize manipulators.

5.1 How Body Language Functions

"You can't conceal your lying' eyes," cautioned the Eagles in their Top forty hit in the mid-1970s. And they were right about it. We like to believe that words are important. But what we do in interacting with other people is at least as crucial as — and maybe more significant than — what we are actually saying. Body language is a strong medium of nonverbal communication consisting of actions of the hand and arm, body posture and actions, and facial cues and eye motions. It pinpoints to others what we thinking, sometimes without them really understanding it.

In the 1940s, psychiatric scholars first started intensively researching body language and since then, they have discovered how important it is. The first four minutes of talking to someone for the first time, our facial expressions represent fifty-five percent of the impression we make. By contrast, just seven percent of the interpretation emerges from our actual speech, with the majority of the details originating from voice tone.

We do much of this talking unintentionally and similarly, many people sometimes perceive our nonverbal knowledge without really noticing that they are doing so. Most of us have no clue our non-verbal indications are having an effect. There are hundreds of these tiny-expressions and people are reading them, even if they only translate these references subconsciously."

5.2 The Reason We Speak With Our Bodies and How We Do It

If you've seen a dog wag its tail, then you know that animals can interact with their bodies. Given that our distant ancestors can date back thousands of years, and that complicated verbal human language likely did not exist until 100,000 years ago, it is a sure option that humans depended on interpreting each other's physical movements, gait, and facial expressions long before they had a language to say what they sensed. In prehistoric times, it may have meant the difference between winning and losing to be able to interpret the mentality and intentions of another hunter-gatherer from a length, before the person got within shooting distance.

That intensity may illustrate why humans have become proficient at forming impressions and making judgment calls based on what psychology professor Nalini Ambady of Tufts University calls "narrow slices" of knowledge, created in the first few minutes of an interaction. Those thin slices are produced, she believes, in the most basic part of the brain, the same place where emotional impulses are stored. That could explain why we develop such strong emotions about someone we just encountered, whether that individual is a potential mate or anyone attempting to sell us a used car.

Researchers argue that body language is a mixture of

Dark Psychology and Manipulation

instinctive, learned and hybrid movement patterns, body posture, and expressions. For example, kids are blessed with the ability to blush and blink, while gestures like wink and salute with a raised hand are learned. Giggling, crying and shrugging are hybrid body language because we are trained on how to communicate them to certain situations while they involve innate movements.

Much like there are hundreds of languages talked/written all over the world, the definition of the body language can differ from place to location. For e.g., in the U.S, a smile implies joy, whereas, in Asia, it may mean agreement. And although Americans regard eye contact as a sign of attentiveness or self-assurance, it is viewed as disrespectful in certain African and Asian countries. In Italy, it is common to emphasize one's words by waving one's arms, but Japanese speakers prevent doing so because it has been considered impolite in their country.

5.3 Body Language Signs of Manipulation

To get their way, tricksters use various techniques, including tricky body language. As we discovered, people may create such movements as an emotional reaction to stressful events. If the person isn't in a tense environment or showing any other symptoms of anxiety, however, this specific behavior may suggest manipulation. In reality, manipulators will use this traditional pacifying to obtain support from you, actively or subconsciously, in order to manipulate your acts.

Neck and hand rubbing

If tricksters want to get their way, they appear to rub their palms together. You can even consider a stereotypical animated villain rubbing their palms together while they chuckle madly. This behavior even Disney realizes as a sign of self-serving conspiring. Neck rubbing may imply the same thing that the manipulator fakes to be nervous or depressed to intimidate you into agreeing. And, by rubbing their neck they experience some remorse for exploiting you and are neutralizing their shame. But they're exploiting you anyway.

Scratching Chin

When a trickster scratches their chin they try to present uncertainty or low trust. Sometimes it is a trick to get them to give up and declare, "It is all right. I can do it. "If you realize that a person is completely capable of doing the stuff you're thinking about and rubbing their chin, you can guarantee that they're attempting to trick you into doing something for them.

Stroking / touching the arm

When an individual rubs or scratches his or her arms, he or she may try to manipulate you. But, of course, there are several reasons an individual might scratch their arms; they might just have a bug bite! But if you doubt that a person wants to

Dark Psychology and Manipulation

influence you, and you find them scratching or rubbing their arms while speaking to you, you can take that as a sign of manipulation.

Tapping the Foot

Manipulators move their bodies in the same manner, they sometimes stamp their foot, or do something identical, like tapping their pen. This may be an indication of impatience or frustration which they may use to convince you for giving in or performing as they want. You are much more inclined to make a rash judgment as people tap their foot and might not necessarily be in their best interests.

Changing body posture

Manipulators often change their body position when attempting to control someone else. This can be an indication of distress or confusion which can be deliberately used by the trickster against you. Normally, our minds are trained to identify when a body is under stress or uncomfortable so tricksters use these behavior patterns to impact your actions and decisions.

5.4 How to Recognize Emotional Manipulation and Tricksters

First and foremost, you have to recognize that when interpreting such body language signs the meaning of the scenario needs to be understood. These nonverbal signals are not clear-cut manipulation markers but they are widely utilized by manipulators. Yeah, they won't tell you straightforwardly whether you're being exploited, however, they will help validate your assumption of exploitation.

Do you feel manipulated at work?

In the business world, the ability to learn body behavior and other nonverbal hints can give an edge. You can steer well clear of the deceitful and self-serving individuals by being able to recognize real feelings underneath controlled actions. You will know how to manage the problem once you understand that the employer is exploiting you, and you always win

How to manipulate and regulate your own body language

Experts believe you can educate yourself to control it by becoming aware of your body language and even use it actively to make your communication much easier.

I recommend making videos and observing the video with the audio off. Use respiratory and mindfulness exercises to soothe yourself before a session so that you are more conscious of your body movement.

Altering your body language in an intentional way to better communicate with another person is also useful. The method, called mirroring, requires understanding and subtly imitating,

Dark Psychology and Manipulation

the facial movements, body position, tone of voice, and other micro-expressions conveyed by the person you're talking to. While this may seem manipulative or fictitious to some, I believe that affecting that kind of synchronicity clearly facilitates you to communicate your true emotions more accurately and avoid misinterpretation.

But be cautious. Specialist and author Janine Driver, who spent the last decade teaching federal agents on how to perceive the body language of suspects during investigations, warns that trying to shape your body language can end up backfiring if it is not done skillfully. A possibly risky mistake is to dwell on any information without caring about how it blends into the overall interpretation.

"Attempting to use body language by perusing a dictionary on the body language is like learning to talk French by reading a dictionary in French. Your behaviors appear artificial; your body language abilities seem to be detached from each other." Instead of attempting to modify or disguise your normal body language, I advise you seek to improve and articulate it, such that it enhances rather than distracts you from the meaning you're trying to express.

- Touching the person you speak to (supportive)
- Twirling hair (shortsightedness, insecurity)
- Slump body posture (boredom, isolation)

- Set, upright (defensive) body posture

- Smiling, lean forward (friendly, if not excessive);

- Language of the body, consisting of hand and arm gestures, body stance and motions, and facial gestures and eye movements, can uncover what we think of other people, usually without our realization.

- Cognitive psychologists claim that the human race formed well before spoken human language, the capacity to read implicit physical signals and to make judgments regarding an individual based on certain signals.

- Like the spoken language, body language appears to change from society to society. Gestures in various countries can have very distinct symbolic meanings.

- By observing nonverbal contact and through teaching yourself, the body language may be intentionally formed to express a desired meaning or perception.

Manipulation isn't negative

- To control is to alter the action or mind of someone

- Manipulation is a conscious force

You may think about nasty stuff immediately when you listen to the term manipulation. Take a break.

Manipulation isn't negative. People with evil intentions are.

Dark Psychology and Manipulation

Example 1: Sneaky deceitful person

Bad guys are evil. Evil Individuals who use manipulation are an issue. For example:

- Cruel Girl tries to reduce Nice Classmate's social status
- She informs the rest of the class that the person was doing something terrible
- Nice Classmate is less liked
- The nice classmate feels bad

Example 2: cheerful trickery

Manipulation can turn everyone in a scene look better.

- Party People are experienced tricksters
- Fun Person hits into someone else
- Party Person disarmingly laughs and says sorry, even if the other individual was mistaken
- Party Person doesn't wrestle and has a fantastic evening

The issue with the instance of Mean Girl isn't manipulation, its malicious intent and spreading lies.

My plea: Have positive intentions

I assume you're going to use the tricks with noble intentions. Please, I request.

Part 1: Body language & mindset

The human brain is judgmental, this is what it is doing. This is what managed to keep us afloat during evolution. In seconds we pass judgment:

- Is that guy a risk?

- Is the man attractive?

- Is that individual user to my survival (social)?

Beware of this drive, but by no means act upon it without effectively understanding the person. The trickeries below will provoke you to act in a manner that is well viewed.

This segment is not solely regarding body linguistic, but such habits influence the body language on a subconscious level.

Every person deserves to be respected unless otherwise proved

Again, by treating others with respect you have everything to acquire, and nothing to lose. That doesn't mean you're supposed to caress boots the whole day; it implies you shouldn't ignore or make anyone feel irrelevant.

Just like anyone else, until they do not deserve it

Outsiders deserve the benefit of the doubt. Anyone can be anything in our universe without having to look like it. I met some kind-looking douche bags and billionaires, who acted like thrilled kids. Look at the book's cover but read a few chapters before you judge.

The douche bag or the billionaire is not 'better' than one another. But being with one made me feel upset and the other left me feeling good and enthusiastic.

Feel confident and express trust

This is particularly crucial that it requires an essay of its own and you could never do that all the time. In addition, there are definitely areas where you may not seem convinced to gain likability areas but the above remains true on average.

With this element you have two possible approaches. Try doing away with things which make you uneasy. Bad skin to me was a problem that I fixed identical to this. One more was the issue of clothes that I addressed when I took a girl with me while shopping. Work out to help yourself feel safe. I understood plenty from self-help audio books. It helped a great deal for me to stay in shape.

All are friends unless otherwise verified. Why burn bridges when you are the one who made them during the first place? No understanding whatsoever:

Don't have to lose anything

You have everything to achieve

If this individual would / wants to be a good buddy, you will realize soon enough.

Always ponder what you can do for someone else

Do not think when you meet somebody else, "what they can offer me? 'But what can I offer them, instead? 'The best way to support people is to make them want to assist you and everyone wins.

Recognize that I'm not saying that you must give unrequested advice to make yourself look intelligent. Assist people if you genuinely and honestly believe the life of this person would be nicer with the information/help/contact you can give.

Offer assistance but do not insist. Keep it short, and let them make their decision.

Part 2: Entering inside a Room

The point in time you enter the room is the period you reveal yourself to the people in that room and their judgment. Make sure to take advantage of that.

Some would suggest more severe techniques such as peacocking, but that's not applicable to every situation.

Smile about how glad you are to be here

Smile whenever you reach a room, no matter where you are. Smile like you really appreciate what you see. Do not overdo it, please do not chuckle loudly. Smile as you walked out and realized the sun was shining.

Accompany the public

Dark Psychology and Manipulation

Not to be explicit. Don't yell "HEY!" Or draw direct attention unless these are individuals who appreciate such conduct. Otherwise, when staring at the individuals in the room, pause a second to stay still or move gradually.

Make eye contact

Don't look over the crowd like it's an object. Look at individuals in the eye and smile at them if someone holds your eye contact. Make individuals feel like positive energy has entered the room.

Take some time

This demonstrates confidence but also means an open approach.

Wave to Friends (illusionary)

Humans are hard-wired to love and/or admire people who have friends. Back that up by nodding to your mates and mouthing anything along the lines of "I'll be right there" as you step into space to perform the normal 'greet the crowd practice.

Here's the thing, to imaginary friends choose to do this. I do this on bigger events all the time. Remember people don't see 360 °. If you wave behind them to an inexistent person they don't know you just waved to empty air.

There are several effects of this:

• People think you know people

• You have more space to gaze around calmly

Dark Psychology and Manipulation

- You'll feel more assured

The key here is to do so with complete faith, don't smile timidly. Wave like your closest buddy is just across the room and that you are trying to tell them you're going to be there soon.

Part 3: Posture

The body is always signaling to the people you encounter. Posture impacts snap second judgment people make regarding you but also what you believe about yourself. Additionally, a decent stance is perfect for the back, so what wouldn't you like?

Stand straight but easy

Attempt this to find a positive posture

1. Stand as wide with your feet as your hips

2. Make yourself as tall as doable and assume your head getting pulled up

3. Hold the feeling of being big but relax the shoulders

4. Loosen up your neck and tilt your head so you don't have to glance up or down with your vision to see a normal human

Few hints:

- Rest when keeping the stance as much as feasible

- Do not puff the chest, it will be straight as though you were lying on the ground

- Steer the shoulders marginally back

Sit up straight but not tight

You can note, as you start sitting up straight, how tiny the majority of people render themselves. When seated at a table you'll immediately feel very tall. Hold the back straight, but remain as confident as possible.

Have a certain tension in the core

When you're standing or sitting, your abs, back, and overall core should never be deflated / floppy. In general, keep the abs and core under certain stress. Not only does it reinforce well on your pose but it also makes moving with grace simpler.

Position your feet apart at around the width of the hip

The feet's stance tells a ton about yourself. It's not an exact science, but normally putting your feet nearer together means insecurity, while a larger stance implies confidence.

Both holding the feet excessively close or too far apart can poorly reflect upon you. Seek to find a place where your feet are at hip width or a little further apart, but not much.

Part 4: Shake Hands

Use a tender but firm handshake

People, in fact, are responsive to how you hold a hand. A handshake with a frail or 'dead fish' would automatically cost you reputation points.

Dark Psychology and Manipulation

- Don't just 'give' your hand, coordination is what a handshake is

- Use the force you'd use to pick up a heavy pan stick

- Don't squeeze too hard if someone offers you a 'dead fish' handshake

Allow eye contact while shaking your hand

Looking away invariably means something negative

- You don't care/respect for anyone else

- There is something you have to hide

Look at somebody's eyes long enough just to memorize color in their eyes. Just watch for a moment, don't stare.

Smile like they're making your day

While taking a look into someone's eyes during the handshake, smile as if you've seen something that makes you happy in their eyes.

Don't laugh loudly, just smile.

Part 5: The Face

The face is a very signaling region. There is currently a lot of work on micro-expressions that people subconsciously create. There is a lot of information that people project without realizing it. You will use your face to mark others with details about yourself.

Turn your neutral face look happy

Have you ever heard of ' resting Bitch Face Syndrome '? Some people tend to look irritated/angry with their face at ease, which lets people view them as a social threat. You would ideally not talk to an individual with an expression of this kind on their face.

However, it does not say anything about the actual individual. Yet it is giving them a detriment.

Make sure your face appears calm, if not comfortable at rest (e.g. while you are operating on a laptop). It's an easy trick to have a look at your face as something is slightly fun for you.

Don't drop eye contact immediately

People are accustomed to pulling away if they meet the eyes of someone. Don't try and do this. Maintain eye contact, and smile. People will often turn down, but there are several individuals who can maintain their attention.

Doing so has several effects:

- People see you as an opener
- You'll feel more assured

Please be aware that you must smile when you hold somebody's gaze. It can be quite creepy to look impassively.

How Can I Smile

Dark Psychology and Manipulation

Smiling is a really easy trick: pretend you're really seeing something that you really enjoy. Smiling isn't about turning your face in a way, it's about feeling joyful and making your face convey the emotion.

Part 6: Positioning

The way you position yourself distinguishes how you are viewed. Positioning and posture merged are extremely powerful.

Opening stance

When you speak to others, place your body so that you're accessible to them. Place yourself ideally in a 'vulnerable' manner. Do not use your arms to protect your chest, do not slouch, etc. This reflects confidence and ease.

Angle your body towards the person you are talking to

It is a small change, but it makes a huge difference to make sure your body 'points' to your conversational partner. Placing your body away will imply anxiety, fear, and distrust.

Do not lean yourself on or against furniture

Leaning on/against an object (for example, a wall) means passivity, and potentially insecure. You should stand with perfect posture as much as you can. Try to develop a pleasant 'neutral stance' using the suggestions from the posture category.

Use posture when you have to lean

If for whatever reason you have to lean against something, hold on to good posture. Don't slouch.

Part 7: behaviors and Techniques

Here I discuss some stuff you should do that mostly require an amount of your conversational / communication data interaction.

Watch your posture

Mirroring is a potent method that has been explored a lot. This means that people feel easier around you and that if you stand the way they do, they like you better. For instance:

- They sit with their legs crossed? Cross your legs
- If they lean on their right leg? You do the same
- If they are holding a drink? You also grab a drink

The secret here isn't to be apparent. The instant they actively notice what you are attempting, the method is losing power.

Mirror moves

You shouldn't be obvious just like with the point above. Yet small things will go a fair way:

- Are you getting a coffee, they grab their cup to take a sip? Do likewise
- Smile right back as they smile (this is a simple one)

Dark Psychology and Manipulation

- Are they coming a little closer to you? Do likewise

Again, don't be blatant, and don't be a weirdo. This method must be used somewhat discreetly, but often.

Chapter 6: How to Spot Manipulators and Manipulative Predators

Manipulators of social (and sexual) contexts had years of experience suppressing their darker characteristics. Several such people share a further dangerous characteristic: they are good enough to succeed with the disguise. I'm going to use the word 'social criminal' here to apply to the stealthiest criminals, while the crime types can fade. Certainly, social predators can engage in sexual misbehavior; on the other side, they cannot do anything that meets the minimum principle for an offense. The commonality is that they are preying on the emotions or assets of victims, either for their own benefit or plainly because they like to do so.

Numerous social predators possess psychopathic characteristics, however, if formally assessed they may fall short of an official diagnosis with an antisocial disorder of character. They may lack the capacity to perceive or care about how their actions affect someone else, contributing them to break promises, disclose personal information, and claim credit for the achievements of others. They get away with this by fawning themselves with victims who attack their pride and particular flaws in an often stretched-out dance.

6.1 How Manipulators Act

Aaron, a senior figure of a media company's editing staff who covers sports activities, turns out to be a research study of present-time chivalry. He is likable and competent, giving way for female coworkers and establishing a guideline to demonstrate that females are never made to cover "overly adventurous" happenings without their clear permission (and mostly a preventative measure, in case they agree). He possesses a strong reputation, as well as a mile-length resume. He is a great listener, mostly spending time assisting work colleagues to brainstorm ideas about stories. His awed attention often inspires them to share more stuff — revealing not only what's in their thoughts but inside their hearts as well. Unfortunately, Aaron isn't just a great listener for them, he's a great manipulator too.

Taking advantage of his work colleagues' insecurity is simple because he has recognized the weaknesses in the walls of each opponent. Matt, who has historically been thought the lesser achiever in his friends, is compelled by the consistent admiration of Aaron for his intelligence — which Aaron pairs with demands to generate pitches that he claims to be his own. Lisa, lately was dumped by her partner, retains her own sense of attractiveness via Aaron's complimenting of her look — which he pairs with demands from her to support him wind up

Dark Psychology and Manipulation

late work in imperative to meet deadlines.

Manipulation by Aaron has been flying under the spotlight for months. When a writer from staff finally objectify that he managed to steal her data of a story about high-tech riddles practiced by Olympic athletes — facts she confidently told him about — her allegations come down to of no use. Hesitant to lose an origin of optimistic attention and assertiveness, coworkers and the other highs are taking Aaron's side — including those who identify his tactics of manipulation.

Just like the other societal raiders, Aaron is charming his way via professional and personal settings, using niceness and optimistic attention to succeed those people who will assist him to make progress. These predators are not breaching the law; they are breaking loyalty. They economically, reputational wise, mentally, and occasionally sexually exploit their victims, carefully trying to cover their paths to prevent any "official" misconduct. They seduce then dismiss a broad range of people they trust.

The veil has been drawn back on abusive and sexual conduct in all aspects of existence due to the # Me-too movement; there's a stronger understanding of such truths more than ever.

This is the moment to expose those who participate in what things are known as "uncharged illegal deeds" or "unloaded harassment," since there's no civil infringement on the law, it may be difficult to explain exactly what crimes these persons perform. Maybe the most worrying part of destructive conduct is its ability to go unnoticed and unlabeled. By comparison, it's easy to identify people who are visibly abusive, hateful, or demeaning — and thus slightly avoidable.

6.2 The Growth Cycle

Grooming comprises desensitizing an individual to unwanted sexual or social approaches by progressive boundary checking while building a trust base. It's a formula for a disparity in power. The primary aim of training is to standardize inappropriate conduct. Whether seeking money, power sex or simply the excitement of imposing mental distress, predators are using victims for their own advantage.

Sexual predators prepare a kid through providing attention and affection to the child desires. Social predators train their manager by offering the respect and admiration they long for. In both situations, predators exploit by concentrated flattery while seeking radically different objectives.

"Wow, Ms. Eric, you've really dismantled that witness. You're such a good advocate. I am certain you're going to make it easy for me." Do you know from whom such praise came from? In fact, it was a perpetrator in some case I was litigating. I've taken to court respondents who consumed the whole trial admiring me about the quick reactions and advocacy expertise, despite frequent admonitions from their lawyer not to speak with me.

Their goal? Obtaining of course a decrease or removal of charges — a demand that they provide with the congratulations. Everyone has places among which they're singularly worthy of compliment, validation, or support. When bathed with overt flattery, some individuals become wary, therefore, predators also seek more nuanced and hidden places of desire or vulnerability. At first, a dishonest manager can appear not much different from a super-attentive manager. Both may tailor the work schedule of an employee to enable her to cater to private needs. But sympathy from the dishonest manager instigates with a tag. Whether it's a romantic or financial motive, she or he considers repayment. And taking into account how they have compensated the private, personal, needs of the victims, they are probable to gratify.

Social predators will not only cater to the needs of an individual however will often take an interest in how much her or his feelings align with them individually, utilizing what researchers Robert Hare and Paul Babiak call a psychotic fantasy to develop untrue resemblance. Perfect chameleons or social predators would be professing exactly the same feelings as their prey, having left victims both relieved and thankful to finally meet someone who understands how they actually feel. No matter the specifics (often blurred due to production flaws), it's promising for them that somebody can connect.

6.3 Individuals during Trial: The Contest for Credibility

Emma loves to spend time with John, a guy she came across at the native library. He loomed her by means of she browsed the Victorian romantic novels, confessing a similar knack for historical romances (after much hawing and hemming). Usually reserved and confidential, Emma is excited to have encountered a guy with such a taste for certain kind of literature, & she feels open to relating her feelings with him. John talks to ask about her upbringing and her potential aspirations and appears to be seriously concerned in her answers. Believing that over several dates they have formed a trusted relationship, Emma voluntarily reveals her desires. And her past regarding sexual matters.

When they knew one another for more than two months, John tells that he has got an ill health mother living overseas whom he wants to bring for treatment to the stateside, and then asks her to lend funds to cover with medical transportation. Amused he'd go back to her to ask for help, and appreciative for his love and affection, Emma wrote a check. Even though she is hesitant to acknowledge that, considering the volume of confidential information he now knows about her, her kindness is partly fueled by choosing to keep john on her positive side.

Dark Psychology and Manipulation

The truth is that the problems raised by John were never meant to gain knowledge but ammo. If he tries to physically, economically, or even reputational wise manipulate Emma more, she would not be able to cope back, in case her confidential information is revealed.

I've been investigating sex offenders for lot more than a decade, and have heard hundreds of victims lament that they think like they're the ones getting accused. Sadly they are, away. An accuser's authenticity is the front and core of a sex-crime case, especially when no eyewitnesses are present. The claimant is still in the answering position of the trial in a he-said-she-said case, prone to relentless cross-questioning from the defense. Most of the concerns stem from the knowledge that a complainant has willingly given to the individual who is currently convicted of the crime targeting her.

Smart predators develop an uneven field of play straight forwardly. Social predators allow greater use of seduction techniques during the grooming cycle. They similarly use reduction strategies-casting criticisms on the legitimacy of the victim. They search and gather personal, revealing details early regarding their victims — to be tucked away and held for intimidation or extortion purposes. The character attack begins when the victim tries to make a complaint.

In these circumstances, a societal predator reveals private facts openly in order to undermine a victim. The naming of an individual as a liar, a greedy employee, an incompetent informant, a troubled drinker, a prostitute, or worse, means that the attacker loses a reputation battle whether a survivor even lodges a lawsuit or even tries to alert us about the true nature of the abuser.

6.4 The Ruse in Mutual Transparency

Andy meets at a workout with Cameron. Considering his place as a national law execution officer he is charismatic, responsive, and remarkably open. He's already communicated plentiful of his lifespan story a few weeks into their causal relationship, swearing Andy to secrecy as he labels many "confidential" revelations.

Andy is enamored with Cameron's glamorous work as she is a single mother operating the jewelry company online from home, particularly considering the regular supply of professional criminality spectacle she sees on television. She is privileged that she is considered praiseworthy of his confidence, and desperate to ascertain that she senses the similar about him. She provides info regarding her health concerns, challenges, & messy divorce to match his transparency. She also shares details about her family.

As Andy and Cameron feast with few of his friends, she learns he has exchanged some of her experiences of living with an abusive ex-husband in conversation. Apparently, Cameron

Dark Psychology and Manipulation

didn't believe her personal records to be private. What would she do in this respect? She can't do anything. Cameron has just shown that he do not have any hesitation about retelling her secrecy. The humiliation, shame, or exposure that could result if Cameron were to react by exchanging more details, would not be worth it.

So, what of Cameron's leaks, which are simply braggadocio of his personal achievements, and it's all secrets? Sharing "in trust" details will not render it more reliable. In reality, if something is apparently confidential, it should be flagged as less credible by the swiftness through which it is provided, quickly in a relation. That is especially true when the latest paramour retains a public value position.

Often the "topmost secret" facts revealed by a serpentine new relation is fake. It's G-rated narrative and the central character who has been suffering for long is practically assured to be a social predator. Unlike the often base revelations a target is encouraged to tell, private information about a predator may be considerate, but it certainly won't be salty. Exploiters never tell outrageous or humiliating stories against them that might be used.

Another warning sign is the exchange of uncorroborated information. Predators of social standing or reputation at the organization are cautious as they do not want to be revealed as liars. Attributing stories of being deceived by a "person who would be kept nameless" ex-business partner guarantees that no true professional or personal contact is contested.

Few of the particular people a predator can divulge information about is her or his latest romantic interest. She or he is "unreliable." Marriage "comes to the end." This is always a play on the victim's part to boost invested interest and passionate attentiveness. The predator bids (usually properly) that victim doesn't face the existing partner directly. After all, when choosing their targets, predators upsize capacity for empathy and conscience.

6.5 The Disguise of Malevolence

A traveling district boss with a compact vehicle is Katie's present guru at the medicinal firm where she is working. He likes to take her to places he visits to like various regional health facilities to "illustrate her the riggings." While they are together in the car, he continuously tries to reach in access of the gloves box, sees her seatbelt and, paws around in the cup holder (and misses) for his coffee, or tends to make other pointless physical movements in her course. Frequently, "accidental" touching occurs. When Katie eventually informs her immediate boss that she doesn't want to follow her trainer to any more sessions, he wonders why? Then she is so ashamed to classify the moment but the actual chain of infringements, so she cites logistical issues instead, allowing her poor conduct to go unnoticed.

Dark Psychology and Manipulation

Elected leaders, senior executives, and the other power figures regularly represent interns, new recruits, and local teenagers as role models and mentors, with the intention of inspiring and motivating them to stand up to understand their potential. Such roles are sought by both sexual and social predators but in a drastically different aims. They leverage the intrinsic imbalance of power present in coaching relationships — in quest of exploitation rather than the empowerment of the victims. If a victim complains about such people to the third party, then the differential of power delivers a ready-made difference of credibility, so that the offender anticipates to "win" each phase.

Predators recognize they must always be plausibly deniable, so that they find reasonable ways to remove a subordinate, for example, having an assistant staying late at work to begin preparing for an occasion the very next day. Efficient predators are wise sufficiently enough that they do not allow anyone into their residences or hotels; other choices are carefully planned. I have impeached sexual predators who make sure that the office building they utilized to make changes on victims was out of the line of exposure from camera systems or windows, so their actions could not be recorded or corroborated.

6.6 Victims Have a Loss of Reputation

Sexual predators have to be extra watchful as compared to social predators because if their behavior is exposed the

Dark Psychology and Manipulation

repercussions are way too severe. Accordingly, they sometimes choose victims that are still deficient in reputation, based on age, socioeconomic standing, criminal history, or other aspects of experience or circumstance.

Sexual predators who masquerade as advisors mostly volunteer to participate with problematic employees specifically consisting a peer-motivating group, or with the disturbed local community. Under such circumstances, increased vulnerability of the victim combined with reduced credibility creates a potent imbalance of power, which also reduces the likelihood of a victim reporting any perpetrator crossing the limit.

I have experience investigating several crimes in which the suspects were deliberately preying on people whose reputations harmed. Such situations included men raping sex workers, inmate assaults, teachers assaulting emotionally disturbed teenagers, and coaches abusing players with documented behavioral issues. The social status of the victims conduces onlookers (and jury members) to the load of the crime and its import.

Unfortunately, there are countless cases that never registered. Many preys of sexual nuisance or harassment still remain submissive and silent, suffering from compromised credibility. They're afraid the victim would reveal their own infamous history or mental problems because they're afraid they'd never be understood regarding a person with considerable control.

Glamorize, belittle, and dispose of in the #Me-too Period

In a society trapped up in alleged global climate change, there's a spotlight on men's actions at work. Men who may have engaged in overt misconduct in a former era will be extra reluctant to do similar to few other predators have often done — to just toy with the emotions of a victim. Victims are made to feel betrayed and shamed — but uncertain whether they were indeed abused.

Website designers Wallace and Laura. Though working for the same huge online business, their contact was restricted to pleasantry exchanges. One day, in the faculty lounge, Wallace approaches Laura where this woman always takes her 2:00 p.m. Break, to praise her on a letter that this woman shared in a forum. Laura is deeply flattered, for Wallace is the single counterpart to consider her contributions, far less to congratulate her on this performance. Laura notices Wallace is as appealing as he is attentive. This positive contact leads to further interactions, which starts at 2:00 p.m. regularly.

Compelled by the noticeable fascination with Wallace, Laura opens up her life to him. She shares private data, goals, and fantasies and images. Since she's formed a liking for Wallace, she gladly complies once he asks if she has pictures of a latest holiday. She sends out a few bikini-clad photos as he states he would love to watch her in a bikini. She chooses to share some more after his positive reaction which she explains as "me in my shorts" She is in lingerie only.

One day, at 2:00, Wallace doesn't show up. He is never coming back again. Laura becomes upset and puzzled. Instantly, she goes through the list to see that his profile name still arises and even goes to check the adjoining campus building to make sure he's still in the company — just to watch him at his counter, working away. The emails she sent him and messages go unaddressed.

She comes back to the building after a week to ask if something is wrong, in person. He smiles politely and explains how busy he is. Laura is saddened and both are never talking again.

Yes, it's probable this is just a romance that's never took off the surface. However, if Wallace is a manipulator, he follows a respected MO of intentionally luring Laura into oversharing in order to gain photos, mostly just to embarrass and weaken her. Predators simply participate in this sort of conduct because it is possible for them. In fact, by rejecting the probability he was ever attracted to her, Wallace will take pleasure in gas-lighting Laura. And provided their technology related roles, every day Laura worries about what Jeffrey's going to do about those revealing photographs.

The darkest elements of human existence will not alter simply because there is inevitably a public spotlight shone upon them. But the increasing understanding of clever predatory strategies can dramatically diminish the possibility that males and females in any field will fall victim.

6.7 How to Stay Below the Table: The Toolkit for Predator

1. Choosy Attention Communal predators display distinctive non-sexual involvement in probable victims' lives, a tactic meant to determine acceptability and generate vulnerability without the use of improper conduct or linguistic. Such conduct emerges after the trickster has earned the confidence of the victim.

2. Too much data predators over share to induce reciprocity, causing people to feel compelled to reveal their own secret, confidential information which could then be utilized for extortion.

3. Effective privacy Predators organize office equipment to establish a safe space away from openings or video monitoring. Beware of places apparently intended to be away from the sight of vision.

4. A moving car is an ideal trick for a predator pursuing to ploy a victim unaided. The minor space within a vehicle is where there are "accidental" touches, yet such tight quarters enable the offender the benefit of the doubt.

Dark Psychology and Manipulation

5. Warning signs after evening. Social predators in managerial roles place restrictions on victims to join "team-building" after-work activities where liquor flows and Smartphone cams seize instants of weakness. These trips are planned to undermine the physical state, character, and essentially, the credibility of victims.

Chapter 7: Identifying Manipulative Behaviors

If you've ever thought like something is wrong about a tight friendship or casual encounter — you're being manipulated, regulated, or just even feel more than normal about challenging yourself — it may be manipulated.

"Manipulation is an emotionally unhealthy coping technique practiced by individuals reluctant to question clearly what they desire and need," explains Sharie Stines, a California-based psychiatrist specialized in violence and abusive partnerships. "Those people who try to deceive others attempt to control others."

There are several common types of coercion, varying from an emotionally manipulative girlfriend to a clingy salesperson — and certain actions are harder to recognize than others.

7.1 How Manipulators Affect Your Behavior

You sense fear, duty, and guilt

Coercive conduct comprises three factors: anxiety, responsibility, and guilt. "When someone manipulates you, you're mentally coerced to do something that you usually don't really want to do. You could feel afraid to do so, compelled to do so, or guilty of not doing so.

Dark Psychology and Manipulation

I refer to two different manipulators: "the abuser" and "the victim." an abuser makes you feel afraid and will use violence, threats, and coercion to manipulate you. The victim instills a sense of guilt in their target. "Usually, the victim acts hurt. But although manipulators frequently play the victim, the fact is they're the ones who created the problem.

An individual approached by manipulators who acts as the victim always attempts to support the manipulator to avoid feeling bad. Targets of this type of manipulation frequently feel responsible for assisting the victim to stop their suffering by doing everything they can.

Strings are connected

If you don't get a favor just because, then it's not 'for fun and free. "If strings are applied then there is trickery.

One manipulator form is "Mr. Nice man.' This person will be supportive and offer other people plenty of favors. "It's really complicated, but you don't know anything that's bad. "But, on the other side, there is a rope connected for any positive deed — an obligation." If you don't fulfill the standards of the manipulator, you'll be forced to feel ungrateful. In fact, one of the most common forms of trickery is to exploit the rules and standards of reciprocity.

For example, a salesman could make it appear like you would purchase the product since he or she offered you a discount. A

Dark Psychology and Manipulation

spouse in a partnership can buy you flowers and then ask for something in return. "These techniques operate as it violates societal expectations. "It's normal to return the favor but we often still feel it necessary to reciprocate and comply even if someone does one insincerely.

You recognize the methods of 'foot-in-the-door' and "door-in-the-face

Manipulators frequently try out one of two strategies. The first one is the strategy of foot-in-the-door, in which somebody starts with a simple yet rational request — like, do you have a moment? — Which then contributes to a bigger request — like I want 10 dollars for a taxi. That's commonly used in street frauds.

The door-in-the-face method is the opposite — it includes somebody making a large request, having it rejected, and then asking a smaller favor.

For e.g., anyone doing contract work can ask you for a large amount of money upfront, and afterward, ask for a lesser proportion after you've refused. This works since, according to me, the smaller appeal appears comparatively rational after the larger demand.

You interrogate yourself

Frequently, the term "gaslighting" is used to recognize manipulation that causes people to question themselves, their

Dark Psychology and Manipulation

actuality, consciousness, or thoughts. A dishonest individual can distort what you're saying to make it about them, hijack the discussion or make you sound like you've done something bad when you're not entirely sure you've done it.

If you're being emotionally manipulated, you may experience a false sense of shame or defensiveness — like you utterly lost or had to do something wrong when, in fact, that's not the case.

"Blame the manipulators. "They are not taking responsibility for this."

7.2 If You Are Being Manipulated, What Can You Do?

How you respond to trickery largely depends on what sort of manipulation you face.

If you believe you or anyone you know is in a manipulative or even toxic relationship, experts suggest seeking therapy from a psychiatrist, or assistance from organizational assistance. A great support group can assist too. "Individuals in toxic relationships need somewhere to understand counterpoints. They're programmed to assume that the behaviors are natural. Somebody needs to help them move away from the belief.

Attempting not to let the manipulative behavior affect you directly for other forms of manipulation. "Use the motto 'Watch not absorb." After all: "We are not in charge of the feelings of anyone else."

Setting borders can often play a significant role in keeping manipulation at bay. "People who exploit have pitiful limits." "As a living thing you have your own volitional perspective, and you need to understand where you end up and where the other person begins. Manipulators mostly have boundaries that are either too stiff or boundaries too enmeshed.

It can also help slow your reaction in a manipulative situation. For example, shy away from signing contracts at first glimpse, do not make a massive purchase without having thought through it, and the first time they are brought up, avoid making major relationship choices. "'napping on it'" is often the finest solution to avoid manipulation.

Chapter 8: Dealing With Manipulation in a Relationship

Did you had a friend that was in your mind so much that you immediately wake up and found that you were willing to do something that you might usually never comply with? Chances are you've fallen victim to a clever manipulator. Manipulation is a huge issue between a good relationship because it is sneaky. Clever manipulators will manipulate your thoughts and acts so that any error you've ever created appears to be your concept. It will made you feel like insane, just because of your emotions and actions are not under the order. And before you realize it is taking place, it can last for long time.

8.1 Signs That You Are Exploited In a Relationship

Manipulation was a massive topic of consideration when I

Dark Psychology and Manipulation

worked with couples. It's a normal tactic that offenders and controlling spouses use as it's impossible to show, it lets the person who is being used seem like it's his own mistake, and it's easier to deal with it. Most people are not even aware that they are being exploited until it is very late. And instead, the issues of trust rises.

Though you do not notice it all the time, there are certain indications that your spouse is holding your mind. It might help to educate yourself to accurately identify when you are being manipulated if you detect them. And hopefully, motivate to get to know a partner that doesn't have to use crooked tactics to control you in order to feel safe regarding your relationship.

Simple Ancient Bullying

It is among the less complex (and more readily identifiable) ways of coercion. Say, your partner starts asking you, for example, if you'd like to clean the car they use. You just don't. You just want to tell no. However, the manipulative look on the forehead and the manner of speech tells you to clean their car better, or bad things can happen. So, you're saying "I would like to", and again you're doing it. The type of person who uses the violence threat to handle you and convince you to do things you wouldn't like to do. They might later claim something like, "You really didn't have to be doing that. You must have denied that." This will make them seem like the nice person, and it's your mistake because you did not get your task finished.

The benefit of home court

Manipulations are all about tests. Taking a individual out of its element is few of the strategies used to take control. Think about where you're living, where you're hanging out, whose buddies you're visiting and where you're going to the date. Are these the spots chosen spots by your partner? Are you living in the life of your partner but they do not reside in yours? That can be a tactic of manipulation intended to boost the confidence of your partner. When you are not satisfied in your environment, you are easier to manipulate.

Where to go: Fair advantage with home court. Fifty-fifty. You and your partner live in the lives of one another. You both are allowed to choose places for dates. Both of you go just places at which you feel at ease. It is a part of getting on a safe, fair relationship.

Devious and mean

That is a difficult topic since it is often easier to do at the moment only as the manipulator wishes and only find out how to avoid afterward. Many criminals take advantage of actual aggression to achieve what they want. But in some circumstances (situations of non-abuse), you can start asserting your "no" and imply it. If in a relationship you can't say "no" without risking your protection, you've got to get out.

Tug Your strings of heart

Dark Psychology and Manipulation

Let us just assume your partner found a cat. The approach that is non-manipulative should be asking your partner that how do you feel about raising a cat, discuss whether you can afford veterinary food and care, finding how your property owner feels about cats, and determine whether or not it is the good option for both the cat and you. The aim of manipulative approach is to nibble on your heartstrings, and if you say no, it makes you seems like a not good person. It goes like, "Take a glance at his short face! He's hungry! Do you even have a heart? Would you want to see him on the roads to die freezing and alone?" There's a massive difference.

What can you do? Do not let anyone make you feels like having the right option for you made you a weak guy. You do not have to carry the cat home to guarantee its safety in this case. You may give it a new house, or send it to a facility for adoption. All of such forms of manipulations have rational alternatives to be found.

Blackmailing Emotionally

Blackmailing emotionally someone is disgusting because it does not contribute towards a healthy and stable relationship. It feels like, "I'm going to destroy everything including myself if you quit." Or, it might even look like, "I'm not going to live without having you in my life." It may be emotional or subtle. It's essentially a strategy that utilizes terror, remorse, and humiliation to hold you under the control of your partner.

Dark Psychology and Manipulation

Decide if you want to stay in a relation just because someone told you that he/she will commit suicide if you did not comply. You are not solely responsible for the complete well-being of another person.

Solution: Don't fall prey to it. It's always a sign of manipulation and it is not a serious sign of self-harm or suicide. But in order to be in the safe place, tell, "If you are feeling depressed, I'm calling the ambulance or cop for the sake of help but I will not be the one to work with it." It may sounds cruel, but it's really the thing you could do.

Playing victim card

Let's portray an example for you. Your companion and you starts to fight. Irrespective of who's wrong, what's been said or what's really happened, your partner's so sad and cannot imagine you'd damage their heart like that. Even though your partner's probably the one who's done bad thing, and without considering how you've responded, you are the one who is always apologizing and your companion almost always is needy of extra attention and love. This way you consider yourself an irresponsible, rude partner and your companion gets away with their actions.

Apologize only for the things you should be apologetic for. Do not give up on the relentless efforts of your wife to pressure you into slipping on your knife. Tell something like, "I'm so sorry that I was angry and increased my voice. It was unnecessary.

Dark Psychology and Manipulation

But I will not apologize for getting mad with what you've done. Here's how it made me think and feel.

Convenient Neediness

If things do not go the way your companion wants, are they weal or ill, or require treatment and support? In reality, this is a manipulation form, even when your companion is very ill. Few examples: your spouse does not really want to go through tough discussion with you because they feel anxious. Your partner does not feel like going someplace and immediately you won't be able to go either since they were looking for you to get help in overcoming their anxiety. Your companion is unwilling to assist you in the work of house since they are suffering from a fever or lack the strength. Your partner do not want to be left alone, because who is going to be worried about them? Or might be possible they have medical issue so you will feel bad for your partner and pay extra attention to them.

Where to go: That is a sign of not so successful relationship, and you're probably going to need to think about. But for now, you should determine how you can care for your companion when you go and do what you have to do. Chances are, they're going to be okay.

Gas-lighting

Gaslighting is the most likely form of manipulation to make you feel like you're losing your mind. Your spouse is doing questionable stuff regularly, including pretending they didn't say something, pretending you didn't say anything, leaving out facts, manipulating the truth, reinventing the history, making you remember things you've overlooked, and having you feel like you're failing them in general.

What to do: Runaway. Gaslighting is a pure, easy, dangerous type of violence.

They're Quiet, Cool, as well as collected

There's something terrible happening to you, there's tension or things appear to be troublesome, is your husband really calm? This could be a trick that can make you sound overreacting. It will seems that you are unconfident in your own reactions of emotions. Your companion regulates the emotional reactions in a way. They assess whether an emotional reaction is needed in a case. If not, you are either being emotional, or dumb. Because they are incredibly calm. They might bring into question your mental well-being or maturity, and with the passage of time you may not even feel that you're trying to look at them for approval to react when anything happens.

If you're an individual often falling for this type of manipulation, you must need treatment to assist you to get back to your genuine emotional responses and trust them. And this abuse may be harmful. The only thing you should do at the time is to go by trusting your intuition and note that you do not have to explain your thoughts to others.

Dark Psychology and Manipulation

They're always kidding

It is a two-sided exploitation. The 1st part of the exploitation is the one they're saying bad things or criticizing you, but it is your fault to get upset because they're just being funny. It does not matter how mean they were, you're always too emotional and can't handle a riddle. The 2nd aspect includes making jokes regarding you in front of people and in general. If you react badly in the presence of others, you will make a scenario, or ruin the fun.

You need not fear about being too delicate or destroying the fun. Confronting your companion when they really harm you may be a hard task, and risking feeling like not so good person, but it's necessary to take a stand for yourself. Even if that manipulative person probably tries to make you feel bad for that.

The better you understand deceptive habits, the faster you will turn them down. However, if you're trying to deal with a major manipulator, odds are your good option is splitting.

The positive social impact should be distinguished from emotional manipulation. A healthy social impact is desired by most individuals, which is part of the give and take of a healthy partnership. One human is used in psychological coercion to the advantage of another. The manipulator intentionally establishes a power gap, then uses the target to fulfill the purpose.

8.2 Deal with Manipulation

Most manipulative people have four common features:

1. They know how to spot the flaws.

2. They utilize your weak points against you, once they have been found.

3. They persuade you to give away something of yourself by their canny manipulations in order to fulfill their self-centered needs.

4. Once a trickster succeeds in taking full advantage of you in a job, social, and family scenarios, he or she will probably follow the violation until you put a brake on the exploitation.

Root causes are complicated and deep-seated for prolonged manipulation. But whatever controls an individual to be emotionally manipulative, when you are on the receiving end of this violence, it's not easy. How can one manage those situations productively?

Understand your basic rights

When having to deal with a mentally manipulative person, the single most significant guideline is to protect your rights, and realize when they are being violated. You have the freedom to speak up for yourself and protect your rights before you hurt someone. On the other side, you can forfeit those rights if you cause harm to anyone. Following are some of the human rights:

Dark Psychology and Manipulation

You've got the right:

• To respectful treatment from others.

• To share your thoughts, your views, and your desires.

• Determining your own goals.

• Telling no without feeling bad.

• To get exactly what you pay for.

• To have differing opinions than others.

• Caring for and defending yourself from physical, behavioral, or emotional attacks.

• Building your own safe and fulfilling future.

Those basic human rights are your ground rules.

Our culture is, of course, full of individuals who do not value those rights. In particular, psychological manipulators want to rob you of your privileges, so they can take full advantage of you and influence you. But you have the strength and ethical ability to say it is you who is in control of your life, not the manipulator.

Do not personalize things and blame yourself

Since the plan of the deceiver is to seek and leverage your weak points, it is easy to understand that you may feel inferior, or even criticize yourself for failing to appease the manipulator. It is necessary to note that you are not the issue in these situations; you are actually being exploited to feel worse about

Dark Psychology and Manipulation

yourself so that you become more inclined to lose your authority and privileges. Think about your relationship with the manipulator, and pose the following questions:

• Am I viewed honestly with respect?

• Are the expectations and requests of that person reasonable to me?

• Is doing favors one way or both ways in this relationship?

• In the end, am I feeling confident about myself in this connection?

Your correct answers give you valuable clues as to whether the relationship's "issue" is with you or with the other individual.

Maintain your distance

Yet another way to identify a deceiver is to see whether a person is acting in various situations and around different individuals with different faces. While we all have a level of this kind of social differentiation, a few psychological tricksters strive to habitually linger in extremes, being extremely polite to one person and totally scary to another — or totally helpless at one instant and ferociously violent at the next. When you regularly witness this sort of behavior from an individual, maintain a good distance, and avoid interacting with the individual unless you totally have to. As described earlier, there are nuanced and deep-seated causes for persistent psychological abuse. Changing or saving these is not your job.

Dark Psychology and Manipulation

Put your spotlight on them by posing questions

Psychological manipulators can eventually render inquiries (or demands) to you. Perhaps these "offers" force you to go out of your way to satisfy their desires. When you encounter an unfair argument, it is often helpful to bring the emphasis directly on the manipulator by posing a few inquiring questions, and see whether she or he has sufficient self-awareness and understand their scheme's inequity. For instance:

- "Do you think this is sensible?
- "Do you sound realistic on what you want from me?
- "Do I get to have a say in this regard?
- "Are you informing me or asking for my consent?
- "What am I getting out of this, then?

You're holding up a mirror as you pose these queries, and the trickster will see the real essence of his or her trick. If the deceiver has a sense of self-awareness, he or she is likely to retract the query and get back down. You're holding up a mirror as you pose these queries, and the trickster will see the real essence of his or her trick. If the deceiver has a sense of self-awareness, he or she is likely to retract the query and get back down.

On the other hand, truly compulsive manipulators (such as a narcissist) will reject your questions and insist on getting their

Dark Psychology and Manipulation

way. If this happens, apply ideas from the below-mentioned tips to keep your power, and stop the manipulation.

Know how to say "no," in a strong way.

Practicing the ability to communicate effectively is to be able to say "no" tactfully but strongly. Expressed effectively, it lets you hold your ground whilst still maintaining a functional relationship. Note that basic human rights include the freedom to choose yourself, the ability to tell "no" without feeling bad, and the freedom to have your own comfortable and safe existence.

Using Resources to Your advantage

In addition to unfair demands, the manipulator would often also demand an immediate response from you, to increase their power and influence over you in the case. At such times, instead of instantly reacting to the manipulator's appeal, try using the time to your benefit and detaching yourself from its immediate impact. You can learn to take control of the situation by simply saying

"I'm going to think about it."

Take into account how effective these few words are from a client to a sales representative, or from a romantic point of view to a keen pursuer, or from you to a trickster. Take a moment and evaluate a situation's pros and cons and take into account whether you want to negotiate a fairer agreement or whether you're better off by saying "no," which leads us to the next aspect:

Confront Bullies, Confidently

A psychological trickster turns into a bully when he or she frightens or harms someone else.

The most crucial factor to bear in mind about trouble makers is that they pick those they interpret as weaker, and as long as you stay passive and compliant, you become a target for them. However, a lot of bullies are cowards on the inside. Once their targets start displaying courage and sticking up for their interests, the abuser always turns away. This is true both in schoolyards and in the home and work environments.

Studies reveal, on an empathetic basis, that often abusers are themselves the targets of abuse. This does not justify abusive conduct in any way, but may make you view the bully in a more enlightened manner:

- "When individuals don't really like themselves, they have to cover up for it. Actually, the classic bully was a victim first. "

- "Some individuals try to be tall by slicing other people's heads off."

- "I learned that bullying never has anything to do with the victim. It's the bully who has underlying insecurities. "

Dark Psychology and Manipulation

When handling threats, make sure to place yourself in a role that you can defend yourself comfortably, whether it's standing alone, getting multiple witnesses there to watch and help, or maintaining a written record about the offensive actions of the bully. In situations of physical, mental, or emotional harassment, communicate with counselors, police departments, or administrative staff.

Set repercussions

If a psychological trickster insists on breaching your boundaries and is not going to take "no" for an answer, implement consequences.

One of the most valuable techniques you may utilize to "back up" a challenging offender is the willingness to recognize and demonstrate consequence(s). Correctly expressed, consequence allows the deceptive entity a pause and causes him or her to move from abuse to appreciation.

PART TWO: MANIPULATION TECHNIQUES

Most individuals indulge in regular exploitation. For example, telling someone you feel "okay" when you are genuinely depressed is technically a type of manipulation because it regulates the responses and attitudes of your acquaintance towards you.

Nevertheless, coercion may often have more subtle effects and is sometimes related to emotional violence, particularly in interpersonal relationships. Most people perceive coercion negatively, particularly when it affects the exploited person's physical, social, or mental wellbeing.

Although individuals who exploit others sometimes do so because they feel the need to dominate their behavior and climate, an instinct sometimes arising from deep-seated insecurity or anxiety, it is not safe behavior. Engaging in manipulation will keep the manipulator from communicating with their own selves, so being deceived will contribute to a broad variety of adverse effects being encountered.

Chapter 9: What Is Manipulation?

The purpose of manipulation is to use manipulative methods to regulate attitudes, feelings, and relationships. Manipulation in certain instances tends to be so strong that it leads a person to doubt their view of truth. One such tale demonstrated in the iconic film Gaslight, in which a woman's husband secretly deceived her until she no longer respected her own beliefs. For example, the husband clandestinely shut the gaslights off and persuaded his wife that the darkening light was all in her mind.

9.1 Manipulation's Impact on Emotional Wellbeing

Manipulation, if left unresolved, can result in negative mental health outcomes for all those manipulated. Chronic coercion in intimate relationships can also be an indication of emotional violence that may, in certain situations, have a similar impact as trauma — especially where the person is made to feel bad or embarrassed.

Victims of persistent manipulation may:

- Feel depressed

- Rising fear

- Build inappropriate management habits

- Seek to appease this dishonest guy continuously

- Lie regarding emotions
- Put the interests of another human before themselves
- Having trouble believing people

Mental well-being and Manipulation

Although most people occasionally take part in manipulation, a severe form of manipulation may indicate a more serious concern for mental health.

Manipulation is more common in the diagnosis of a personality disorder like emotionally more unstable personality (BPD) and narcissistic personality (NPD). Manipulation can be a medium for many with BPD to meet their emotional needs or get validation and often happens when the person with BPD feels insecure or deserted. As several individuals with BPD have encountered or endured violence, coercion may have evolved implicitly as a tool for dealing with their needs.

Individuals with a negative personality (NPD) can have different explanations for coercive behavior. Because those with NPD may fail to establish intimate partnerships, they may turn to coercion to "win" their spouse in the partnership. Features of manipulative abuse can involve bullying, accusing, playing the "victim," problems of dominance, and gaslighting.

Munchausen syndrome due to Proxy, through which a caregiver turns another adult to become sick for sympathy or love, is another disorder marked by deceptive behavior.

9.2 Relationship Manipulation

Long-term manipulation, such as those between friends, family members, and romantic partners, can have severe effects in close relations. Manipulation may weaken a relationship's wellbeing and contribute to the poor mental stability of those in the partnership or even relationship breakdown.

Manipulation may lead one person in a marriage or relationship to feel threatened, lonely, or useless. Also in stable partnerships, one spouse can exploit the other unintentionally to prevent conflict, or just to try and protect their spouse from feeling burdened. Some individuals might already realize that their friendship is being exploited, and prefer to ignore it or downplay it. Manipulation in romantic relationships can take multiple shapes, such as exaggeration, remorse, gift-giving, or the selective display of affection, secrecy, and passive aggression.

Adults who manipulate their kids can set up their kids for shame, depression, anxiety, eating disorders, and other psychological problems. One research has shown that parents who use coercion techniques on their kids may actually raise the risk that their kids may use coercive actions. Signs of coercion in the partnership between parent and child that include having the child feel bad, a parent's lack of responsibility, downplaying the successes of a child, and a desire to be active in certain facets of the child's existence.

People may even feel exploited when they're part of a dysfunctional relationship. One individual can use the other in deceptive partnerships to satisfy their own needs, at the cost of their friend's. A dishonest friend might use remorse or manipulation to gain things such as issuing loans, or they may approach the person only when they need to fulfill their own emotional needs, and may make excuses when their friend needs help.

Examples of Manipulative Conduct

Often, individuals can unintentionally influence others without becoming completely informed of what they are doing, whilst others can deliberately seek to improve their coercion techniques. Several indications of manipulation are:

- Passive- Violent Actions

- Associated threats

- Injustice

- Withholding facts

- A person alienated from loved ones

- Gas-lighting

- Taking advantage of gender to achieve goals

Dark Psychology and Manipulation

- Verbal abuse

Given that the intentions behind manipulation can fluctuate from unconscious to deceitful, it is vital to recognize the manipulative circumstances that are taking place. While breaking it down can be crucial in harassment cases, a psychiatrist can help you learn to cope with or tackle certain people's abusive behaviors.

9.3 How to Treat Misleading People

If manipulation is harmful it may be difficult to cope with certain people's behavior. Workplace manipulation has been shown to decrease performance, and loved ones' manipulative actions can make reality appear questionable. If you feel exploited in some kind of partnership, it may be beneficial to:

- Shutdown. When someone wants to get out of you a specific emotional reaction, prefer not to hand them one. For example, if you are known to impress a manipulative buddy before asking for an overstepping favor, don't play along — rather, respond kindly and change the discussion.

- Show confidence. Manipulation may also involve attempts by one individual to allow another to question their ability, instincts, or even truth. When this occurs, keeping to the narrative will help; but, if this happens regularly in a tight relationship, it may be time to quit.

- Stay on topic. If you point out conduct that leaves you feeling manipulated, the other individual may attempt to limit the situation, or muddle the scenario by bringing other issues. Remember and stick to your point of principle.

- Handle the issue. Point out the deceptive conduct as it happens. Maintaining a focus on how bad the behavior of the other individual affects you instead of beginning with a judgmental statement may also help you come to a resolution while stressing that their manipulative strategies won't work on you.

Tackling Therapy Manipulation

Treatment and counseling for manipulative behavior may greatly depend on what underlying problems are resulting in the issue. For example, if the manipulation is a result of an underlying mental health problem, personal therapy could help that person realize why their conduct is unhealthy to themselves and others around them. A therapist may also be able to assist the manipulative individual to learn skills to interact with others while honoring their limits and addressing underlying emotions that may contribute to the behavior.

Some mental health problems, such as borderline personality, can trigger people to feel insecure about relationships, causing them to behave manipulatively to feel healthy. In these situations, a therapist can help the individual overcome their mental health problem, which may in effect minimize their distress and make them feel comfortable in their partnerships.

Chapter 10: Covert Emotional Manipulation

Several of the dark psychology tactics that you'll find use this type of emotional manipulation in one way or another. You will recognize signs of CEM as you learn more about the world of dark psychology, and it's various forms. And knowing precisely what CEM consists of is a crucial first phase towards recognizing the nature of manipulation. Covert emotional manipulation is one person's way to manipulate another's thoughts and feelings in an underhand manner which is undetected by the manipulated person.

10.1 Concept of Covert Emotional Manipulation

Breaking down each of the three terms in the title is a perfect

Dark Psychology and Manipulation

way to get a grip on the simple concept. Covert refers to the way in which certain manipulators can conceal their intentions and the true nature of their actions. It is not possible to categorize any emotional exploitation and power as hidden. However, targets of the hidden sort usually do not realize they have been exploited, do not recognize how coercion has been done, and may not even be able to infer the motive of their manipulator. CEM is a dark Stealth psychology bomber, avoiding detection and defense until too late. The mental aspect of treating relates to the manipulator's personal emphasis. Other possible forms of manipulation require the attitudes, values, and motivation of the individuals. Focuses on CEM Specifically influencing the mental condition and perception of an individual.

This area of influence is the focus of manipulators as they know that an individual's emotions are central to all other facets of his or her personality. Manipulating the feelings of others is like breaking their jugular vein. In case a Person has emotional control, they have control over their feelings. The final piece of this mystery is the word "coercion." power and manipulation are similar things is a widespread misconception. This isn't the case. Manipulation refers to the dirty tricks and hidden process of influence occurring outside of the consciousness of the person being regulated. Another big distinction is the purpose behind influencing somebody else, as opposed to the intent behind manipulating them. An influencing person has the mindset of "I want to support you make choices that are beneficial for you." A manipulator has the mindset of "I want to subtly manipulate you to favor me." Therefore, knowing the purpose of any action is simply a question of determining whether or not it is an indication of hidden emotional exploitation. Now you've had an explanation of just what is hidden emotional coercion and whether it's distinct from other types of control. I will now explore the most likely situations to find arising covert emotional manipulation, as well as the major types of manipulative characters that occur time after time again.

10.2 Manipulators in Different Situations

Broadly speaking, there are four main situations where indirect exploitation of emotions may occur. Professional, personal, romantic, and family. By far the most common situation is romantic covert emotional manipulation, and can also be the most fatal. However, less apparent forms of CEM can be seen almost everywhere. Once you know the idea and its practical applications, you'll be able to defend against it, regardless of the circumstances you're in. Just as there are popular scenarios where covert emotional manipulation can take place, there are prevalent kinds of people who develop the ideas that underlie CEM. Being able to link the CEM theory to real, individual portrayals of its concepts is an important element of fully

Dark Psychology and Manipulation

understanding it. A dictating life partner is a frequently noted illustration of CEM principles. When someone is in a marriage, and their husband is clearly attempting to control them, the individual is expected to be disgusted with what's going on and is looking to find some way out of that. Because of this, many regulating partners exert their effects in the most secretive way possible. Their girlfriend or wife tends to end up becoming a target of utter sexual abuse, without even knowing that it is happening. This gives the manipulator the power they want without any threat of being detected and having lost the other person for better. Also, a so-called "buddy" could use CEM to get the result they want out of their connection with someone else. One of the more popular forms of manipulators in this specific category is someone who deliberately triggers in a person the emotions of remorse, compassion, and responsibility toward them. The person manipulated in this way will not be aware they are being affected. They won't be able to demonstrate why they feel and act toward their "friend," the manipulator, the way they do. Further prevalent play area for covert emotional tricksters is the professional field. Numerous people have tales about working for a supervisor, or some powerful figure, that appeared to cause unexplained feelings about remorse, anxiety, or obligation in them. People who have been exploited in this way have never been able to identify why those emotions exist and where they originate. Within the CEM world, family situations are among the most troubling. A skillful manipulator who can locate a victim within his or her own family is probable to be very harmful in terms of their influence. That is because CEM is an effective tactic particularly though the manipulator and target do not have a truly strong relation to one another. The degree of power and leverage will rise dramatically when the true bond of the blood link is applied to the mix. Why are familial situations so suitable for using CEM? To put it plainly, people are now experiencing a sense of moral responsibility to support people out of their own families to "go the extra mile" and ensure that their needs are met. The hidden emotional manipulation activities contribute to the current predisposition to control, and the effect is a rather soft target. So how precisely do clandestine mental manipulators continue to instill the power of their victims at these levels? They have a variety of techniques that are challenging to spot, yet much more difficult to avoid.

10.3 Methods

You already understand the concept of covert emotional manipulation and the types of circumstances in which it will happen. This is a strong general overview of the topic, but it is also necessary to consider some of the different techniques that manipulators use to gain power. This form of emotional abuse has the entire function of having it as untraceable as possible.

Dark Psychology and Manipulation

This segment is aimed at blowing this underground universe wide open for all to recognize.

Love bombing

Love bombing is a tactic commonly used by relational manipulators at the outset of their relationship with a target. It includes the serious, unexpected, and aggressive show of good feelings towards a victim. Which can at first appear counterintuitive. If someone wants to injure others, why do they immediately behave so intensively positive? Because it has its own purposes! The idea behind love bombing is that it generates an overwhelming feeling of confidence, intimacy, and loyalty towards the manipulator from a victim. The severity to which love bombing is used, and the individuals from whom it is used, depends on the situation assessment by the manipulator. A target who is alone, depressed, and needing help and consolation will definitely be more deeply and freely bombarded with affection because the manipulator thinks they will be responsive to it. Likewise, a more rooted target would need a less severe and subtler positivity assault. One can learn two valuable lessons about CEM from the description of the technique of love bombing. First of all, it beautifully demonstrates the hidden existence of CEM. Imagine trying to understand the bombardment of love as something bad. "Okay, this guy was really sweet to me and made me feel pretty happy." It's doubtful that such a comment would cause any alarm bells or warning signs of violence. This is a textbook example of how anything that has a bad impact may be interpreted as optimistic. The second clear message we should gain from knowing love bombing about CEM is how CEM is tailored to the particular circumstance that each target poses. Experienced manipulators in their history would have secretly manipulated other men, and evolved through the encounter. Therefore in any particular scenario, they know the best strength and pacing of any specific CEM technique. For example, every person responds to different "loving" gestures differently. Compliments function well on some, while gifts affect others more than others. If someone who has not been trained in the CEM sector has attempted to love a target, it is doubtful that they would have a lot of success.

This is because it requires knowledge of the exact extent to which a victim reacts to certain methods and not to others. Just as a Dr. can recommend the right dose, so the dark manipulator can use the correct amount of manipulation.

Reinforcement

Intermittent constructive reinforcement is a commonly practiced procedure that follows love bombing. It is a means of controlling a victim without them realizing what is happening to them. The standard sequence of a CEM scenario in the textbook includes love bombing accompanied by optimistic Strengthening and intermittent positive attention. The

Dark Psychology and Manipulation

justification for this sequence is now being clarified. Love bombing in the early days of their relationship is the pure, unearned, and extreme show of optimism from a manipulator to their target. It is meant to weaken the defenses of a survivor, enhance their dependence on the individual who manipulates them, and establish the context of a supportive partnership, intimacy, or whatever other shapes the contact takes. After love-bombing the next move is always constructive affirmation. That is a conduct reversal, through which the manipulator no longer displays unending, pure positivity towards their target.

Instead, the manipulator withholds some sort of positivity until a period when the target demonstrates a desirable action. So, for instance, if the manipulator wants their victim to regularly call them, the manipulator will only exhibit a better answer when that happens. The target may be uncertain of the strategic manipulation with positive feedback toward them but will subconsciously agree with the manipulator's desire to enjoy the pleasant feelings on display. This positive strengthening is then substituted by intermittent positive strengthening or IPR. IPR requires avoiding positivity gestures, even though a positive activity is seen.

If the manipulator wants that the victim asks them for things, and the victim agrees, the manipulator will only validate the desirable action with a pleasant emotional reaction sometimes. This unpredictability triggers a strong, hidden wish for good publicity on the victim's behalf, without the victim even being mindful of what is going on.

So the target can start seeking out a successful manipulator response by whatever means necessary. The manipulator makes their target behave in a certain manner so the person may have no idea what they do or why they do so. The preceding sequential technique of love bombing, positive strengthening, and finally intermittent positive reinforcement illustrates one way in which a covert emotional manipulator can deploy positive expression and cold withdrawal to sculpt their victims' emotional response. Truth denial is a strategy of CEM which initially affects the victim's mind, instead of the emotions. The effects though, as you are about to see, will devastate the feelings of a survivor.

Denying reality

One of the most painful moments a human can endure is the sense of losing his or her own sanity. This is bad enough if something obvious, such as mental disorder or the temporary by-product of pressure can explain it, but is even more unsettling if an emotional manipulator has covertly induced the feeling of madness. Reality denial applies to a variety of CEM strategies that both share the same purpose — the undermining of the conscience of a person to fulfill the personal interests of the manipulator. The ways in which the denial of reality takes place and its impact will now be further explored. Gradualism

Dark Psychology and Manipulation

is one of the key concepts underpinning the rejection of truth. Instantly, manipulators are unlikely to strive for complete degradation of the wellbeing of a target, because such a result is difficult to accomplish without being identified. Rather, the professional manipulators appear to pursue the method "slowly but steadily." This involves the gradual erosion of a person's health until the flimsiest of foundations are placed upon their confidence in their own faculties. And how does an underhand manipulator continue the cycle of eroding the wellbeing of a victim? This often starts with small scale weakening of the confidence a person has in their own memories. The manipulator can create various circumstances where a survivor is forced to doubt their own memory of events. The manipulator must also guarantee that the one who ends up looking the most convincing is their own representation of what really occurred. This slight trust loss cycle essentially serves two overlappings, covertly deceptive ends. Second, it reduces the victim's trust in their own forces of comprehension and recollection. Next, this trust is passed over to the manipulator. It's important to remember that at first, this may never feel like a huge deal. The manipulator will literally come across with a slightly better memory as the person. The victim would be also grateful that they have somebody they can depend on for their memory!

Over time, the covert emotional manipulator will elevate the risk of the events that they cause the victim to question. What starts as innocent-looking and meaningless can be transformed into a person who lacks all faith in his own cognitive abilities. The most dangerous part of this cycle is the propensity of the survivor to blame the lack of capacity on his own mind. Professional manipulators would always be the people who manipulate the trigger so rarely make the target fully conscious of what's actually going on.

Chapter 11: Manipulation Techniques

To accomplish their ultimate aims, manipulators use bribery, mental manipulation, bringing the other individual down, deception, and building an illusion. Blackmail, lying, creating a hallucination and putting others down are the techniques used by manipulators. These are the core of every manipulators tool box so they can get the victim into doing what they want.

11.1 Blackmail

The purpose of utilizing this sort by intimidation is relying further on the subject's emotions. In regular blackmail, the target has a danger to cope with, often involving physical damage to themselves or anyone they love. For the

Emotional coercion, the manipulator must strive to evoke feelings powerful enough to motivate the victim to action. Although the target may believe they are supporting out of their own goodwill, the trickster has managed to ensure they are having the assistance and drawing out the emotions whenever required.

Blackmail is the first strategy that a trickster would use. Blackmail is deemed to be an act that involves irrational threats to make a certain benefit or cause a loss to the target unless the manipulator's demand is met. It can also be described as the act of intimidation including threats of arrest as a convict, threats of taking properties or money from the subject, or threats of physical damage to the subject. There is a long tradition of the word blackmail; initially, it was a phrase that implied payments paid by the settlers to the region surrounding Scotland to the chiefs in charge. This payment was intended to shield the settlers against the marauders and robbers that went to England. Since then it has adapted to represent something different and in some instances, it is an offense in the U.S. For the purpose of this section, blackmail is more like a challenge to the target, whether physical or mental, to intimidate them into doing what the trickster needs.

In certain instances, Blackmail is often known to be extortion. Although there are instances when the two are typically associated, some differences do exist. Extortion, for instance, is when someone takes another's private possessions by risking to do future harm if the land is not given. In comparison, blackmail is where intimidation is used to discourage the recipient from participating in legal behavior. At times, these two things must work together. The individual will intimidate others and demand money to be held at bay to not do damage to the victim. To achieve what they want the manipulator will be able to use this tactic. They will take the chance to analyze the details of their subject of personal nature and then they will use it as a form of leverage against them. By threatening to reveal an unpleasant secret or messing their chances of having

Dark Psychology and Manipulation

a new promotion at work, they could blackmail their target. Or the manipulator may function more threateningly by attempting to physically hurt their target or the families of the target before they decide to go along with the manipulator. Whatever the blackmail could be, it is used with the aid of the target to help the manipulator reach their final goal. And often they'll be ought to trigger the target into the action the manipulator needs. The manipulator will take advantage of the situation to get the thing they want; they will use the sympathy or remorse they excite to coerce the target into cooperating or assisting with them. Often the extent of sympathy or remorse is blown out of proportion, which makes the target even more inclined to help out in the scenario.

11.2 Putting Down the Other Person

The manipulator has other choices should they decide to persuade their target to help achieve the ultimate objective. One method that does have quite a bit of success is when the manipulator can put his subject down. For most situations, where the manipulator uses verbal skills to bring a target down, they may face a strong risk of having the subject feel as though they have been exposed to a personal assault. When the subject feels that they are being targeted, they would bristle and not be able to support the manipulator in the manner they like. We will be more careful with the procedure to find a way to do so without creating or ringing alarm bells.

One way you can achieve that is by humor. The comedy will lower obstacles which would otherwise exist because comedy is humorous and helps us feel nice. The manipulator will turn their indignation into a joke. Given the fact that the put down has transformed into a joke, it will function almost as well as though the humor were not there without creating the obvious marks on the subject. Often, the manipulator may channel their put down in the form of a 3rd person. This lets them disguise what they're doing more conveniently along with offering a simple means to refute causing damage if it comes back to haunt them. They think they are somehow smaller than the manipulator, for example. This uplifts the manipulator to a higher stage and leaves the target feeling like something needs to happen. The target is most likely to want to do it right and correct whatever errors they have made. This will bring the manipulator in a place of authority and will make it easier for them to get the target to help.

11.3 Lying

No matter what the manipulator's ultimate purpose is, lying is something they are a specialist at and can do all the time to obtain everything they want. There are many various types of lies that the manipulator will employ to help them reach their

Dark Psychology and Manipulation

final objectives. Another being that they are spreading full lies while some are omitting portions of the facts from their targets. If the manipulator lies, it's because they realize that the lie would travel far further easily that the reality will. Telling anyone the reality could render them unable to support the manipulator out and that would go against their plans entirely. Alternatively, the manipulator would say a lie and persuade the target to do something for them because it's too late to correct the problem by the time the subject found out about the lie. The manipulator may even want to withhold some of the facts of the lies they say. They're going to say some of the reality in this approach, but they're going to leave out other details that are unsavory, or that could impede the progress being made. These types of lies can be just as hazardous as telling what the reality of the story is and what the lie becomes increasingly difficult. It's important to understand that when you're dealing with the manipulator, anything they say to you can be a lie. It's not a safe decision to believe what the manipulator does because they're only attempting to manipulate and exploit their targets to accomplish their end objective. The manipulator can do and say whatever imaginable, including lies, to get what they want and they won't feel bad for it. Because soon as they get what they want, they're not really concerned about whether it impacts the target.

11.4 Creating a Hallucination

The manipulator will not only lie but also be an expert in the creation of Illusions are more successful in achieving their ultimate target. They must try to construct a vision they like and then persuade the target that this image is really a reality; whether it matters to the manipulator or not. To achieve so, the manipulator must put up the facts required to make the argument that functions against their objective. The manipulator must plant the theories and the proof into the subject's heads to launch the deception. If these theories are in motion, the manipulator would be willing to step aside for a few days to encourage the abuse to take place in the minds of the targets during that time. By this point, the manipulator would have more opportunity to get the subject to go through with the plan. Manipulation is a type of mind control that the subject has trouble resisting. With the exception of brainwashing and hypnosis mentioned in the preceding paragraphs, deception may occur in daily life, and in certain cases, it may occur without any awareness or influence of the subject. The manipulator must operate discreetly to accomplish their end objective without making the target becoming paranoid and disrupt the operation. The manipulator won't think about who they're harming or how someone may feel because most of them won't be willing to consider their targets' needs. They only think they want something because the target they've selected would

Dark Psychology and Manipulation

help them get to that objective. The methods mentioned throughout this chapter are intended to better illustrate what's going on throughout the manipulation phase. It's always better to seek to stay clear of someone who may be a manipulator so you can prevent this type of mind control.

Chapter 12: Emotional Influence

Our emotions lead us in our day-to-day strategic thinking, often without even noticing it. We all have primary instincts that affect our choices. While we are hungry we are searching for something to cook. When we're exhausted, we nap-or consider another cup of tea. We want to play, cuddle, or keep a little animal or new kid when we see it. These are all instinct-in-action forms of emotional reactions that impact our decisions without much additional thought.

Many influencers and marketers are familiar with all these emotional reactions and recognize when to use them to market effectively for potential customers. They use pictures and videos which inspire our emotions, make us feel pleased, comfortable, thrilled, or wanted – and not just an item, they "sell" these emotions to us. Such emotional reactions can shape our purchasing decisions.

12.1 What Is The Influence Of Emotions?

Emotional states are what gives our regular lives color: thrilled, sad, frustrated, and many more variants; and every one of these affects how we look, what we do, and yeah of course, what we purchase. And the emotions we experience once we make a choice, or buy a product will determine whether we will make that decision again. A great emotional experience can quickly generate customer loyalty or a customer who will exchange those optimistic feelings with friends, convincing more consumers to buy your product.

Marketing experts know precisely how to use these positive reactions to promote buying and keep customers coming back for the product. Find the scenario below of 2 coffee bars. Shop number one is a central cafe where you can grab a cheap doughnut and an instant cup of coffee. Shop number two has a large range of nice, though pricier, coffee varieties and options, cozy sofas, trendy music streaming, and a feel that says, "All the young kids are hanging out here." Even with the lower prices of shop number one, more customers are flocking to shop number two for the young-kid feeling and relaxing environment. This is a perfect illustration of emotional influence playing its part.

Reason emotions are so important

Although consumers may think that they use their rational mind to make choices, the reality is that many of these choices are influenced heavily by emotions. And the theory is recorded and researched well. Evidence in ads reveals that our buying decisions are more affected by the emotional responses than by the marketing material itself – often two or three times more. Other work has also used functional magnetic resonance imaging (fMRI) to demonstrate how we use our emotions to make purchasing decisions over knowledge, including evidence.

Utilize emotional influence

Ok, we know that emotional motivation is crucial to explain how decisions are made by customers, so how can we tap into that? Smart advertisers respond to these feelings by building an identity for the products. Rather than simply providing information regarding a company or business, infusing a personality gives the business life which can make it far harder to draw customers who identify with certain characteristics. From visual ads to labeling, environment, and the vocabulary used to characterize the company, these characteristics can be reflected in anything.

Forming Personas

One of the keys to understanding how emotions influence can be utilized is to create people for your final target clients. A persona is a crafted-up customer profile, which can also be outlined in the specific qualities and traits of each consumer. Having to know the people you want to approach in your branding assists you to understand customers, humanize, and help explain how to cater to their feelings.

You get a better understanding of who your targets are once

you establish the people you want to target (and yes, you can – and should – have more than one. Your online profile will

Dark Psychology and Manipulation

include such items as age, gender, location, employment/career, relationship status, and other variables. You really should name them, and assign a stock image to them. What are their goals in life? Their points of grievances and discomfort? Their motives? Write bios for every single person you generate and you want to approach. Many of the marketing workers will use these profiles to unify the squad to ensure sure everybody is on the same page.

Marketing to your likes

You can customize your strategy when advertising your services or products once you have set up your ideal people to market to. Ask what the needs are for your character. What are their weak points, and how can your item cater to them and propose alternatives? Consider these people to be actual humans, and find some way to attract them in using their emotions.

Think further than your product, and take into account the feelings your product gives buyers. Consider how the new technology innovation makes a customer look – delighted and enthusiastic, but probably also part of a crowd "hot," clever and hip. They may be comforted to have resolved or modified a problem from an earlier version of the device. Now, you sell a way of living, not just a model, and it appeals to the emotions of your consumers. In this way, advertising sells the emotions your device provokes and will lead to increased sales success.

Initial Impression

First experiences count, whether it's to make new friends or watching a new commercial for the first time. Repeated studies show that in split seconds we establish these first impressions utilizing our intuition and emotional responses. Which is why it is so crucial to know how to advertise your product. A consumer's first exposure to an item, or its marketing, will have an instant effect on their feelings towards it and will generate favoritism in the long term.

The first feeling will be deeply emotional. Take into account using color's mental power, as well as storytelling. Motivate your consumers, help build trust, and plan a suitable product image and way of living that it supports.

Chapter 13: How You Can Use Mind Control?

The mind is the sanctuary of one individual. You can lose everything else to someone, but the sole owner of a human mind is the person itself. Absolutely correct? No!

People want to think that they have complete control over their own ideas and behaviors. That their brain is as much in control of themselves as their dominant hand is. But is that the case, really? When you're imagining, are you monitoring your dreams with care? If you can't focus, do you choose to distract your ideas? In reality, our minds are extremely sensitive to command and power. Just think about watching a scary film.

The soundtrack, lighting, and camera angle choices are guiding and influencing your mind and feelings. Although you understand you're watching a film, your mind still reacts to the cues its being given. If something that we have selected and are conscious of, can impact the mind so intensely, how powerful would the impact be of a talented, dark, and psychological trickster?

13.1 Each Type of Mind Control Does Not Go Unnoticed

Undetected regulation of mind is the most dangerous form of control of the mind in nature. If somebody is aware that their brain is being impacted then cognitively, physically, or verbally they can react to it. They can prevent dealing with manipulative people. A number of people will flee to take charge at the slightest hint of a bad individual attempting to get into their head. If their mind controller is unnoticed, like a stealth bomber, then the victim cannot put up their efforts in time. There are two types of strategies to take over an undetected mind of a person — social communication, and media utilization.

Traditionally, control of the media mind was only necessary for big corporations and only relational control of mind was left to individual mind controllers. That is no longer the case, today. Computers and mobile devices have directly placed media mind manipulation powers in the hands of the coldest tricksters who walk the Earth. Before we know about the actual techniques that are used to gain undetected power over the mind, we need to think about the manipulative individuals who use these strategies. Undetected mind controllers, as with all dark psychological manipulators, have a wish to influence those around, usually for their own advantage. However, undetected mind controllers are much more lenient and practical than other manipulators. Unlike reckless psychopaths, only after careful consideration, undetected mind controllers are inclined to act. It's no simple task to manipulate someone's mind in a manner that stays undetected. It requires conscious awareness and use. Mind controllers are cautious and clever creatures, regardless of that. They also worry about being spotted out so they target to hide as much as possible of their techniques. They're like secret puppet masters, pulling the strings of their victims from behind a veil.

13.2 Undetected Tactics of Mind Control

Let's understand about the particular methods manipulators use to regulate an undetected way of thinking of a victim. We will discover the interpersonal and television techniques which constitute the toolkit of a manipulator. Examples of how these strategies may be used on a person or larger collective scale will be given.

Dark Psychology and Manipulation

Finding the Victim

One of the first and most significant psychological concepts of undetected regulation of mind is to identify a victim with a goal. Scientifically as well as anecdotally, it has been proven that an individual with an urgent need or desire is more vulnerable to unrecognized control of the mind than someone who feels at ease and comfortable. This can range from a simple, physical target like feeling thirsty and wanting a drink to a big, psychological objective like needing love and affection. Reckon of someone in a crowd seeking someone else. They'll succeed in filtering out all the people who aren't their goal and fine-tune the one who is. The brain is akin to that. If there is something that it wants or needs, it can direct an individual toward it, even if they are unsure that there is any control going on. The greatest mind controllers will distinguish discreetly what the goals of a victim are, and will try to manipulate people with these goals in mind. One textbook example of the vulnerability of people with a target is a subliminally conditioned experiment. Subliminal influence is yet another term for undetected control of the mind. A movie with a hidden picture of an iced tea was shown to two sets of people. One group of people was thirsty, but the other was not. When given the chance to buy a particular drink from a collection, the thirsty people purchased the iced tea in larger numbers than numerically would have been anticipated. This is proof that when a person's brain becomes hungry for something, it would happily come up with ideas of what to pick. So how does that principle work on an interpersonal, individual scale? If a mind controller discovers a victim who craves something desperately in their life, usually the satisfaction of some deep emotional need, the manipulator will be capable of controlling their mind more easily. For starters, if a person has recently experienced a breakdown of a romantic partnership, it is possible that their psychology is needing a friend. The mind controller will impact their victim into thinking they are the hero of the victim when they are probable to be their ruin in truth. Some of the most common spaces of need for a manipulator to exploit will include a person's need for monetary stability, their need for belonging, and their need for friends. An experienced manipulator can exploit these vulnerabilities for a range of purposes. The manipulator may try to exploit their victim, either sexually or economically. They may seek to gain loyalty to some form of cult or extreme ideological movement. For their own sadistic pleasure, they may simply toy with the victim.

Restricting selection

Restricting options is an undetected spoken method of mind regulation. It's a really sophisticated type of dark manipulation, as it offers a number of built-in "get out provisions" for the manipulator should their target become suspicious. The best approach to this specific form of mind control is to remove any

Dark Psychology and Manipulation

real choice a victim has about a specific circumstance while creating an illusion that the victim has been in control all the time. The choice restriction is comparable to a common and effective selling strategy known as a close option. I will use a way to show this process, correctly identifying the distinction between somebody behaving in a psychologically normal manner and a dark manipulator who only wants to satisfy their own motive at the cost of others. Take a lady who's getting asked out for a date. A regular guy might be brave enough to ask his question, lacking confidence or surety, and finally stammering out an open-ended question like "Do you want to go out with me?" "Such a query leaves a clear chance for a" No "response. This is the standard way things go for people unfamiliar with the use of dark psychology rules. However, somebody who knows how to control somebody's mind in an undetected way will engage in the same situation quite differently. They like to tempt their victim with confidence and smoothness, to get them to chuckle and to lower their guard. Then, the manipulator will ask with complete confidence and assurance "So, am I taking you out on Wednesday or Sunday night?" The restricted choice given to the victim, who because of the elegance is in a mentally soft state, will mostly result in the victim selecting between Wednesday or Sunday night. Answering 'no' has never been a choice. The devilish aspect of the above method is that there is no real evidence of the words an individual has spoken, unlike many other forms of mind manipulation, including those assisted by the media. If the victim, miraculously, picks up on the manipulator's restriction of options, the manipulator can react in two ways — a rejection or reconstruct. A rejection allows the manipulator to insist that they do not offer a limited selection and that the victim memorizes things incorrectly or is too concerned. A reconstruct can allow the manipulator to put the victim on the rear leg by saying something like "I can't believe you're doing so much analysis of my words. This really hurts me and makes me unwilling to open up to you. "Both the rejection and the reconstruct are effective emergency escape strategies for the spotted manipulator.

13.3 Mind Control through Pictures

As the five senses in life are our guidance, so too can they be our opponents and traitors. Our sense of sight and the brain's visual processing facilities are very potent. We almost always fantasize visually, even if there is a lack of a different sense, and we generally picture anyone we remember, instead of aligning some other sensory input. This allows imagery and mental distortion an especially effective media mind management tool. Advertising development has historically remained in the possession of institutions and corporations. These deceptive forces were able to advance the creation of visual, subliminal influence of thought. Examples include split-second images of a product or person being inserted into an apparently innocent

Dark Psychology and Manipulation

film. These split-second photos, which the viewer perceives as nothing but a blur of light, are capable of taking effective control of the emotions of an individual. They were used just as recently as presidential elections of the 21st century. These devastatingly effective imaging methods are in the control of individual manipulators now, worryingly. To make matters worse, these strategies may now be adapted to a single person. If the victim has a specific fear of something or avoidance of it, the manipulator can use the frightening image subtly to access and distort the emotions of a person without knowing. Let's consider the example of individual mind control with imagery. We are living in the Mobile and Video era. Everything at the contact of a screen can shoot full HD clips and deliver them to others at blistering speeds. Therefore, high-tech manipulators can refer to images that are feared. For instance, if a manipulative husband is conscious that his wife is deeply afraid of insects, during a video chat, he may "mistakenly" place a book with an insect image on its cover in the background. The wife is unlikely to deliberately register the position of the book but she will feel its effect on a delicate, emotional level.

13.4 Mind Control through Sound

Sound is another way a person is prone to untraceable control of his or her mind. That will be confirmed to you by both studies and personal observations. Have you ever felt that a song I stuck

Dark Psychology and Manipulation

in your mind? Is it easy to get rid of it? Even though you realized it was present, the audio had a strong influence over you. When it is undetected the strength of audio manipulation becomes even greater. Studies have shown that if cafe customers are introduced to music from a given area, there are more chances that they will order wine from that country. When asked they had no clue that their choice had been steered by something as basic as sound. The cowering of words and expressions in music as well as other media that contain background music is one renowned example of media mind manipulation using sound. There have been court cases aimed at proving that performers in their work conceal occult references, and to restrict them from doing so. That has also occurred beyond the television media world, with a more significant impact. Audio mind manipulation is often used by governments as a form of brainwashing. In North Korea for example, people are forced to listen regularly to patriotic songs. These are deeply embedded within a person's mindset and affect an unknown influence. Think commercial jingles, for a less serious illustration. If a person is triggered by a popular jingle's song, such as the melody of the McDonald's "I'm loving it," the individual normally repeats on autopilot the promotional message. Specific manipulators can often utilize the audio undetected mind power. There are a number of techniques of behavioral manipulation utilizing different forms of auditory mind regulation. Even if you understand the strategies, you still have

Dark Psychology and Manipulation

difficulty recognizing that they are being implemented. This is because of their sneaky, submissive nature. One of the creepiest forms of audible mind control is to unconsciously influence a person as he sleeps. Have you ever seen such CDs and videos that are used to help people avoid smoking through sleep? The evil equivalent of such products is an experienced mind controller. The manipulator will take this opportunity to inject their gloomy and deceitful commands into a person's ear and let them submerge into the deepest part of the brain when a victim is at its most vulnerable when they totally let their guard down by falling asleep. The masking of phrases with similar-sounding phrases or noises is yet another form of interpersonal auditory mind control. Have you seen the movie American Psycho? Though it is fiction, it shows true methods of mind control. The main character, serial killer Patrick Bateman, openly informs his targets what he is doing: "I am in executions and murders." When confronted about what he said, he answers simply, "I am in acquisitions and mergers." The subliminal effect is already in the psychological recesses of the individual. Sounds outside the spectrum of human hearing are a type of auditory mind regulation and can be utilized by both individuals and organizations. Such sounds, which are specific frequencies, instill deep fear, dread, or uneasiness to those who are unintentionally exposed to them. Although widely used in horror movies, such sounds have been successfully used by some innovative mind controllers to impact their victims' emotional stability and well-being.

Chapter 14: Persuasion Techniques

The problem with this method is that there are often so many various types of persuasion found in daily life that it can be impossible for anyone person to reach through to the target and create a change. While persuasion serves to alter the target's thinking and perceptions like the other types of mind regulation, it feels as though everyone is attempting to convince you over something such that it is easier to resist the suggestion that comes to the target. For instance, when an argument is going on, the advertisements on television, or even when a debate is going on, a sort of convincing is taking place. People also use persuasion without knowing, to their benefit. This chapter would go into more depth on persuasion and how it can be used successfully as a method of mind control.

14.1 What Is Persuasion?

We start with the concept of persuasion. As people talk of persuasion, several specific responses can also come up. Some might think about the ads and advertising they see all over them that promote the buying of a certain commodity over another. Some might think about political persuasion and how the politicians might seek to manipulate the decision of the people in order to have another vote. Both are forms of persuasion because the message attempts to change the way the subject thinks. Persuasion will be seen in daily life and it's a very strong

Dark Psychology and Manipulation

tool and has a huge influence on the topic and culture. Advertisement, mainstream media, legal rulings, and policy can also be affected by how persuasion functions which in effect will attempt to persuade the target as well. In order to transform their attitudes and personality, brainwashing and hypnosis would require the victim to remain in solitude. Coercion will also operate with only one individual to achieve the ultimate target. While persuasion can be executed on just one target to change their minds, it is also achievable to use persuasion on a wider scale to persuade a whole community or even society to think differently. This can make it all the more effective and potentially fatal because it has the opportunity to alter many people's minds in one go instead of just a single subject's mind. Moreover, most subjects should be able to resist the advertisements for purchasing TV and luxury vehicles or the newest item in the market. Other occasions the method of manipulation can be even more discreet so it will be more challenging for the target to shape their own views on what they are being informed. They'll think about a dealer or conman who's attempting to get them to alter all their values and who'll pressure and annoy them before the transition happens. While that is definitely one form of talking about convincing, it is also important to use this method in a constructive manner instead of just a negative. For starters, public service ads may persuade citizens to avoid smoking or recycle and provide convincing ways that will enhance the subject's existence. It's all about how the convincing process is used.

What is persuasion composed of?

As for the other methods of mind regulation, when it comes to persuasion, there are some things to look out for. These elements help define exactly what persuasion is to make it more acknowledged. Persuasion is described as "a symbolic mechanism in which communications attempt to encourage certain people to alter their attitudes or behaviors about a problem by transmitting a message in a free-choice environment."

It is one of the aspects that separate persuasion from the other methods of mind control; the individual is always able to make their own informed decisions about the matter, regardless of the fact that persuasion techniques are going to work to move the mind of the individual in a certain direction. Whether they choose to purchase a product or not, or whether they believe the reasoning behind the argument is compelling enough to shift their minds, the respondent will choose which way they want to believe. There are a few aspects found in the persuasion that help to better describe it. These factors include: persuasion is visual because it includes noises, pictures, and phrases to bring the point across. Persuasion requires the person to actively seeking to persuade the target or community. Self-persuasion is a central aspect of the face, web, radio, and television. The

Dark Psychology and Manipulation

communication may also take place either verbally or nonverbally. Let's look in a little more depth at each of these issues. The first factor of convincing is that a symbolic picture is necessary.

To persuade others, you ought to be willing to convince them that they can adjust their mindset, or behave in a certain way. It will involve utilizing phrases, sounds, and pictures to communicate the new message. To prove your case, you will use the terms to launch a discussion or statement. Pictures are a great way of showing the evidence needed to convince someone to go one way or the other. Few non-verbal cues are available, but they would not be as successful as utilizing the words and pictures. The second point is that manipulation should be done in a calculated manner to affect how people behave or think. This one is fairly simple, if you don't want to Influence others deliberately, you don't use coercion to alter them. The persuader will use various strategies to convince the target to believe the same way they do. This may be as easy as either holding a conversation with them or providing facts that confirm their perspective. But on the other side, it could get a lot more involved and consist of more complicated ways to alter the mind of the victim. Much of the methods utilized in persuasion will be addressed later in this segment. The interesting aspect of persuasion is that it provides a sort of free will to the target. The victim should make his / her own decision

Dark Psychology and Manipulation

in the manner. For the most part, they do not have to go for it, no matter how hard somebody tries to convince them for something. The topic may listen to a thousand advertisements on the best car to purchase, but if they don't want that model or don't need a new automobile then they won't go out and purchase one. If the person is against abortion, how many individuals come out and say how big abortion is won't matter, the participant is unlikely to change their minds. This enables much more free choice than is found in the other aspects of mind manipulation, which could demonstrate why when asked, many people don't see this as a kind of mind control. Persuasion is a type of mind control that can take place in a variety of different ways. While brainwashing, hypnosis and manipulation must occur face-to-face, and sometimes in total secrecy, persuasion is unable to occur otherwise. Examples of persuasion can be found all over the place. For several years Persuasion has been around; in reality, it has been around since ancient Greece.

That doesn't suggest the craft and reasoning methods are just the same as they were back then. In reality, quite a few modifications have been introduced to the art of persuasion, and how it is used in present society. This section will look at the key elements of modern-day persuasion. Richard M. Perl off spent a good amount of time researching new manipulation, how it is being done, and how it will influence the entire society. He has written a novel, The Persuasion Dynamics.

Communication and behavior of the twenty-first century, and describes the five aspects in which the application of contemporary persuasion is distinct from those used in the past. Such five forms include: The amount of communications found convincing has increased by leaps and bounds.

The argument was seen in ancient Greece's times only in literature and in elite debates. Convincing was not a major deal so you wouldn't see that too much. In modern days, taking you around is hard without any sign of persuasion. Think about the different methods and forms of commercials out there; the average person in the U.S. will find up to 3000 of these every day. Besides that, there are always people banging at your door trying to get you to purchase something, believe their suggestions, or try something new. Persuasion is far more a part of modern life than it has been in the past at any other time. Persuasion moves really fast: back in ancient Greece periods, it might take months or longer to get from one point to another for a persuasive message. This restricted the effect of persuasion since most people could not get the signal. Most actions of persuasion had political candidates reach constituents in just secs at once and any message can be quickly transmitted. Persuasion takes on a much greater role when it can spread so fast.

Dark Psychology and Manipulation

Persuasion can imply a great deal of money: now that businesses have uncovered the influence of persuasion, they are doing whatever they can to make it work. The more effective they are in convincing customers to purchase their goods the more money they receive. Some businesses solely exist due to the persuasive system, such as public relations firms, marketing companies, and advertising companies. Other firms will be able to use the persuasive methods offered by these firms to reach and exceed the sales goals they set. Persuasion has become cleverer than in history: at the start of persuasion, the operator would announce their viewpoints loudly for the whole group to listen in the hope of getting them all to change their opinions. These days are gone as the method of convincing has become even more discrete. While it is common to see actions of convincing that are often very overt and in your face, like with certain types of advertisement, many others take a more discreet route. An indication of that is where companies build a certain impression of themselves, such as being nice to the customer, in order to encourage people to purchase the product. You might also note that instead of participating in a conversation with your mate about going to a dance, they're trying to use social pressure or maybe mention a few things to try to convince you to come along. Despite being more sophisticated, persuasion is just as useful today as it has ever been. The persuasion process has become more and they have to make many more decisions. For example, when previously a person has only gone to the one supermarket in town to purchase anything they need, now they can choose from various shops for their requirements from the hardware store to the food store to the clothes store. Besides this, there is also more than one choice available in the area for any of these consumer categories. All those choices make it harder for the operator to find a strong message of persuasion for the customer or some other topic.

14.2 Different Ways to Persuade Someone

Techniques of persuasion may also fall under certain terms and are referred to in forms such as tactics of persuasion and techniques of persuasion. There is not just one approach that can be used to convince someone to believe or to behave in any way. The operator may be able to discuss the matter while submitting proof in order to change the mind of the target, they may be able to use some kind of force or pull against a target, and may offer the target a favor, or use another tactic.

Using Power

Depending on the context, the agent can conclude that using

certain coercion to get the target to think that way is a good idea. This can happen when the ideas don't match accurately, the regular conversation doesn't work, or when the operator becomes frustrated or annoyed where the conversation is going. Often force is used as a sort of fear tactic as it gives the target

Dark Psychology and Manipulation

less time to rationally think about what happens particularly in comparison to when a reasonable discussion takes place. Generally, a force can be used when the operator has had less effectiveness using the other available modes of persuasion, although sometimes it is also done starting with the use of power. At other times, the force can be used when the operator feels like they are losing track or when the target is capable of presenting counter-evidence to the operator and the operator becomes angry. It is often not the smartest choice to use force when it comes to feeling more likely to be in danger. If the target is challenged, they're less willing to respond and hear something the operator does, and the cycle won't move forward. Due to all of these factors the usage of coercion in the practice of persuasion is usually prohibited and avoided; unlike the other methods of mind regulation mentioned.

Tactics of influence

Another technique that can be used to convince the target to lean a particular way is to utilize the available weapons of influence. Robert Cialdini developed those six influences in his book Influence. This book explores the art of convincing and describes the six tools of control that will render the person effective with their aims. Reciprocity, loyalty and continuity, social verification, interest, power, and scarcity are the six tools of control. Such six tools of control are very important to the operator because they are a part of their targets' shift mechanism. Each of these six arms will be addressed below. Reciprocity The concept of reciprocity is the first tool of power. The theory implies that if one person, the operator, gives anything of interest to the other party, the target, and then the subject must seek to compensate the agent in return. It simply implies that, as the agent provides a sort of service to the target, the target may believe that at that stage they have a duty to provide a comparable service to the agent. Although the two services will not be equivalent, they have the same kind of meaning such that the responsibility to both is equal. The rule of reciprocity is very effective because it helps the agent get the subject into the right frame of mind for the act of persuasion by quieting and overpowering the subject with a sense of duty. The agent may be more likely to convince the subject to do or act in some way because the subject will have that sense of duty hanging over them. The agent won't have to think over whether the target should have the correct moral code to have transform the favor. Unless the subject will not feel the need to do so, the investigator should have certain means at their fingertips to drive it into action. Yet when it was required the topic never gave it back. Now, by telling the favor, the agent has forced social standards on the subject, making it even more likely that they will be able to persuade the subject to do something. For the most part, the subject will be happy to reciprocate with the agent without needing any outside forces. When the favor is granted, the subject will begin to look for ways to repay the agent so that the score is even and they don't appear greedy or selfish. The agent will then be able to provide the subject with an easy solution on how to repay the debt; the subject will feel gratitude for having this easy solution and will be more likely to go the way the agent wants.

Consistency and engagement

The next weapon of influence to be debated is engagement and consistency. If they want to persuade anybody to change their perspective, the operator will need to use these. When things seem to be consistent, they are simpler to comprehend and can help the target make better decisions. It's not fair for the operator to constantly adjust the details they're using, or alter any things required to support the target interpret the evidence. Instead of helping the

Mechanism of persuasion, always moving away from continuity, can render the negotiator appear like a thief and someone who cannot be believed, culminating in the collapse of the method of persuasion. Continuity is one of the most critical facets of the process of persuasion.

Consistency is widely respected in society: people want stuff to continue a particular way much of the time. Although there is a lot of variation in daily life, people are comfortable ensuring that stuff should be fairly stable generally.

Dark Psychology and Manipulation

This helps us to understand what has occurred, to know what to expect, and to be informed should any adjustments arise. When continuity was not present, it would be very difficult to schedule anything and there would still be confusing problems running on. When you decide to persuade a person about a certain topic, so you have to be sure that the statements are clear and important to them.

Feeling consistently like a disaster. People prefer continuity as it allows them to recognize when to do and when to do. We recognize what it's time to sleep when it's time to function, and what those items are going to happen all day long. Consistency provides a really useful shortcut, due to the complications present in modern existence. Life is complicated enough without contributing to certain items that don't make sense. When individuals will have stable lives, it makes it even easier. Consistency is a wonderful asset since it helps the person to make the best choices and manage knowledge. When the operator wants to be effective in their efforts to convince the target, they must guarantee that their argument is accurate. There is little space for misleading proof that could then surface to spoil the whole operation. Hold the evidence accurately and descriptive to convince the subject easily.

The process of communication is one that blends in with continuity. It is necessary to have a sort of agreement in order and recognize that the target is genuinely convinced and that the initiative has paid off. In advertising, this can imply that the subject will buy a product or in elections, it can mean that a target will vote for a specific candidate. The commitment made will vary according to the type of persuasion. As per the concept of consistency, if a person commits, either in writing or orally, they are far more prone to uphold the commitment they have made. It's been discovered that this is even more accurate in case of written agreements since the target will be psychologically more specific and there will be some hard evidence that they agreed to the commitment. That makes good sense; many people are going to guarantee orally that they are going to fix or do something, only to flip around. Sure, some people are going to do what they say and they are more probable to do that if promising verbally than not promising whatsoever, but often it's still hard to get the outcomes you want in that way. Moreover, there's no way to back up that claim as an oral agreement just becomes a disagreement he said she said and no one will eventually win. From the other side, if the operator could get a written promise, the target can move ahead to continue participating in self-persuasion for the purpose.

They must have numerous justifications and explanations for supporting the undertaking along with others to prevent any problems with the operator. If the operator can bring the target to that level the agent would have even less research to do.

Social proof

Dark Psychology and Manipulation

Persuasion is a means of social contact, and so the social rules, when it happens, would have to be observed. The subject will be influenced by the people around them; they will be more likely to want to do what everyone else is doing, instead of doing their own thing. The subject will base their actions and beliefs on what others do around them, how they behave, and how they think. For instance, if the target grows up in a neighborhood, they are more apt to behave like people from that neighborhood; on the other side, those who grow up in a very religious society will invest a lot of their time studying, educating, and supporting others. Under this belief, the phrase "the crowd's influence" may be very powerful. The target will want to understand what individuals around them do all the time. In this world, it has become almost an addiction to be willing to follow what others are doing and fit in, considering the idea that individuals are trying to tell that they choose to be special and be an individual. An explanation that is offered of whether people are going to do things if others are doing something can be seen on a phone a thon. If the host says something like "Operators are waiting, please call now," then the subject might feel like there are operators sitting around doing nothing because nobody is calling them. That would make the target less apt to respond because they feel that if no one will call then they will not call either. If the host changes just a few words and instead says "If operators are preoccupied, try calling again," a really different outcome can be achieved.

Dark Psychology and Manipulation

The target will now believe that the operators are preoccupied with many other targets' calls so the company must be nice and valid. The target will be much more inclined to contact in if they get through immediately or have to be put on hold. The method of persuasion of social proof is by far the most accurate in scenarios where the target is unsure of what they are going to do or where there appear to be many resemblances in the situations. The topic would always prefer to adhere to what people around them are doing in unclear or unpredictable circumstances that involve several decisions or options to make. This is because of the way it should be. If there is anyone similar to the subject in charge, the subject will probably listen to them and follow them more than if the person in charge is very different from the subject. The operator will be able to use the idea of social proof to help with their art of persuasion. The first way they will do this is to

analyze the language they speak.

Chapter 15: Understanding Deception

Deception means the act— huge or small, toxic, or kind— of motivating followers to accept data that is not true. Lying is a popular type of deception — the statement of something identified to be false with the intention of deceiving.

Though most people are usually honest, there are times when even those who adhere to honesty participate in deception. Research suggests the typical citizen lies multiple times each day. Some of such lies are major ("I've never betrayed you!") but more frequently than not, they are tiny white lies ("That suit looks perfectly fine") employed to escape awkward circumstances or to protect the sentiments of someone.

15.1 Forms of Deception

Trust is the foundation stone of all types of social life, from the love story and parental involvement to government. This is often compromised by deceit. Since truth is so necessary for human company, which focuses on a common vision of reality, most individuals have the general assumption that everyone else is sincere in their connectivity and dealings. Many traditions have strict societal prohibitions against deception.

There are several forms of deception which may occur. There are 5 specific forms of deceit discovered, according to the Interpersonal Deception Theory. Some of these have been

Dark Psychology and Manipulation

demonstrated in other aspects of mind control, showing that some overlap can occur. The 5 major types of deception usually involve:

Lies: this is where the operator makes up information or offers data that is totally opposite from what the reality is. This information will be presented to the target as fast and the target will see it as the reality. It may be risky because the subject is not likely to know that they are being given fake facts; if the target realized the facts were inaccurate, they would certainly not speak to the operator and there would be no deceit.

Equivocations: this is where the agent renders comments which are inconsistent, vague, or conditional. This is executed to lead the target into confusion and not to know what's happening. It could also help the operator to save face when the target returns later and wants to accuse them for the misinformation.

Concealments: This is one of the most prevalent forms of deceit used. Conceals are when the operator omits data useful or relevant to the setting, or they purposely engage in any conduct that would hide the information relevant to the target for that specific context. The operator may not have lied explicitly to the issue, but they would have assumed that the crucial knowledge that is required will never reach the target.

Exaggeration: this is where the agent overestimates an aspect that twists the facts a little, to transform the narrative the way they want. While the operator may not be telling lies directly to the target, they are trying to do the complete opposite of the method of exaggeration in that the operator will understate or lessen elements of the reality. They'll tell the target that an incident isn't that big deal when it could actually be the factor that defines whether the target gets to graduate or gets a very nice raise. The operator will be ready to look back later saying how they didn't even realize how big of a deal it was, letting them look good and the target looks just about petty if they whine. These are all just a few of the kinds of deception that could be found. The operator of the deception will use any method available to them to reach their ultimate goal, much like what happens in the other types of mind control. If they can accomplish their target using another approach against the target, then they can do so and the above list is not unique in any way. The deceit operator will be very harmful as the target may not be able to recognize what the reality is and what is an act of manipulation; the operator may be so experienced at what they are doing that it would be nearly difficult to decide what is the reality and what is not.

15.2 Reasons for Deceit

Researchers have shown that three major motivations are

involved in deceptions detected in close ties. These would involve motives focused on partners, motives focused on oneself, and motives fixated on relationships.

Dark Psychology and Manipulation

Let's look at the motivations that centered on the partner first. In such a motive, the operator may use deceit to prevent hurting the subject or his spouse. They can even use the manipulation to secure the subject's friendship with an unknown third party or prevent having the target worry about something, or hold the subject's self-esteem preserved. This kind of deception ambition will often be seen as both relationally beneficial and socially friendly. This kind of deception is not as terrible as some of the others. If the operator learns something negative that the best friend of the subject says about them, then the operator may choose to hold it to self. Although this is a type of deceit, it lets the target preserve the relationship thus preventing the target from feeling sorry for itself. This is the most commonly noticed type of deceit in partnerships, which does not do too much harm if it is detected. Most couples would want to think of their own self-image and also how they feel. In this intent, the operator uses the deception to safeguard or enhance its own image. This method of deceit is used to protect the person from scrutiny, humiliation, or frustration. Typically, when this manipulation is utilized in the partnership, it is viewed as being a more serious problem and transgression as compared to the partner-focused deception. It is because the operator chooses to act in a selfish manner rather than acting to protect the marriage or another partner. The operator will use this deception with the aim of restricting any damage that could come to the relationship simply by ignoring the distress and dispute in relation. This type of deceit, depending on the circumstance, often benefits the relationship while at other times it can be the source of hurting the relationship as it can make it more difficult. For e.g., if you want to mask how you feel about dinner because you don't want to get into a confrontation, the relationship might benefit from it. But on the other side, if you have an affair and instead choose to keep this story to yourself, it will ultimately only make the situation more complicated.

It doesn't matter what the deception is intended for, it is not recommended in a relationship. The operator holds knowledge that might be relevant to the target; if the target finds out about it, they tend to lose faith in the operator and question what else the operator is withholding from them. And for the purpose behind the deceit, the target won't be too worried, they'll just be frustrated that something has been kept as a secret from them and that the relationship will start to break. Often it's better to adhere to the relationship's loyalty strategy and associate yourself with others who don't pursue deceit in your social circle.

15.3 Monitoring Deception

If the person is involved in preventing deceit throughout their life to prevent the games of mind that come with it, it is always a smart thing to know how to recognize deception as it occurs.

Dark Psychology and Manipulation

The target often finds it hard to determine that deception occurs unless the operator slips up and either says a lie that is evident or outrageous or contradicts something that the target already knows is accurate. While it may be challenging for the operator to deceive the target for a long period of time, it is something that will usually happen between individuals who know one another in daily life. Identifying when deceit happens is always challenging, as there are often no ways to say when deceit happens that are absolutely accurate. Owing to the pressure of holding the tale correct, the operator is often more prone to spill details to alert the target by either verbal or non - verbal or verbal signals. Researchers claim that identifying deceit is a perceptual, dynamic, and nuanced mechanism that also differs based on the communication being shared. The actions of the operator will be interconnected with the actions taken by the target after receiving the message. During this swap, the operator will expose the visual and verbal information that will pinpoint the deceit to the target. At some places, the target may be able to say that the operator lied to them.

When the operator is being dishonest, it's not always easy to say. According to Warn Vrij, a renowned researcher of deceit, there are no especially correlated nonverbal conducts of deceit. Although there are some nonverbal actions that may be associated with the act of deceit, such signals may often appear while certain activities are occurring, and it becomes impossible to decide if the person utilizes deception until they commit a direct lie. Another researcher of deceit, Mark Frank, offers another definition of manipulation that involves whether it may be identified at the emotional level of the participant. When there is deception, it needs mindful conduct that is intentional on the part of the operator so listening to phrase and paying enough attention to the body language and facial expressions that are going on are both crucial when trying to determine if someone is misleading you. If someone poses a question and the operator is not prepared to answer it directly, instead of using some type of disruption, has an inadequate logic structure, keeps repeating words a lot, he is probably lying. There are some non-verbal signs that may be visible when someone is misleading, but they may also have some other issues like anxiety or shyness. These are components that will be recognized later if the operator uses the deception process in the correct manner. Camouflage, disguise, and illusion are the three primary elements of deceit.

Camouflage

Camouflage is the first element of deceit. That's when the operator works to conceal the facts in a different way so that the target does not understand that the information is missing. This method will often be employed when the operator uses half-truths when they tell details. The target will not recognize that the camouflaging took place until afterward when these facts are in some way disclosed. The operator will be talented in camouflaging the reality so that by chance the possibility of target finding out about deception is really difficult.

Disguise

Disguise is yet another element that can be observed in the deception procedure. When this happens, the operator works to create an impression that he is something or someone else. That is where the operator masks everything about himself from the target, such as his real name, what they do for a career, who they were with, and what they are up to when they're out. This extends beyond just altering the costume that someone wears in a play or film; while disguise is utilized in the process of deception, the actor tries to alter their whole appearance to confuse and manipulate the target. There are many scenarios that may explain the usage of disguise in the cycle of deception. The first is disguising themselves in relationships with the operator, usually as another individual so that they cannot be recognized. This could be achieved by the operator to get back into a pool of people who don't like them, alter their personality to have others like them, or for some purpose to fulfill their objectives. The term disguise can in certain situations apply to the operator disguising the true essence of a plan in the hopes of avoiding an influence or motive incompatible with that request. Often this type of disguise is noticed in propaganda or politics because it hides the real nature of what is happening. If the agent hides who they are from the target, then it can be very hard for the target to assess who they really are. When data is withheld from the target, it clouds the way they can think because they do not have the correct knowledge to make rational decisions. While the target may think they make rational decisions of their own free will, the operator has taken away critical details that can change the mind of the target.

Simulation

The third part of the deception is called simulation. This comprises of displaying false information to the target. There are 3 methods that could be used in the simulation, such as distraction, fabrication, and imitation.

In mimicry, or imitating another system, the operator will unconsciously portray something similar to itself. They may have an idea similar to somebody else's and instead of giving credit, they're going to say it's all theirs. Sometimes this type of stimulation may occur by auditory, visual, and other means.

Fabrication is yet another tool that can be used by the operator while using deception. What this implies is that the operator takes something found in actuality and changes it to make it different. They could tell a story that hasn't happened or add adornments that make it look better or worse than it actually was. Whereas the center of the story may well be true, yes they got a bad grade on a test, it's going to have some modification like the teacher deliberately gave them a failing grade. The truth is that the operator did not study and that's the reason they got the bad grade in the first place. Ultimately, distraction is yet another type of deception simulation. This is when the operator tries to get the target to concentrate on something other than the reality; generally by baiting or providing something that could be more enticing than the concealed reality. For instance, if the husband cheats and feels the wife is beginning to find out, he might carry a diamond ring home to divert her from the problem for a brief moment.

The problem with this method is that it often doesn't last long and the agent has to find other ways of deceiving the target to keep the process going.

Chapter 16: Seduction Techniques

It all depends on the victim of your seduction. Analyze your prey extensively, and select only those that will prove vulnerable to your enchantments. The right targets are the ones you can fill in a void for, who see something unusual in you. They are mostly isolated or miserable, or they can be quickly made so — because it's almost impossible to seduce an entirely contented person. The right target has a certain quality that triggers intense emotions within you, making your seductive moves seem more normal and fluid. A perfect target allows ideal pursuit.

16.1 Seduction Tool Kit

Generate a greater sense of safety

"If you're too plain forward early on, you risk building up a resentment that's never going to be extinguished. At first nothing of the seducer has to be in your form. The seduction should start at an angle, not directed straight so that the target only becomes aware of you slowly. Haunt the outskirts of the existence of your target — approach via a third party, or appear to develop a fairly neutral connection, progressively moving from colleague to lover. Lure the target into feeling safe, then strike.

Appear to be a desired object-create triangles

"Few are drawn to the individual evaded and neglected by others; crowds gather around those that have already lured interest. In order to attract your victims to make them desperate to have you, you need to create an illusion of desirability — of being needed by many. Being the favored object of your interest will make them happy, to win your heart in an audience of admirers. Make a reputation that precedes you: There must be a reason if many have failed to resist your charms.

Sending out mixed signals

"Once individuals are conscious of your presence, and maybe slightly fascinated, you ought to spice up the curiosity before it falls on another person. Most of us are way too obvious — be difficult to sort out, instead. Send confusing messages: harsh and delicate, both religious and worldly, harmless as well as devious. A mixture of characteristics suggests depth, which also fascinates as much as it confuses. A mysterious, mystical atmosphere can make people crave more knowledge and pull them towards you. Generate such authority by suggesting something conflicting within you.

Creating need

"It is almost impossible to seduce a person who is perfectly satisfied. You need to instill tension and disharmony in your target's mind. Stir up feelings of dissatisfaction within them, resentment with their conditions, and with themselves. The sense you create of inferiority will give you the space to assert yourself, to start making them see you as the solution to their issues. Pain and fear are the right predecessors of satisfaction. Learn how to produce the need you can fill up.

Step into their minds

"Most individuals are locked into their own realms, which makes them stubborn and difficult to persuade. Moving into their soul is the way to draw them out of their isolation and set up the seduction. Live by their guidelines, have fun doing what they love, adjust to their feelings. You will massage their deep-rooted narcissism and reduce their defenses in doing so. Take part in every move and whim of your targets, offering them nothing at all to react against or resist.

Master the technique of conceit

"It's important to make your targets feel frustrated and require your help, but if you're too clear, they'll see through you and become defensive. However, there is no established protection against insinuation — the art of injecting ideas in the heads of individuals by dropping hints which take hold days later, sometimes looking to them as their real concept. Develop a sublanguage — big claim accompanied by discharge and apology, vague comments, banal conversation combined with seductive glances — that enters the unconscious of the target

to express your true meaning. Get it all provocative.

Generate Temptation

Dark Psychology and Manipulation

"Tempt the victim deep into your seduction by building the perfect temptation: a glance of the delights to arrive. As the serpent persuaded Eve with the guarantee of prohibited knowledge, you must generate an urge in your targets that they cannot govern. Discover their weak spot, that fantasy that has yet to be understood, and indicate that you can lead them toward it.

Use the devilish power of words to generate confusion

Convincing people to listen is hard; they are filled by their own opinions and needs, so they have no patience for yours. The way to make them care is to suggest whatever they want to know, flooding their ears with anything they want. This is the core of seductive words. Use loaded words to stir up feelings, flatter them, comfort their anxieties, envelop them with lovely words and promises, and not only will they pay attention to you, but they will also end up losing their will to oppose you.

Holding them in anticipation- what's next?

"The moment people believe they know what to anticipate from you, the hold over them is shattered. More: You have lost power over them. The best way to control the seduced and retain the advantage is to build anticipation, a measured shock. Attempting something they don't anticipate from you would offer them a wonderful feeling of spontaneity — they won't be able to predict what's next.

Look out for information

"Lofty expressions of affection and nice movements may be suspicious: why are you striving so hard to impress? The nuances of a seduction — the discreet movements, the offhand stuff you do — are much more enticing and surprising. You have to learn to confuse your victims with a multitude of fun little routines — personalized presents suited to them, clothing, and accessories crafted to satisfy them, actions that demonstrate the time and energy you are giving them.

Make your presence felt

"Significant stuff happens when the victims are alone: the faintest sense of relief in your absence and the whole plan goes in vain. Predictability and over-exposure will trigger this response. Stay mysterious, then. Intrigue your victims by varying a thrilling existence with a nice distance, joyful instances accompanied by computed absences.

Relate yourself with romantic pictures and items, so they continue to see you as a charming person. The more you figure out what's in their minds, the greater the seductive illusions they wrap you in.

Confuse need and reality

People spend a lot of their time dreaming, envisioning a future full of wonder, achievement, and romance to accommodate the challenges in their lives. If you are able to develop the illusion that they can live their fantasies out via you, you will get them at your grace. Target at secret desires that have been thwarted or silenced, inflame inexplicable emotions, cloud their reasoning powers. Lead the seduced to a stage of confusion where they can't distinguish between illusion and reality anymore.

Disarm through tactical weakness and insecurity

Far too much maneuvering on your aspect can give rise to distrust. The finest way to hide your paths is to make the person look special and powerful. If you seem to be feeble, vulnerable, enthusiastic about the other individual, and unable to regulate yourself, you will make your conduct look quite natural, less orchestrated. Lack of strength — crying, bashfulness, pale skin — will help to build the influence.

Victim isolation

A lonely individual becomes fragile. Through gradually isolating the victims, you render them more prone to your power. Bring them apart from their usual life, peers, families, and house. Give them the feeling of becoming oppressed, in limbo—they leave one world behind and join another. When alienated like this, they have little outside help, so they become easily deceived in their uncertainty.

Generate a Desire

People who have had some form of enjoyment in the past will try to replicate it or revisit it. The most deep-rooted and pleasurable experiences are typically from early childhood, which is sometimes unintentionally aligned with parental figures. Bring your victim back to that point by putting yourself in the triangle of the Oedipus and branding them as the needy kid. Unconscious of the reason for their emotional reaction they will be in love with you.

Prove yourself

Many people like to be seduced. If they oppose your efforts, it's certainly because you haven't gone that far to alleviate their suspicions — about your intentions, the intensity of your emotions, etc. A prompt intervention demonstrating how much you are able to go to prevail over them will dissipate the suspicions. Do not think about looking stupid or getting it wrong — any type of deed that is self-sacrificing will overwhelm your target's emotions, they will not realize anything else.

Mix the taboo and the transgression

Whatever one can do, there have always been cultural limits. A few of those, the most basic taboos, travel back decades; others are shallower, identifying appropriate polite behavior, for example. It's immensely seductive to make your victims feel that you are guiding them ahead of either type of boundaries. People are anxious to explore the dark side. If the impulse to violate attracts the victim to you, they would have trouble

Dark Psychology and Manipulation

avoiding it. Bringing them further than they might imagine — the common sense of guilt and obligation generates a strong connection.

Pleasure and discomfort blend together

In seduction, the main error is being too sweet. Maybe your generosity is sweet at first, but it quickly becomes tedious; you're trying too much to please, so you seem nervous. Try to inflict some discomfort rather than overwhelming your victims with friendliness. Let them feel nervous and guilty. Incite a breakup — now a negotiated settlement, a switch to your previous kindness, will bring them down to their knees. The lower lows you build, the higher the ups. Creating the anticipation of terror to heighten the sexual effect.

Use the Lures of Spirit

Everyone seems to have suspicions and anxieties — of their own looks, self-worth, and gender identity. If your seduction caters solely to the looks, you will stir up those concerns and make your victims self-aware. Rather, by attempting to make them concentrate on something exquisite and spiritual, tempt them out of their anxieties: a spiritual experience, a noble piece of art, the occult. The target, lost in a divine mist, will feel refreshed, and carefree. Reinforce the impact of your seduction by attempting to make its sexual culmination appear as the two souls' true partnership.

Give them room to fall

If your victims get used to your aggression, they will offer less of their own energy and the pressure will slacken. You ought to get them up and switch the tables around. Pause for a moment when they are under your trap and they'll start coming after you. Give a hint that you're getting bored. Show interest in someone else. They would eventually try to literally control you and modesty would fly out of the window. Build the impression that they are seducing the seducer.

Chapter 17: How to Take Full Control of Your Relationship

Any sort of partnership has power dynamics at play. Then it should be no surprise that your loving relationship will also feature a power dynamic. There is a fair amount of control and reverence in some relationships and one party has more influence on others. The authority can shift at various points in your relationship to make things even more difficult. Maybe you both never spoke about control and reverence at the outset, so it was spread evenly. But then you found things changing as days progressed on and you started to feel like your wife or husband kind of had more authority.

17.1 Tips on Gaining Upper Hand in the Relationship

Hold on a second ... weren't you the couple's Beyoncé?

It's common in a relationship for the power balance to shift. There is a lot that could have changed the partnership structure. Yet if it's moved toward a different path (the one you do not adore), how can you stay on an equal playing field? If your guy got somewhat too "Kanye West" on you, how would you gain greater power and authority in the marriage? How can you turn this boat around and head into a safer, healthier sea?

Dark Psychology and Manipulation

1. Speak.

Using your speech is one method to become more effective. Be transparent on your desires and your wishes. If you're not speaking up for yourself, who else would? Understand, he or she cannot read your thoughts. Then you must use the vocabulary to convince him/her everything you want and need in the relationship.

2. Have restrictions

Every person has their own list of norms and boundaries they're at ease with. You're going to have limits in your marriage and it's vital that you maintain them. For you, there are several things that will step over the line and you need to have the ability to draw that line strongly.

3. be more autonomous

Being independent and strong does not really mean you don't need your spouse in just about any way, it just means you, as a competent individual, you are able to do things yourself. It is crucial that you are able to be self-sufficient in a relationship. Your spouse will thank you and so will you for this sovereignty.

4. Stay true to your words

Saying stuff and doing the contrary is one way to ruin your respect very quickly. Actions tell a bigger picture —, particularly in relationships. Therefore, if you inform your partner that something will have certain consequences and you don't stay true to your words, he or she will not take you seriously. And even if you make a slight commitment to your partner, you have to honor the pledge.

5. The Golden rule

Rather than trying to follow the bricky yellow road, what if you follow the golden rule. A simple way to gain power is to treat your partner just the way you want to be treated. If you want consideration and respect, then you also need to give it to your partner as well.

6. Rest assured

If you're not respecting yourself, then why do you expect others to? It starts with you. You need to show how you want to be treated. This will be determined how you treat yourself. The manner in which you talk about yourself? Will you give some authority to yourself? What do you think of yourself? Take a minute to talk seriously about whether you regard yourself.

7. Don't just settle

For someone who understands what he or she deserves, there is nothing more comfortable and desirable. If you're in a partnership where your mate thinks he or she can get away with something, you have already lost respect and authority. Take a stand for yourself and don't care about walking away from a relationship that doesn't help you.

Chapter 18: Signs of Being Manipulated

Toxic individuals are exhausting, and physically wipe you down "They really need you to feel pity for them & to be accountable for all one's issues, and then they also want to solve these things.

The smartest gauge is to know that how you feel upon dealing with someone — our emotional and physical responses to individuals are our biggest drivers, noting that you must consider if you're more anxious, tense, or frustrated upon seeing this human, commuting with them, or speaking to them over the phone.

18.1 Dealing with a Toxic Person

Other indications to keep a watch out are if the individual is constantly condescending, compulsively in desire, and/or unwilling to take accountability or say sorry for one's behavior.

"It may be anyone who regularly takes narcotics or alcohol, lies, or wants you to lie about them, regulates or demeans what you've been doing. A toxic man's life is always personally, emotionally, financially, physically, and/or inter-personally out of balance.

Effect of Toxic People on Your Life

Toxic individuals can impact all aspects of people's lives and we are always oblivious to that. We feel sympathy for them. The myths they inflict on us are accepted and rationalized. And this, in exchange, changes how we look about our values and ourselves. Toxic individuals are happy to drive happiness down from the stuff we previously enjoyed, such as jobs, relationships, interests, and even our self-love.

Setting Boundaries to Eliminate Manipulators

"If you feel unnoticed or misunderstood and feel manipulated or compelled to do stuff that is not even 'you' then you may be affected by a negative human. "Toxic individuals can make you question yourself or unconsciously do something that you wouldn't normally do—you might feel a need to be fit in or cool or get approval. Every situation is different but by influencing people to do something, toxic individuals may have a detrimental effect on others. They try to generate turmoil by negative behaviors: to use, to lie, to steal, to control, to criticize, to bully, to manipulate, to create conflict, and so on.

18.2 Signs of Being Manipulated

Most people do not realize whether they are being deceived until it's quite late. You know when you start to do, say, or believe things that serve them, you're being exploited as contrary to you. Good people inspire you to do the brightest and motivate you. Manipulators convince people that they know what's best for you.

Then which are the warning signs – the real, clear indications if someone out there tries to manipulate us?

Blame Game

It does not matter how many times a toxic individual places you in painful scenarios on purpose, they are never going to excuse you for that. They are always finding reasons to keep you accountable for your acts.

Remember, for starters, the Xmas party where Sally the toxic person got wasted, made an embarrassment of herself and spoiled the entire night — then you blamed yourself for not controlling her alcohol consumption, suggesting that the whole thing was your fault?

Isolation

Did you notice you don't splurge time with friends and family anymore? A toxic friend will expect your undivided attention and make you feel guilty if they feel they don't give you enough of themselves.

For example, John a toxic person gets to control your entire time, to the large extent that he blurts out because he notices on social sites that you are trying to hang out with the other fellows and friends — that also without him. You realize then that you spend almost all of your leisure time with that kind of

individual and have completely overlooked how your other mates are like. This is not nice.

Always making you Guess about Them

One day they'll be absolutely delightful and then another day you'll wonder what you have done to get them upset. There is often nothing evident that will justify the shift in attitude-you know that there is something wrong. They may be prickly, cold, sad, cranky, or cold, and if you question them that there's something not right, the response is likely to be 'nothing' – but they'll just give you enough to make you realize that something is there. The 'just enough' could be a shuddering gasp, an eyebrow raised, a chilly shoulder. You may find yourself trying to make justifications for them when it happens or doing anything you could to keep them happy. See why that's working for them?

Quit trying to make them happy. Toxic people have long since figured out decent humans would go to exceptional measures to keep happy the individuals they value for. If your efforts to satisfy don't succeed, or if they don't last for long, then it's time to give up. Step back and return once the attitude has changed. You really aren't accountable for the emotions of someone else. If you really have executed anything to hurt someone unknowingly, ask, discuss this and apologize if need be. You don't have to conjecture at any cost.

Manipulative

Dark Psychology and Manipulation

If you feel like you are the only one that contributes to the friendship, you are probably correct. Poisonous people are capable of attempting to send out the feeling that it's something you are in debt for. Those people also have the means to take something from you or do things that upset you, and then maintain that they did it all for you. This is especially common in places of work or friendships in which power equilibrium is already out. Statements like these- 'I left you with that 6 months' value of filing. I thought you would praise the encounter and the chance to know your tasks for the filing containers.' Or, 'I'm hosting a dinner party. Why don't you bring a meal here? It will give you the opportunity to exhibit your kitchen expertise. You owe no-one any of it. If it is not feeling like a courtesy, it is not.

Do Not Own their Feelings

They will behave as if the emotions are yours, instead of possessing their own emotions. It is termed projection, as when they project their thoughts and feelings on you. For instance, you might have been accused of being upset with somebody who is frustrated but can't be held accountable for it. Could that be as dramatic as, "Are you all right with me? 'Or a little more straight forward, 'What's the reason for being mad at me,' or, 'why you have been down all day.' You're going to find yourself explaining and securing yourself and often that's going to happen constantly — because it has nothing to do with you. Be absolutely clear about what is about you and what is about them. If you feel like you are defending yourself far more times previously against baseless accusations or unfitting questions, you might be projected onto that one. You don't have to clarify, validate, or fight to protect yourself as well as cope with an allegation that was misfired. Bear that in mind.

Eggshells

Negative people prosper in trying to keep people on their toes and taking advantage of irrational tantrums. You never really know what kind of mood they're going to be in, so you're going to have to monitor what you're doing to them — or you're going to get 15 instant messages regarding a molehill of an issue that's resulted in a peak, including a lengthy list about all the excuses you're a bad guy, your life goes nowhere, and you are not as good enough as they are.

You may have a buddy such as Sean a toxic person who is unable to deal with an informal meetup. And there is a whole intense moment every time you see him, he brings up a problem you've caused or needed to fix, or necessitates you in an exhausting return that pressurizes you over and tends to make you doubt oneself and one's personality.

Makes you Prove Yourself to them

They will place you in a situation where you'll have to pick among them and some other thing on a regular basis – and you will always feel inclined to pick them. Poisonous people would wait till you have an involvement, therefore the drama would then emerge. 'If you ever really cared for me, you'd be skipping your exercise lesson and spending quality time with me.' The problem with this is that never enough is enough. Several events are deadly-unless its living or mortality, it's likely to be waiting.

Always trying to make you Feel Low

They're trying to pursue excuses why the interesting news is not perfect news. Examples are: For a promotion – 'Money is not so great for the type of work you are going to do.' For a vacation on the beach – 'Well weather will be hot. Do you think you would like to go? On becoming a Universe Queen– 'Well you know the Universe isn't that big, and I am sure that you're not going to have breaks.' don't let someone discourage you or reduce you to their own size. You do not need their authorization anyway – and for that issue anybody else's.

Never Says Sorry

Before they really make an apology they would then hide the truth, so there is no reason to argue. They're going to spin the words, alter the way it occurred and so persuasively re-enact it

Dark Psychology and Manipulation

they're going to believe their own baloney. People don't have to excuse themselves to be incorrect. And you do not need to go ahead with an apology. Just go on-without others. Don't give up your facts but don't carry on with the reasoning. There is really no point here. Some individuals would like to be correct more than they'd like to be delighted and you have got better stuff to do than providing the right-combatants with fodder.

No Closure on the Issue

They are not going to pick up your phone. They will not respond to messages and emails. and among the sessions of their voice mail, you may discover oneself attempting to play the discussion or reasoning in your head again and again and again, speculating about personal life, wondering what you've done to hurt them, or if they're deceased, lively, or even just neglecting you – which can all experience this at key moments. People caring for you are not going to let you feel total crap without going to figure it out. It doesn't imply obviously that you are going to sort it out, but still, at a minimum, they're going to try. If they end up leaving you 'out there' for long sessions, take that as a signal of people's assets within the interaction.

Irrelevant Things while Conversing

When you are attempting to solve things that are essential to

Dark Psychology and Manipulation

you, harmful people come up with insignificant stuff from five justifications before. The issue with it is that you are attempting to argue on something you appears to have done 6 months ago prior to you understand it, also defending yourself instead of dealing with the problem. Not only, has it just seemed too often end up with what you did to them.

Toxic tone- non-toxic words

The tone may be ignorant enough and much more is conveyed in the tone. Things like, "what have you been doing today? 'Can mean something different regarding how it's said. It might mean something from 'I think you have done nothing - as normal' to 'I'm certain your day went great than mine. Mine was horrific. Just horrifying. And you haven't even noticed enough to ask.' When you ask the tone, they're going to be back with, 'What I said was what you did today,' which is true, but not really.

Altering the main focus while conversing

You may be trying to fix the problem or get clarity, and before you know it, the conversation/reasoning has relocated away from the topic which was essential to you and then onto the way you talked about – whether there is a problem with your way of doing it or not. You'll see yourself justifying your attitude, your movements, your word usage, or the manner you move your belly while you take a breath – it doesn't really have to make any sense. Your original desire, whereas, has gone well on the heap of unresolved discussions that continue to get larger day by day.

Exaggeration.

'You never ...' you always' ...' It's impossible to protect yourself from this abuse. Poisonous people have a habit of trying to draw on the yet another time you did not or the one you did as proof of your inadequacies. Don't let yourself into the reasoning. You are not going to win. And then you just don't have to.

Judgmental.

Quite often we all have it wrong and people who are harmful would then make it sure that you have got it. They are going to demean you and point a finger at self-esteem that suggests you are much less since you made an error. We are all permitted to have it mistaken now and then but no one has the courage to stand in judgment unless we've conducted something which impacts them.

Chapter 19: How to Win Friends with Persuasion?

To me, it is not for beauty to be "appealing." It's about the whole vibe of a person — are they fascinating and interested, are they making me chuckle, do they appear kind? And a huge part of figuring this out initially gets down to what other person is communicating via body language.

Now I'm not saying that you can figure out everything else about yet another individual just by how they do it or by not tilting their heads. All I'm saying is that accessible and welcoming body language creates a big difference when it comes to how relaxed I feel when I get to know someone that creates it far simpler to find out the important bits, like whether we have common beliefs, or not.

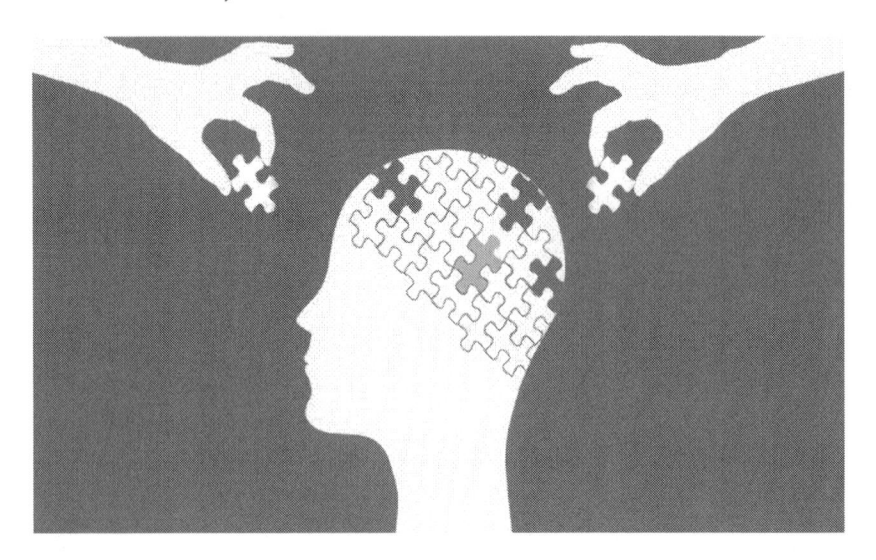

19.1 Techniques to Win Friends

Smile (But Not Right Away)

Have you really observed that somehow smiles are highly contagious? When you smile it's hard to not smile back for others. Well, now, science supports that assumption.

When people glance at an image of someone else happy, they find it incredibly hard to frown. It's just too easy to return a smile that conducting something else takes concentrated effort.

One of the greatest things you can do anytime you walk into a room is to place a sincere smile across your lips. In return, you'll build a successful chain reaction that will take you throughout the day.

Smiling influences the way we perceive the feelings of others from another report by analysing the electrical impulses in the brains of volunteers, the team has found that smiling makes we view the individuals around us as more optimistic.

They found, specifically, that when people don't smile, they interpret "neutral" faces as "neutral." even so, once people smile, they misinterpret "neutral" facial expressions as "glad."

So the world has become a happier place when people smile. Do you think that looking more optimistic at the folks around you would start making you quite common to speak to them?

Dark Psychology and Manipulation

It's really not a secret we love being around happy people. We feel comfortable when we see somebody with a sincere smile or happiness on their lips. We also naturally see individuals smile as relaxed, which is a very attractive characteristic.

Did you realize that your brain produces healthy chemicals while you smile which can help boost your mood? With more dopamine running into the bloodstream, you will feel better for yourself and have a higher likelihood of helping others.

Smiling is effective amongst many others. If we smile more often, then we want to talk to others as well. The more individuals we speak to, the more relaxed we are. The more assured we feel, the far more organic it becomes to smile.

Then, why not check it out. Be all smiles at the pedestrians on the road you walk. Smile into the mirror to oneself. Watch each morning just a few mins of comedy. To smile often, do anything it requires. Your body and brain will thank you.

Use Eye Contact to Create Better Relationships

Do you ever question why many individuals seem so quick to find new friends when others consider it hard to establish productive new relationships?

It's the appropriate use of eye contact in several cases that makes the distinction!

Researchers have found how one of the most significant

differences among people who are relatively self - assured and who make more friends, and those who are quiet and reserved would be that self-assured people make eye contact with their listeners far more often.

There are many introverted people that avoid eye contact when they talk to someone. They prefer to glance away or downwards rather than glancing at the individual they're referring to.

If you've been far less popular in trying to make buddies than you really want, by trying to make this one easy shift in your conduct, you might become ready to be more social and outgoing.

Do Not Criticize, Condemn, or Complain

Any fool, yet most fools can condemn critique or whine. For being forgiving requires self-control and character, this practice would then give major dividends throughout the relationships with other people.

Eye Contact

Learn how to efficiently use eye contact while you are trying to talk to someone. Some of us rarely allow eye contact while we are interacting with our discussion companion. This can make others think of us as anxious and dishonest. Many of them, on the other side, make much more eye contact and look too deeply. This also renders our partners in conversations uneasy. Follow the correct balance of eye contact as well as gaze away. Most of North Americans, particularly the Caucasians, chose to get a great deal with eye contact while talking to somebody. When a person fails to build eye contact with them, they tend to think something is fishy about that person. The mere term "shifty-eyed" denotes an individual whose eyes move about the room, which means they are unreliable. When talking to someone who's from either a cultural value that chooses a great deal of eye contact, be careful to keep trying to look at that individual regularly while speaking, even as you think what to say after that. A penetrating gaze you don't have to use, a pleasant stillness will do. If it always upsets you to stare straight at the eyes of another human, you should gaze at the expression of another human without relying entirely on the eyes.

When you usually point at the region of the ear or the nasal bridge that is near enough to get to the center of the head to glance into that person's eyes.

You can think it's calming your own anxiety by having your view go somewhat out of sight. If you are talking to others, hold the attention on the other person for the most part. If you look too much around the room or look at other people too often, your friend may assume you're annoyed, or you're

Dark Psychology and Manipulation

looking for somebody else you'd prefer to talk to. If you have trouble knowing precisely how to start making eye contact, you could even receive support from exercising before a mirror, or with someone else.

But don't stare too intensely at others!

A very intensified, gaze start could even make your partner being very uneasy with the conversation. To be on the other end of an extreme glare, especially at close distance, can be quite uncomfortable. You can lighten your impression by smiling more frequently, nodding, and gazing at the whole face and also the eyes. You may also regularly look away for short periods. Try staring at the expression of your discussion partner when you talk, and add in plenty of smiles and gestures, sometimes turning away as you chat and listen. It will demonstrate you are polite, involved, and open. If other people have the perception that you really actually listen to them and happily talk to them, they'll be far more probable to choose to have more discussions with you.

19.2 Protect Others' Pride and Win Big

While success may seem to come by uplifting yourself over others, in fact, the perfect way to succeed is to establish a sincere interest in others. Defending the dignity of others through trying to avoid criticisms and clashes is the very first move to win them over and persuade the others to listen to your viewpoint.

You should really be courteous, applauding your listeners instead of critiquing them as a basic guideline, in order to build someone else up as well as change their views. Everyone believes one's own name is the "loveliest voice" they've ever listened to, so a true leader believes first of all on how to uplift others around him. Analyze and make gentle, kind suggestions, instead of challenging or directing the people with whom you lead or collaborate. By trying to make others believe that your own great, honorable concepts are in fact their own, you are far more likely to build trusting relationships than if you are continuously disagreeing or trying to show superiority.

Likewise, accept your own errors, and accept them. It might seem intuitive to the contrary as empowerment is frequently represented as somehow about superiority and demonstrating your toughness. But ignoring responsibility and trying to downplay your own mistakes while pointing out others is in fact an indication of vulnerability. If you are honest and open about your imperfections you will become more convincing.

Listen More, Talk Less

How to succeed in making buddies and influence other people is at its core regarding communicating effectively. But rather than mastering the art of trying to argue and propaganda, carefully establish the skill of good listener. When you approach people with open-mindedness and friendly attitude, they are much more inclined to share as well as collaborate with you than to try and compete with you.

Listening to someone, we know so much about them: for starters, their goals, aspirations, expectations, value structures, beliefs, and perspectives. Realizing what helps make someone else tick is the very first move to convince them and lead them.

An attitude of silent but effective listening is better, rather than trying to control every discussion. Motivate individuals around you to speak about yourself and their priorities and you will be much more likable. And when you're talking, you must talk more about your discussion partner's interests and less concerning yourself. Whenever it comes to persuasive, charismatic dialogue, smaller is better. Talking is cheap but able to listen is absolutely priceless. Remembering the name of a person, having to ask individuals questions to motivate them to speak for themselves so that you can find their passions and interests is what makes us believe that you really like them, and they like you in turn. In two months you start making more friends by becoming honestly interested in people than you could ever in 2 years by attempting to get some other individuals taking an interest in you." If you strip it down, you must hear to 75% and speak only 25% of the time.

Know the Value of Charm

Dark Psychology and Manipulation

One thing people don't talk a lot about in the job hunting sector is that much of having the chance isn't really about skill, in which university you went to university and whom you recognize, its people who like you. A decent cv that brings you through the door, but charisma, social abilities, and potential can hold you there because people would usually pick the person they enjoy staying around over an applicant they wouldn't appreciate staying around very much but are much more skilled. Become someone like people would want to talk to, be truly curious about people because that will enhance your living and create many more options than you ever imagined possible.

Be Quick To Acknowledge Your Own Mistakes

Nothing can make you less hostile and more friendly if you are patient enough and fair enough to accept your inner weaknesses. Having good and healthy professional and personal relations depends on you, particularly your shortcomings, taking full accountability of your acts. Nothing would help ease the stress or conflict on your part more than a simple acceptance and apologizing.

Chapter 20: Watch the Behaviour of People

Everybody is distinctive; everybody has different behaviors. What would be more enjoyable than in a café, resting in a park on a bench, or on a terrace, watching other people pass by? Movements, gestures, verbal and nonverbal behavior-you will track anything.

It's interesting to watch people, see their behaviors, and look at their productivity, for many reasons. It's enjoyable but it's very interesting as well. Realizing what inspires people, why they do what they do, and how they respond to the impacts around them would only lead to life quality enhancements.

20.1 People Observation

We called this "people observation" technique because it explains effectively what it actually is. Some of you might think that the language of the body is this.

Perfecting the Body Language: how to notice People's Mind Non verbally

Of course, the purpose of body language is to track and interpret the gestures, but the interpretation of people is not restricted to only that.

Observation of persons builds from the following measures:

Dark Psychology and Manipulation

Body moves

Expressions on face

Language-Conduct

Way of Thought

Political views

Correlations regarding the above

Observation of the People: why and how to do it

Let's say you haven't been so social in the past. You had recognized your issue and was wondering what your choice would be to change that.

You always needed a number of friends. Rather you might be more defined as boring. So for me to become more enjoyable and unexpected you had to modify your own attitudes.

Dark Psychology and Manipulation

First, you began reading regarding body language and habits of action which can show what people think. You got to learn many trends and tried to recognize them in others each time you would go out.

One's greatest challenge would be forcing your eyes wide open each time. You see, it was a little difficult to hold your concentration on other people's gestures, particularly at the start.

You must be cautious to not get too centered while monitoring someone else because you're going to give a weird person's impression. Also, to make associations among their motions and their phrases you must notice what the other people have been saying.

There are two important components of body language. The main body movement (legs, hands, posture, etc.) as well as the expressions.

You could only identify basic moves at the start of the observation. When you were with someone who had performed a specific pattern at a given time, try to confirm their feelings and thoughts at that time the next moment.

You only needed to make sure their actions were relevant compared to what you had been researching. Of course, you did not question people what they felt directly; merely informal questions...

As you are outside keep watching the men. Reach a level at which you could concentrate on your observation at the same time and give full focus to everything else the person told.

Finally, understand that this technique had become a talent stored in the memory system of the procedures. As you practice the technique, you would then understand the process and your subconscious will be able to understand the response of other people even if your focus is not aimed at the strategy.

That's great because you'll have a perpetual instinctive reflex regarding the persons you encounter that will always be right. In conversations with others, you should have an edge and connect easier.

Now we'll see the stages of the technique as well as how the method can be implemented in your daily life.

The "Observation of the People" technique

Expressions

That's the second most popular type of body dialect. Seek to grasp the features of the hands. It can offer you far more info about other people's inner world. Yet they too are more difficult to spot.

One must confess that it really is challenging to understand trends in facial expressions. Initially begin with the fundamentals using the same techniques as the body gestures.

Dark Psychology and Manipulation

You will finally be able to detect various expressions. You have to take the very same measures as you appear to have done with the phase of the movements.

If you achieve a point at that you can interpret other people's body language then you can know how much you have improved your curiosity towards others. This expertise will give a competitive advantage when you interact with others.

A helpful tip to help you understand the language of your body better is to examine one's body movements and sentiments, and how the two to correlate.

This could be your initial body language practice; to interpret your body while communicating with others.

Body moves

Base your attention on many acts, as described earlier. The very first 2 are body language sections.

You have to identify some specific body language moves. Purchasing a good book associated with it will be doing the tactic.

First, learn the main body's movements, so they are easy to identify. That would be an easy starting point. Each time you are outside, strive to remember similar behavior.

Gold is what patience is. There's no purpose in reading the entire book in a week and intending to immediately implement its strategies. That is clearly not feasible.

Note, this is really a process and it involves time and practice for the mind to learn and consciously or unconsciously utilize it. Trust your instincts, then.

Slowly you will be identifying identical patterns every day in different individuals. This situation will cause the linkages between the movement patterns and the feelings in their mind.

When you feel that all the directed movements can be detected easily, continue towards the other one. This is a good way to enhance all body motions and eventually, you'll also be capable of detecting numerous motions and clusters of movement.

The hint is to be patient. It is a People Observation requirement.

Language

Let's use psychology now. Observation of certain people's language and attitudes will give you useful knowledge regarding their personality style.

Notice when they talk to those who use a lot of "me" or "I." That shows a likely focus on one's ego. And also glance for "defensive" expressions because a "defending" behavior may result from the accentuated ego.

People with poor self-esteem are seeking to conceal their actual selves. You can spot them by the dialect they are using.

Dark Psychology and Manipulation

In a fictional scenario, they usually exaggerate and stress how they might react. The reality of course is distinct in several cases.

Observing the words people are using, you will tell that they are healthy, evil, emotional, or just if they have psychological problems or a traumatic childhood background.

You have to relate all those characteristics to the language they use.

20.2 Watching the Behavior

Have you really sat and watched in a restaurant that has different people tables? It will not only be fascinating people observing, it may even be analysed into human patterns. Will an individual at one table control the discussion, raising their arms in violent hand motions while another participant sits mutely, listening to and absorbing what other person is saying? Do people at a different table appear to be drenched in a conversation that might cross on an assertion? What does all of this mean?

It is important to consider the various behavioral styles first, in order to better understand the complexities in play. Most individuals are on a lifetime search for one of the following things: outcomes, communication, reliability, or factual information, and this search influences how they most of the time behave. This doesn't imply someone who is pushed by results also doesn't appreciate interconnection or reliability; it just means that people often have one style of behavior and attitude which appears to be more dominant than others. Public observation of these styles can give you a pretty good idea of how particular persons are connected and how they act the way they do.

Real-world experience in a restaurant

Identifying a few of the cognitive patterns in effect can be relatively easy at a normal restaurant. The immersive individual will ask them their name when the server first welcomes them, want to know a little bit about them as well find out for how long they've been working here. They will connect with the server. They tend to talk quickly with plenty of gestures and always, first and primarily, consider the individual they are communicating to. While they're going to interact a lot and lead the discussion, they're going to be mindful of having the other individual in mind, preventing any contact that's too overt.

This is the doers that are motivated by performance. They directly communicate, are fast-paced as well as appear to have been task-oriented. Those people would typically be there on the phone pre or post buying their meals, emailing, or text attempting to increase their performance. Chances are, instead of full sentences, the messages will be given with simple sentences or bullet points because results-oriented individuals would like stuff done now. They'll definitely know just whatever they like to consume before the waitress comes to the table so they'll be eager about placing the order.

The calm person is going to be respectful and comfortable, not hasty. They're going to make the waiter chat about food offerings, regular sales and they're going to have some informal talking. Not wanting to offend the server, that much if they know it already what they will be ordering, the consistent individual might ask the server's opinion on a meal. Communication could even start with phrases like "if you don't bother," "if it isn't too enough distress," or "I absolutely despise disrupting" with others at the table in an attempt to lighten the straightforwardness. The seekers for stabilization and doing anything in one's control not to toe the line. They are stagnant directed than in the first 2 categories but they target the people like the engaging group. if this had been a sports betting table rather than a cafe, those will be the individuals to witness even though they prefer to keep one's emotions under control and typically show one's devilish smile.

The individual based on facts seems to be task-oriented as well as operates at a moderate speed, involved with knowing the appropriate details before continuing. This person should be one of those at the table to question what components are in any meal, side dish and sauce and how they could be replaced, changed, or omitted or not. They are trying to ask why a certain seasoning is being used with a certain meal and, oddly enough, they are going to be the last person to order at the table, taking their chance to create their ideal decision. Since these decisive conversationalists are far less worried about inconveniencing someone than to be wrong, those who will pose questions till they feel at ease that they have all the details they need to resolve a scenario, even if it is merely placing an order.

The discussion will probably be fascinating with those 4 personality types sitting at a table. The participatory person will significantly contribute the discussion obviously but would then do so ideologically in an attempt to earn acquaintances. The facts and results will be more straightforward and will be the candidate most likely to say stuff that could be considered rude either to the participatory or reliable person. The outcomes individual may analyze a great thing they have during a discussion and the conspiracy theories-based individual will ask several more "why" queries to effectively understand the subject of the discussion. The queries may get annoying for the result-oriented individual who really doesn't wish to have to clarify their self in this

detail.

The steady speaker will place everyone else first and notice their social skills, doing their finest at the table to listen to it and comprehend the other viewpoints. The person guided by the results would be the first one to look at their watch, curious to know when the meal will eventually be presented.

Tolerance is not a core value for the person guided by the outcomes. The participatory individual would have to contend with the desire to control the discussion. By now, the person on the basis of facts has calculated their meal's calorie count yet to show up.

Mannerisms

The results-driven people's body language is easy to identify: standing hand in pocket, going to lean forward, walking briskly and speaking with tons and tons of the over-emphasized hand movements. Now, those who want the details and the very first time they would like to listen to it right. The participatory person tries to switch his weight a lot and in a discussion, his hands seem to be everywhere. This person will most likely bump into someone or something when strolling, and they're too busy to look at all the individuals around. Expect plenty of large movements and facial expressions from such jovial people while having a conversation.

Body language signs for the stable person involve slouching with the hand in the pocket, strolling at such a comfortable, constant speed, and the infrequent gesture all through discussion. For the reality-driven person, body language indications include having to stand with their arms rolled up onto their chin with one hand whilst they process the information. They walk in a specific horizontal path and when interacting they have next to no hand gestures, rather opting to stay very restrained as they soak up the details around them.

20.3 Conflicts between different types of behavior

The individual who enjoys to actually debate larger picture notions can quickly become irritated by the person asking a lot of follow-up questions (generally the fact grabber), needing a much more clear analysis of how everything is in the manner it is. Fact seekers will ask lots of questions and feel stress unless they fully answer the questions to their satisfaction. Likewise, based on their pace, the slow and gradual individual may well be placed off (and conversely) by the outcomes thoughtful person. The person who results wants answers right now, and when it feels right, the stable individual gets around to the catchphrase. The intensity of each person will generate unease for other individuals.

Dark Psychology and Manipulation

When it comes to discussion two participatory individuals at the very same table will start competing for superiority. Like two dogs struggling for alpha dog position, the other persons involved, such as the server, would find it challenging to get a word in mid-sentence.

The individual who is high in solidity would generally get along well with somebody who is social since they respect people and appreciate them. And it produces a complementary dynamic because the engaging individual likes to chat and when the urge hits, the calm person is fully satisfied tossing into a thought.

The person focused on the evidence would possibly also get on well with a stable individual well. The steady person does not need to pose a ton of queries; they become difficult to comprehend. The truths-based individual will directly communicate, while the calm person will try to smooth the discussion with comments that render the contactless straightforward. Possibilities are, both, just like social and calm individuals, would be complimentary too.

Chapter 21: How To Get Rid Of Manipulative People?

Some people in this world only exist and flourish because they are constantly using someone to their benefit in order to get ahead. Manipulators have the capacity to make someone else feel as if they've been supposed to pay something, but often pounce on hard-working, unselfish people who are more likely to be manipulated in their job. If you're in a situation where somebody is attempting to sway you, notice: You all are your own individual. Don't let anyone leave you feeling any differently.

21.1 Techniques

Addressing the Issue

The very first strategy for dealing with a devious person is to realize that you're being exploited, either in a job or in your private life. Such people will consider you to drift everything that you do when they need help and are extremely overwhelming in their requirements for help. They don't see your requirements in the least bit while they require you to do something, and they see their requirements as the highest concern. If you realize co-workers or so-called mates putting their own needs ahead of yours, then immediately start to take measures to sabotage their efforts.

Dark Psychology and Manipulation

Inquire

Manipulators will try to even get you to do things with hardly any questions raised for them. So when you ask them a question it changes the power balance to your side so very marginally. Ask them how or why a quest would help all interested participants, or whether they really believe it is fair what they are looking for. If they are honest they will have to admit they are a little irrational or nonsensical. If they choose not to be truthful, you've shifted control even further to your own side, as there's no justification to do something for someone who is less than true to you.

Retain Strong

In older person clothing manipulators just are pricks. They are preying on those they feel would not speak-up for themselves and they think they will still get whatever they want. Manipulators, however, lose power completely once their perpetrator is standing up for their rights before them. They're so used to getting their bidding accomplished for them that they also have no clue what to do if someone disregards their requirements. They will often try and influence your decision by standing firm against such a manipulator. Don't let them do it. Only you can control yourself; compromising just once can lead to a slippery slope where aggressors are constantly victimizing you.

Use your time to benefit

Manipulators start making demands as well as enforce time limits which cause major pressure to their perpetrators. But it's your time. If someone you know tries to take benefit of you, demands that you complete the task over a certain amount of time, inform them that you will "think about it." Doing so is as useful as completely tearing them down. In reality, going to string them along turns the table on the deceiver entirely, because they would be the ones looking for you to learn. Of course, you do not want to be the manipulator, but allowing the aggressor a dose of their very own medicine can't harm your own purpose.

Set repercussions

The demands that manipulators enforce on others who are mandates which must be fulfilled in their eyes. They're going to be doing their utmost to make it feel that you owe something to them, and have to do what they're doing. In fact, it's they who might owe you when you do such individuals this massive favor. Make that absolutely clear to those people. This works particularly if you do have other regulations that need your urgent attention. If they find that they are going to end up getting to do something in exchange for you, they would more than likely retract their demand. Although they will possibly try and find another target instead of actually

finishing the work on their own, you have at least managed to get them off you.

Conclusion

Dark psychology is a concept of human cognition and an analysis of the human experience as it refers to the psychological essence of people to prey on others driven by psychopathic, psychopathological or deviant criminal impulses that transcend intent and basic principles in instinctual forces, scientific theory, and evolutionary biology. Most of mankind has an ability to victimize many living beings and humans. Although a number of people suppress or sublimate this urge, certain people regularly execute such urges. Dark psychology investigates the personalities of deviants, terrorists, and people doing cybercrimes. Dark psychology is the capacity of manipulating the emotions of people. We also have this power and consciously and unknowingly make use of it too. This is a mental game where we compete with the emotions, desires, experiences, etc. of certain individuals in order to fulfill oneself by attaining desirable goals. We can say, for example, that a salesman is very genuinely enthusiastic about selling his products to the client while using dark psychology to influence the clients. He is deliberately doing so. On the other side, an egoistic person plays the game of one's subconscious to unknowingly satisfy the needs of others. Dark psychology which occurs unknowingly can be quite dangerous as it can deeply affect the feelings of others. It's not healthy to deliberately refer to someone, too.

Dark Psychology and Manipulation

Manipulation of darkness is an incredible weapon that can control darkness or mist. That is the reverse of the Manipulation of Light. This superpower's users can build, form, and control the shadow or darkness for different degrees of results, shapes, sizes, and intensities. Based on the degree of energy, one can easily use this amazing force to shroud an entire region, nation, or even this planet in everlasting darkness for the whole time. Besides that, this capacity is as productive as one wishes and relies on the consumer for its control.

We are knowingly seeing dark psychological strategies in our daily lives. The manipulators secretly strike us and we couldn't even know it. Manipulators use techniques in that matter, consciously. Some secret manipulators deliberately say and do stuff for influence and leverage to have what they want to get.

The methods of coercion include implicit violence, narcissistic bullying, criticism, and indirect kinds of emotional harassment. These are the guns that are commonly used:

Having the remorse and the embarrassment sound

Comparing you against another

To deceive and refute

What you favor

Complaining about you

Should not think

Dark Psychology and Manipulation

Emotional blackmail

Showing sympathy

Playing around in your subconscious

To apologize

Those techniques are used for awareness by manipulators. These toxic tricks can be traumatic to you, and can also harm your self-worth. We will figure out how to negotiate with selfish and challenging people for our own self-protection.

There are good and bad aspects of any single event in this universe. If we can use dark psychology to influence the minds of people for the betterment of human civilization, that's going to be great. There are too many sinister psychological strategies for someone to exploit. We can use these techniques with ease and of course knowledge. We have to remember that while using tricks, not to be the reason for any kind of harm to others.

Below are a few tactical strategies and suggestions for controlling the minds of the people. Let's use them for craft:

Smile While Speaking: It will make people feel relaxed with you and open up to you.

Eye contact: This helps to make you sharp and smart in front of others. People are going to be treating you and your expressions seriously.

Dark Psychology and Manipulation

Being nice to others: Say "hello" to your neighbors as well as others you know and maintain yourself as a well-behaved person before them

Making people happy: When you intend to manipulate someone's mind you will be able to make them happy because laughing makes them comfortable.

Keep quiet: If you don't ask for more information, keep silent then the other individual will automatically fill your thirst. On the other side, if you decide to resist others while being quiet, he/she will quit bothering you.

Help others feel comfortable around you: Say the names of others with love when communicating. Do not ever make a circumstance humiliating. Give them an opportunity to try to understand.

Start arguing: Don't really attempt to reason because you realize he/she is thinking anything, don't mention anything outright. Let them stop and try using constructive terms to get them to realize the truth.

Handling a hostile person: Stay silent and only use the very thing that would explicitly assault him/her. That way he/she is going to be monitored.

So the deep ideology and deception can function like this.

References

24 Rules Used In The Dark Art Of Seduction. Retrieved from https://www.businessinsider.com/robert-greenes-the-art-of-seduction-2014-5#choose-the-right-victim-1

4 Ways To Psychologically Manipulate Someone. Retrieved from https://www.lifehack.org/306016/4-ways-psychologically-manipulate-someone

Retrieved from https://www.shapironegotiations.com/what-is-emotional-influence-and-how-does-it-affect-sales/

Clark, D. How to identify someone's behavior from a distance. Retrieved from https://blog.ttisi.com/how-to-identify-someones-behavior-from-a-distance

Dark Psychology & Manipulation: Are You Unknowingly Using Them?. Retrieved from http://drjasonjones.com/dark_psychology/

How To Regain The Upper Hand In Your Relationship. Retrieved from https://www.yourtango.com/2015267725/8-ways-regain-the-upper-hand-in-your-relationship

Manipulation: Recognising and Responding to It - Counselling Connection. Retrieved from https://www.counsellingconnection.com/index.php/2019/06/28/manipulation-recognising-and-responding-to-it/

Manipulative people: 6 things they do (and how to handle them). Retrieved from https://hackspirit.com/manipulative-people-6-things-they-do-and-how-to-handle-them/

Mullin, S. Emotional Persuasion: The Advanced Guide | CXL. Retrieved from https://cxl.com/blog/emotional-persuasion-guide/

The Stealthiest Predator. Retrieved from https://www.psychologytoday.com/us/articles/201805/the-stealthiest-predator

Three of The Easiest Ways to Manipulate People into Doing What You Want. Retrieved from https://lifehacker.com/three-of-the-easiest-ways-to-manipulate-people-into-doi-5953183

Three Techniques to Read People. Retrieved from https://www.psychologytoday.com/us/blog/emotional-freedom/201402/three-techniques-read-people

Us, A. Dark Psychology - Dark Side of Human Consciousness Concept. Retrieved from https://www.ipredator.co/dark-psychology/

Win Friends & Persuade People With Help from Dale Carnegie. Retrieved from https://www.blinkist.com/magazine/posts/how-to-win-friends-persuasive-techniques

Dark Psychology and Manipulation

Dark Psychology and Body Language

How to Explore the Secrets of the Mind, NLP and body language, dark psychology and emotional manipulation

By

Stephen Tower

Dark Psychology and Manipulation

© Copyright 2020 by (Stephen Tower) - All rights reserved.

This document is geared towards providing exact and reliable information in regards to the topic and issue covered. The publication is sold with the idea that the publisher is not required to render accounting, officially permitted, or otherwise, qualified services. If advice is necessary, legal or professional, a practiced individual in the profession should be ordered.

- From a Declaration of Principles which was accepted and approved equally by a Committee of the American Bar Association and a Committee of Publishers and Associations.

In no way is it legal to reproduce, duplicate, or transmit any part of this document in either electronic means or in printed format. Recording of this publication is strictly prohibited and any storage of this document is not allowed unless with written permission from the publisher. All rights reserved.

The information provided herein is stated to be truthful and consistent, in that any liability, in terms of inattention or otherwise, by any usage or abuse of any policies, processes, or directions contained within is the solitary and utter responsibility of the recipient reader. Under no circumstances will any legal responsibility or blame be held against the publisher for any reparation, damages, or monetary loss due to the information herein, either directly or indirectly.

Respective authors own all copyrights not held by the publisher.

The information herein is offered for informational purposes solely, and is universal as so. The presentation of the information is without contract or any type of guarantee assurance.

The trademarks that are used are without any consent, and the publication of the trademark is without permission or backing by the trademark owner. All trademarks and brands within this book are for clarifying purposes only and are the owned by the owners themselves, not affiliated with this document.

Introduction:

Dark psychology consists of various mental-control, manipulation, and coercion techniques. Some consider it a concept of human consciousness that can be used to control and manipulate others for malicious, devious, and narcissistic reasons. Some recognize it as an acquired skill utilized by humans since ancient times, just before known history. The people in this following category find this ability set to be one that comes beyond the usual spectrum of human actions and which will profit human beings from knowing more.

In addition, dark psychology really not so normal to the abused individual. Many individuals who are exploited from a narcissist or someone else performing the dark psychological practices are wary of being intruded upon. This is also the secret to recognizing the dark psychology: to realize that the vulnerable individuals are predators whose desires and well-being are deemed subordinate to those of the abuser. That dark psychology reflects a common form of human activity is a question that needs to be more discussed because that is the premise on which many professionals of this dark work rely to argue for their activities.

Dark Psychology and Manipulation

The fact is, only pure manipulation and intimidation come under the dark psychology umbrella. It is the simple gadgets practitioners use for comical purposes in their work. One of the very first aspects readers should find is that in an analysis of this topic, semantics is becoming a quick problem. Practitioners of dark psychology take part in the persuasion that some might consider not so harmful or sick-intentioned just like manipulation, so why is there a difference? Indeed, most interpretations of coercion left the difference in muddy waters between this word and coercion.

Have you ever gone into a meeting thinking so sure in yourself, then come out feeling frustrated again having no good explanation of why the other party should believe you? Did you ever come out from a discussion and decide to do it with someone, just couldn't work out why you first accepted? Probabilities are, you manipulated. If you were acting with your impulses by use convincing terms, you were conditioned to act on or behave on what you originally were not completely comfortable with. Until you started the discussion, you should be completely persuaded and so certain of yourself, but halfway, you noticed yourself forgetting thoughts, frustrated, disoriented, and frazzled.

Manipulation may sound as if you're being manipulated, and left your own skills in question. Being constantly manipulated can end up leaving you upset, demotivated as well as

Dark Psychology and Manipulation

despondent and wonder how you have not seen this coming. Nevertheless, have you really avoided it if you realized how to evaluate the signals that show that somebody might not be good?

Manipulators exert their power by taking advantage of your feelings and altering your mental experiences to manipulate and achieve advantages. They are preying on your flaws and going to take benefit of the reader through effective communication meant to mislead you enough so that until it's too late, you don't see what they are. Identifying whether you've been tricked to defend yourself from manipulating is important, and facilitating a healthy power balance in interactions. And it starts with teaching how to evaluate the people.

Another method of telling if you're being tricked would be through facial expressions. The strong, non-speakable, and subtle signs that raise doubts when you understand where to look for. By observing the transmitted movements, facial expressions, and postures, one may recognize and appreciate the full meaning of what somebody is trying to convey -or not trying to say. Learning how to evaluate someone will provide some interesting discoveries, and most significantly, open your mind to the indications that you might be taking advantage of so that you may take action to avoid or fully stop the advancements.

Chapter 1: Delving into dark psychology

All living creatures would look at each other out in a utopian world. Neighbors will be mates, business rivals would not be fierce with their competition, or strangers would be all good. There will be no kidnapping, robbery, or even assassination. Only peace and unity will be fine. You even go about the business without having to think that somebody was trying to use you. You may put your card details unmonitored, and no one will attempt to rob you. It would be the standard to sleep with your open doors and windows as well. There would be no identity theft. Prisons will become unusable, and women would be able to walk throughout the middle of the night without fear of being attacked.

Sadly, this isn't the type of universe in which we live.

In the actual world, people are constantly using and abusing one another. It seems almost like there's every time someone lined up to take benefit of you every spin. In the present era, where an Internet and various other innovations have wiped out geographical constraints, you may be at that much higher risk of becoming prey to other human beings. Not only are the individuals you interact inside the material universe prey on you, and there's also the extra threat from virtual predators. Just enough to think that people have become much more predatory than animals.

Most citizens would have wanted to accept the great of those they know unless proved differently. Just assume about all this. Do you ever believe in them as a great person or a nasty person when you come across a new person? High possibilities are, hopefully, everybody has as kindhearted as you. Which are they won't do any damage to you or to anybody else? If you've been through life thinking everybody is as nice as you, you're at a really high risk of being manipulated as well as the taken benefit of.

Let's just roll back a bit.

When an individual being is raised, it is raised with those intrinsic characteristics that are vital to its existence. For example, a kid came to this world with the potential to cry and get another human to satisfy their requirements. That's why the child actually needs some other individual to cater to them, and they're too small to do anything individually. As such, when it needs to be fed, a baby will cry, cry when it gets to rest, cry when it requires comfort ... cry for almost anything. No one has trained his or her baby to cry — it's a survival technique that came straight out of the womb. When this baby's parents may not set specific limits so far as to respond to the requests of the baby, the child is learning that by crying, it could get almost anything. Thus, it begins manipulation. That is not to say parents are directly responsible for manipulator breeding. While mother and father lead to the improvement of controlling

Dark Psychology and Manipulation

behavior by nature of genetic factors and the type of care provided to children, or absence thereof, there are many other variables at play. We are greedy creatures at the very heart of our existence. Second, we seek the better for us, and then, for others. There's a trend between certain individuals as between the degree of which they're able to move and achieve the greatest for their own. The path is blurry for others, and even sometimes in barely existent. That is when dark psychology starts where the boundary is blurred or doesn't exist.

Dark psychology involves the science of exploitative human behavior in the simplest form. In other phrases, dark psychology uncovers humans to their own advantage, just like they prey on certain human beings. It falls into the far deeper aspects of human nature, where unheard of is empathy, compassion, and kindness. Dark Psychology tries to identify why certain humans seem to have no reservations about causing harm to others as far as they hope to benefit from it. Dark psychology recognizes that not everybody is a good person, even then inclined you could think so, but instead attempts to reply to why that would be the case.

Human predatory action is something that has existed since the start of time. Individual beings have also been preying on one another. That is a consistent fact; just the predation methods alter. Through their predation, human beings usually use two primary networks: intergroup or intragroup, respectively, which are external and internal networks.

1.1 Intergroup vs. Intragroup predation

There are usually inferior and superior parties in any category of individuals, including a family, culture, state, or area, where there are mutual similarities. Often, the supremacy or inadequacy is calculated with what the group of individuals defines to be the same criteria. It could be the economic force, or the social class, for example, or so on. You may always note that the higher groups are preying on, the smaller ones with their own progression. When that happens, the predation of the intragroup is at play. An indication of intergroup predation is a group of businesses developing industry in a suburban area populated by the poorest people. In this case, there are no reservations from the richer segment of society about endangering another less lucky section that is susceptible and easy to prey on.

When a group believes itself equal to some other group and (externally) preys on them, this is considered intergroup predation. It was predation among two groups or more. That is basically what occurred during the conquest when, for their own gain, European countries conquered certain nations that they found weak and uncivilized.

Dark Psychology and Manipulation

You might not even note the predators between you in your daily life. Human prey is indeed very able to blend in with the majority of the people. They seem like ordinary people who lead ordinary lives. Whenever a killing or any other unlawful incident occurs in a community, you'll often hear a community member say about the offender: he really was a decent person, excellently-liked by everyone in town. We would never have suspected he was responsible for such a horrific act. The fact is the suspect wasn't really a good man. He was more frequently than not a pure evil guy dressed as a decent man. The words poor and decent, of course, do little justice in describing the dynamic and sometimes confounding dynamics that play a role in having one want to become a rapist.

Although the creatures may not often be visible in your world, there are a few easy ways to recognize a threat. If you are attentive to the individuals for whom you connect, you'll find it easier to say apart from the positive from the poor ones. This is particularly true when you listen rather than talk. When you listen to and watch, you know more. So, what are the human predator's distinctive trademarks?

1.2 Uncovering a human predator

Your favorite work colleague maybe someone you actually get alongside or anyone who tries to pretend to get along for their advantage. How do you spot a difference?

Dark Psychology and Manipulation

They are extremely cute

Often, the most powerful predators are incredibly cute. They understand how to do the best stuff and tell the right words, and they come off as appealing to anyone else. Relying on their capability to get into the good books of anyone by means of a few excellently-placed smiles and compliments, they come off as extremely likable. When you meet a charmer like that, they'll make you believe you're the core of their world. They would pay attention to you, make you feel unique, and will pull all the breaks to please you. This is an art form learned for many charmers. They had years of experience to render Mr. Charming act great.

When two ordinary humans meet without hidden agendas, the communication that is taking place is natural, occasionally uncomfortable, and often simplistic. That is, rather than deep, sincere conversations, there is probably to be a complete lot of small conversation to fill the silences. The following conversations come after you got to know someone a little deeper. Be aware of someone who tries to divulge charmingly any non-relevant information that prevents them as a perfect human who is unable to make a wrong move. Be aware of anyone who has a great answer to every question. Finally, be careful of someone who appears to pass through social encounters easily. This sort of person could be an excellently-meaning people pleaser, but there's also a risk they're putting on a performance you have to pay a lot for.

Possession is the rule of a day

Have you really come across as someone who acts as though they are owed anything by the world? That kind of person has to have at whatever cost what they want. They'll have a tantrum if they don't, and make us suffer for that too. Human predators are also humans responsible. That explains why they always have no trouble having at any expense what they want — even though it means harming others. The world is in its debt, after all, and this mortgage must be paid back, although it means walking on some or multiple toes along the direction.

At the workplace, privilege is expressed in the case of a friend who thinks they merit a reward for whatever purpose they show back with. This sort of employee would go to considerable efforts to guarantee that the manager offers them the reward they think they've won even though they're barely pulling their loads at the department. They are going to want to make everybody involved feel poor and disrespectful of the promotions. If they don't get their way, and the promotion ends up going to somebody else, they'll take that individual their enemy throughout their life. How can that person take their promotion off after all? It'll never happen to this greedy person because they'll actually have to strive more to increase levels.

They love to be controlled

Dark Psychology and Manipulation

Many people like to have some power over certain parts of life. Wanting to be prepared to contact the shots is natural, within fair limits. The trouble begins when a specific individual feels they have to call all the decisions in their lifetimes and in the lives of others. Many manipulators are Freaks of Control. Many of them would have delicate ways to express that control, but others can't really be bothered to keep it less apparent. If in your life you've got a control freak, you will already realize it. Power freaks are also impossible to ignore due to their tendency to become interested in just about everything at everything. Control freaks in the work environment have a very difficult time deferring to everyone else, even when they need to. They would like to run every show because they understand it's theirs to receive the reward.

The refusal to recognize once they are incorrect is another indication of the control freak. Human beings are subject to mistakes and accepting you are wrong, necessitating a certain amount of graciousness. There is part of a quality that other freaks in power ignore. One explanation people who enjoy being in charge find it challenging to accept mistakes is because they see it as an acknowledgment of being poor, which undermines their idealized version self-visualization that they have been stronger than anyone else. If you are ever involved in a safety obsessed debate, don't hope to succeed. They every time win in every battle that involves the control freak. If they don't win, the victor will become the latest enemy to be vanquished, whatever may come.

Control freaks like to quibble anyone and everyone, too, judging them by the major power they set for oneself. The control freak would have a viewpoint under the sun about anything, even if that opinion is rude and unnecessary for or even unrequested. Their criticism is harsh and frequently makes someone else feel worse. This is a way for them to gain control; if you start making somebody feel inferior and tiny, you have a greater chance of achieving them to fulfill your requirements, whatever they may be.

Command personality is not, as you might have expected, the standard psychiatric word for such people. Rather, it is a word used in casual contexts to define someone who has an intense compulsion to force others to agree with it or to manipulate others. While a requirement for manipulative authority over others motivates this abnormal requirement for control, there are many major causes for this sort of behavior.

Freaks of control also have mental conditions that trigger them to act as they do. A character disability is characterized as a behavior pattern that differs from what is deemed standard practice. To recognize this kind of conduct as a behavioral condition, it must happen regularly, to the point that it is deep-set throughout the existence and everyday decisions of the victim. From time - to - time, everybody has the bad days where

Dark Psychology and Manipulation

they make poor decisions; every day, an adult with a mental illness has a terrible day. Adolescents are also identified with personality issues. For certain cases, it may take longer to arrive at a diagnosis.

There are 3 personality issues that are sufficient to result in a person becoming concerned with being in charge of others. These consist of antisocial personality disorder, personality disorder with histrionics, and personality disorder with narcissism. People with antisocial mental illnesses also have an inflated feeling of self-worth and, if at all, very little concern towards others. Even so, they are also inclined to dominate people without having any type of remorse or empathy. Conversely, people diagnosed with histrionic mental illness crave publicity. They're going to go to whatever extent to compel us to pay heed. They have to be in complete control of the display even though it means hurting to get this type of attention about anything in their lives. Interest is the method to and the result of their control over the others. In short, it's a melody they could even enjoy forever.

Narcissists love power because they think that they are smarter than anyone and that they have the right to control that. There's simply no way a narcissist can get your way. If you're engaging with such a narcissist, whether at a job or in a private partnership, the only thing that you'll ever be able to give is yes.

Narcissists depend on dominance as it nourishes their limitless urge to be the best star of whatever space they are also in.

1.3 Their feelings aren't real

Have you ever met somebody else who looks very generous and kind, but you were told by your instincts not to believe them? It's presumably that the sixth sense might tell that it wasn't all that goodness and empathy. While the mind and heart can be deceived, the keen eye is often able to select out the facts from the lies.

Human predators understand that relationships are beneficial to certain emotions. They know children are very well-liked, and they take generosity to mean a man is good at heart. Predators won't care much about generosity but will go to extraordinary lengths to color the image of perfection they require. They'll show up with home-baked brownies for public meetings. They will get the biggest check at charity events. They always get the brightest, warmest laughs. On the surface, they will become a picture of friendliness and kindness in the community. That's why when they want to unleash their other hand, they still catch people who are unaware — the one that isn't as sweet and not as gracious.

Take a pinch of salt with you when trying to deal with someone who is going to great diameters to defend; they are a very nice person. Beware of what your gut is saying about this individual.

You may be deceived by your eyes and ears, but that internal voice of sanity can still have your back.

1.4 They like sacrifices

One of the effective methods to distract people from your misdeeds is to switch the spotlight on the wrongdoings of another person. Human predators perfected the art of victim playing. It allows them sufficient time to demonize another person while distracting everyone else. An individual playing the victim would never offer an excuse for something they do. Whether they are late, it's because anyone else submitted the invitation to the wrong meeting. If they cheated, this is because their team member wasn't paying enough attention to them. If they hit a further person, it is as they were made so mad by that person that it ended up driving them to brutality. It is always a story or something else.

The fact of the matter is the abuser never becoming the survivor. They also neglect the capacity to be the perpetrator. After all, their livelihoods, as well as those of others, have been orchestrated to suit everyone's own interests. But predators are also aware that some people want to feel sympathy for survivors. As such, as long as it serves them, they should play the victim.

With this awareness of how predators appear, you can wonder what precautions you should take in order to defend yourself.

First of all, it's necessary to remember that this 1st chapter just hits the layer of mind control and the players in it. The chapters that follow should dive further into stripping away the more complex problems at stake. You'll have developed a much greater appreciation at the conclusion of this deep analysis of how manipulators or other mysterious characters work. This knowledge can help you protect oneself and turn the tables accordingly, if necessary. You also can safeguard yourself, that being said, as early as now.

1.5 The basic principles of defending yourselves from human predators

The very first thing to understand is how to recognize the props the predator uses to conceal from you their true personality. That, in the case of lavish presents or unwanted love, maybe artificial goodness and hospitality. Watch out for anyone who finds himself too ideal. A smart man once explained that you might think wisely if the contract is too nice. If a person finds himself to be flawless as well as perfect, it is likely because they wear a mask. If the mask comes off, you're going to be in a lot of trouble.

Dark Psychology and Manipulation

Second, learn oneself in and out so that you can never be fooled by another human. Everyone has its weak spots. If you do not know where one's blind spots are, human predators will be fair game. Predators are just like sharks — one spot of blood, and they're like white on rice all over you. Get to learn where you are bleeding from and hold this awareness locked well away within of you till you are one 100 times confident that this detail can be trusted to a human.

The third way of defending yourself from predators is to use time with your benefit. According to World Bank statistics, the average lifespan in the US in December 2017 was 78, while that figure in Canada was 80. That ensures you have a pretty strong probability of surviving beyond the age of seventy if you stay in one of those areas. So why is everybody so hurried about? By, Unfortunately, we 're living in a society where everybody is in a hurry to get something or go somewhere. In

Dark Psychology and Manipulation

the middle of all this rush, predators are preying on the desperate ones to keep up. If you hurry through stuff, you'll look back and think about all the errors you've made that you might have prevented. Use the moment to your advantage of knowing someone or the ability to understand an expenditure. Predators want to inculcate terror in their victims by letting them believe they are out of time. You really don't run out of energy. Space is with you. Using them wisely. If you stop to contemplate any time you're confronted with a choice, you'll find yourself going much smarter choices and escaping the various pitfalls that the predators around you have developed for you.

Chapter 2: A brief history of dark psychology

Human mythology is riddled with tales of ghosts and creatures that behave in such drastic ways that the very description of them sends chills down the length of the adults that listened to such tales as relayed by past musicians and bards. The creation of monsters advises us that perhaps the universe is not as secure as it might seem from within our window. Beasts live between us and render our lifestyles as something to be protected against, as anything to be protected.

Maybe a creature crawls out from the closet while you rest in your room or slips in from a backdoor that you failed to lock. Maybe you assumed you were over there, but as it enters your door, you listen footprints crackling upstairs and a soft voice roaring. You see a bushy, tail-like foot poking out beneath the bed or a claw. You notice a heavy, malevolent laugh while running for life. You sprint into the shower, and the door is locked. It's not necessarily a stellar exit strategy as there is no window in your toilet, but you didn't know where to get off. Maybe the beast is on the escalators. You don't know where everything actually is. But after that, you push the above head bathroom light chain, and see that you are the monster.

Monsters exist among humans and are medically related to as H. Sapiens ... sapiens. Aliens from some other world did not

Dark Psychology and Manipulation

commit actions of murder, theft, and ruin. They were living things who decided to commit these crimes, and today they also live between us. There is indeed a term in behavioral genetics, the so-called dark chord. This word, which we will later discuss, applies to the three characteristics of psychopathy, narcissism, and sociopathy. Such characteristics are deemed especially harmful, so distinguishing such people from the general public is necessary, or would it be?

An argument could be done that since ancient times human beings were accepting the horrific components of their character. Today we believe of common practices of the ancient history such as orgiastic religious practices, human sacrifice, and ritualized murder as barbaric acts of the past that indicate a better forgotten time, but it has been argued that these acts represent social and cultural outlets for the black universe that lies beneath the beautiful surface of the human outside.

Societies then were organized specifically. This would be up upon you to determine whether things are easier today, or if they are bad. As garish as the aforementioned past practices may have been, their career status within their living area represented an acknowledgment that human beings had a bad side to their personality, and it was great to give outlets to this dark side than to let it explode and simmer in unexpected ways. For what do today's gang stalking, serial murder, cybercrime, and narcissistic as well as antisocial acts portray, but living

Dark Psychology and Manipulation

things give in to ends of themselves because they have previously expressed themselves in other ways?

The argument is not to assert that living things must consider giving in to their so-called dark tendencies of singularity but to recommend that the contemporary art of mind control represents a variety of activities expressed in ancient society in unique ways. Although the conversation of societies' tradition of providing into their character's dark sides may seem incidental to the conversation of mind control, few things could be more essential. A significant phase in planning for defense lies with the understanding that anyone you know may be the perpetrator of these black arts. It could be someone you already understand.

2.1 History of Dark Psychology Study

The 2 social scientific patterns that proactive solutions-day dark psychology are undoubtedly anomalous psychology and psychology for individuals. Irregular psychology is a branch of psychology experiment concerned with psychological illness-related habits of behaviors, emotion, and behavior. These emotions, thoughts, and behaviors can precede a psychiatric disorder and are usually thought abnormal. As psychology tends to construct a relatively linear dichotomy between regular versus abnormal behavior, a sociological factor will come under the scepter between irregular or atypical behavioral forms as opposed to actions assumed to be inside the usual spectrum.

Person psychology is the psychological theory system founded in the early late nineteenth century, centered on human conduct as driven by purposeful activity as compared to latent libido and sex impulses that describe Freudian psychoanalysis. While we have already addressed in some depth the degree to which individual acts are not consciously driven and may thus be viewed as non-purpose, person psychology allows for implicit or involuntary motives, it just appears to recognize them when non-Freudian, benevolent, and even not always implicit.

For example, as a motivating factor for action, Alfred Adler focused many of his texts on superiority complexes. He found that people who handled the situation in angry or otherwise unbecoming ways were generally inspired by a sense of inadequacy, which is a certain sense caused them to "act out." Now in some people, an inferiority complex as an enthusiastic may lie beneath the surface, although others may be fully aware that they have a feature of themselves with which they are not completely satisfied and which they are trying to compensate.

When creating dark psychology as an outgrowth of internal mental ideas as compared to Freudian psychoanalysis concepts, it may be simple to assume that human beings usually act with conscious, deliberate motivations as opposed to being

Dark Psychology and Manipulation

consciously or unconsciously inspired by sexual urges, such as the well-studied complex of Edipus (the desire for a man to kill his father and sleep). In order to truly comprehend the historical growth of dark psychology as a research field, it is crucial to realize that the philosophy of individual psychology requires the form of non-completely aware motives that are required to explain why human beings tend to act in such a cruel fashion. Even so, the theory of dark psychology supposes that humans are capable of a dark universe, engaging in harmful actions that have no purpose at all.

The research and therapy of psychological disorders have been around as a field of study since the Ancient Egyptians, at least. We have more data from the Greek period, partly because we are closer to the Greek philosophy period in time than we are from the Egyptians, and this group just seems to reach the concept of pathology with a fascinating avidity. The research of what we term pathological psychology today existed in the 18th and 19th centuries and earlier in the context of asylum and hospices that diagnosed people and women with irregular mental disorders, but the discipline as we now know it dates from the 20th century in fact.

Indeed, previous to the 19th century, trepanation, exorcism, and being burnt on the stakes as a witch were the standard remedies for pathological mental conditions. Trepanation relates to drilling a hole in the brain to expel malignant spirits

Dark Psychology and Manipulation

from their grip over the head, and it is claimed by others to be the earliest surgical technique we have historical evidence of. Trepanation was already performed in the 19th century, and still today, there are proponents for the procedure, though their appeals usually fell on deaf ears.

Exorcism also looks at how society viewed odd habits and emotions in the current age. Indeed, many habits that we take into account to fall inside the normal range today have been considered mental diseases up till the early 1980s. Exorcism, although maybe less brutal than trepanation, represented the perspective that an evil force or demon inhabited the individual who possessed the weird thoughts and actions. All this really did had been a transmission from the individual's malevolent encouragement to anything else, whether something else was an informant of evil or an agent of evil.

One line of thinking recognizes Satan as the manifestation of human potential to act in a manner "strange" or, more accurately, evil or cruel. It is hard to say as to if their ideas of ghouls, demons, values, or even of Satan himself embody a true fact that people beings were produced to commit acts of possession, or whether they could be better described as stories intended to fool children or to teach them valuable life lessons of good and evil. Of course, exorcisms are still happening today; there are individuals who really assume that evil acts come from ownership.

Dark Psychology and Manipulation

If you believe that the evil committed by human beings comes from a source outside the human being, then dark psychological theory because it currently stands may be somewhat contrary to what you believe. A locally important in dark psychology, however, is the idea that humans are able to behave without purpose in a remarkably violent and cruel manner, simply as an augmentation of something obscure that dwells inside us. It is up to you to ascribe this type of conduct to Satan as a component of your religious views.

Of course, 19th-century and later abnormal psychologists did not fully recognize this idea of an independent factor for the conditions they were seeing, and so treatments such as trepanation or exorcism would've been disconcerting or at least pointless to them. As we commented on earlier, this is a time in which scientists were shifting away towards the doctrinaire beliefs that dominated their careers, ideologies that mostly had more to do with theology than with the professions' own empirical compendia. There is nothing intrinsically inconsistent with religious belief, of course, but a practitioner who is inexperienced with human anatomy if he is not permitted to examine q cadaver is probably to follow a religion that is not advantageous to him (or herself) or you.

Abnormal psychologists started to question why humans were inspired to behave in an abnormal manner, and the Devil or the

Dark Psychology and Manipulation

Demons were not entirely acceptable responses. Most of these research groups in psychological disorders were psychiatrists, as well as psychoanalysts who undertook detailed studies of these subjects on the basis of a new, more free understanding of health matters. Though the word dark psychology did not emerge until later in the mid-twentieth century, narcissists, sociopaths, and those who we might identify today as possessing mental illnesses were conducted already throughout the 19th-century studies.

Abnormal psychology of that time would have followed the trend of what we now understand as Freudian psychoanalysis, with Alfred Adler 's writings representing one of Freudian's first major departures. Although Adler is today a virtually unknown figure, his biographies from the generations 1912-1914 provided the basis of many of the concepts that pervade the psychological field today. His writings were translated into English in 1925, and his personality beliefs and where they derive from predominate in advance psychotherapy and psychoanalysis.

Adler focused on resignation, compensation, and over-compensation as the 3 external factors that shaped the development of personality. His theories parallel those of another essential psychologist, Abraham Maslow, who acknowledged Alder 's influence on his own work. Although Adler himself didn't even write about "dark psychology," his theories helped shape this topic's development as a departure from pre-existing psychoanalytical theories

The analysis of dark psychology can be new, but it reflects a spectrum of habits that have been associated with individuals since the very start. Even so, the dark area of psychology provides the illusion of a transient domain of research, as the word and the principles connected with it are more widely available to the people. This has turned dark psychological into a topic that remains quite beyond the radar of those that may be the victim of perpetrators exploiting their resources to damage impact. Dark psychology is an uncommon field in that it includes both those professionals who teach their art as a sequence of tools that can be used by manipulators as well as narcissists, as well as those minds who seek to arm possible targets in defense.

2.2 Famous historical manipulators

History is riddled with stories of people and women who have exploited what we all know for dark psychology to inflict tremendous power and hurt over others. In fact, these skills are so prevalent and so outdated that may be the most proficient professionals must remain nameless at all times. Although the narcissist may try to announce the tremendous harm they have performed to others as a means to flaunt their own superiority, an entity behaving of the dark universe, or a person talented

Dark Psychology and Manipulation

enough in dark psychology to recognize when to remain quiet regarding their methods, such persons may usually not be identified to the public.

But it helps to know how dark psychological instruments can take effect by analyzing those who used them and those who fell, the victim. These practitioners' names are numerous and easy to quote, although one may get into the pitfall of decreasing complex individuals to one-trick ponies with the description 'narcissist' or 'sociopath.' Grigorii Rasputin, for example, was certainly a practitioner and manipulator of dark psychological art par quality, but he was a 'mystic,' 'holy,' 'lover' and maybe one of the most interesting.

Rasputin is, of course, an interesting case because he wasn't personally accountable for the kind of relevant death tolls a Ted Bundy or indeed a Jim Jones is. Some are willing to draw publicity into dark psychology by figuring men like these out as illustrations of the art as it enables them to draw interest in the topic. Most people are keen to learn how men like Ted Bundy, as well as Jim Jones, are produced in society. Ted Bundy himself said famously that males like him were like husbands, brothers, sons, and the like all around him. This is the kind of statement designed to send shivers down the leg of American citizens who have to arrive to see the world as tense with every kind of danger outside of their window.

Dark Psychology and Manipulation

In truth, the universe is fraught with risk, but the manipulator needs to stain in your mind just this kind of paranoia. As we mentioned in our discovery of the psychological foundations of dark psychology, this art practitioner may have an intentional desire to ruin you or act from a depth well of violent behavior. Whatever their inspiration, instilling so deep into the victim a paranoia that the victim sees each interaction as a dangerous and unpredictable opponent is one of the most powerful tools in the toolkit of the manipulator.

This technique works very well because every interaction is a possibly dangerous one, but every person you meet may be an opponent ready to attack, but it's a psychotic idea that doesn't really arise with the goal but is harmful to the target. Being ready to defend yourself against dark psychological techniques doesn't mean behaving like having a psychological symptom or another severe anxiety condition. If this is how you act, therefore the predator has managed to win. They've turned you into prey that's always thought, and that action stems from worry. They can detect and love this fear upon you.

It was thought Grigorii Rasputin had the ability to hypnotize and heal. He was able to cure his hemophilia's Tsarevich Alexey simply by putting his hands on the boy. While some historians contested that Rasputin currently possessed this ability, others asserted that he might well have possessed the ability to hypnotize and that he'd have placed the prince in a kind of

Dark Psychology and Manipulation

trance-like state that triggered relaxation and basically represented control of the mind. Because of his capacity to repair the inherited affliction of the head of state, during the darkest chapters of Russian imperial events of world war I, Rasputin was able to gain influence over the Russian state. Since the Tsarina might have considered itself responsible for the hemophilia of her son as she had carried the mutation to him via her Hanoverian ancestors, it would have been specified.

As will be further explored in the next section, individuals in a weak state run the risk of being attacked by a narcissist and manipulator who can precisely size a male or female up. While we may not believe in narcissists, psychos, or manipulators as mentally smart individuals, these kinds of individuals do have emotional awareness that allows them to be attuned to other people's subjective emotional responses. What all these people lack is self-regulation and compassion with the emotions. It is this lack of compassion that prevents a meaningful identification with you by the Machiavellian, narcissist person, or psychopathic person. This emotional barrier enables them to consider you as a prey to their attack.

It's vital to know that prey is just that prey in the dark psychological game. Just as a gorilla, lion, and perhaps other wild animal prey to individual members who are weak, young, injured, and otherwise at an unfairness, so does the deceiver help to recognize these aspects of others and use them to

Dark Psychology and Manipulation

determine who would make better prey who could not. The connection here is simply that of predator and prey in the end. Even though one may well be inclined to see others that one fulfills as people with a harmless benefit in you, during these interactions, the predator dimensions you up to determine what prey you are doing and how best to strike.

There is a question as to whether Rasputin was truly a manipulator, or whether history has unfairly maligned him. Figures similar to the Russian government believed that Rasputin had improperly limited access to the Romanovs and that he was privy to that information that somebody in his condition – that is, a serviceman with no role in government – should not be private to him. Rasputin came to an end his days by killings at the grip of Prince Felix Yusupova as well as Grand Duke Dmitri Pavlovich, Tsar Nicholas II's cousin. Although Rasputin was probably a hypnotherapist, narcissist, and usually unfriendly person, history will never know whether he still influenced everyone else to behave in a sinister manner or taped himself into a well of dark singularity.

There are some that are less disturbed about this evaluation. Jim Jones that inspired his followers of cults into an act of public execution, is considered a powerful narcissist and manipulator who maybe represents the kind of narcissism that is considered Machiavellian. The Machiavellian type appears to believe he or she is above the ordinary human cut, and thus the

Dark Psychology and Manipulation

law does not apply to each other as they would implement to somebody else. This is a Napoleonic sort who is always possessed of tremendous wisdom and skill, and often assumes that the capacity to reshape the universe or life in some form has been delegated to them by nature.

These people are extremely harmful because their intellectual powers, capacity, or charisma can trigger someone to have followers who act as they bid without ever really comprehending that these rulers are, in fact, narcissistic or antisocial individuals who are motivated on a major level by intentions that are only clear to them. This is one of the quandaries of mind control, an area that may well be shed lighter on by those researching it in the future. An individual who is motivated to manipulate others or force them into harmful actions is behaving with a will, not with destructive energy represented by dark singularity. But the people who often follow them are inspired by the dark energy they've tapped into so that the evil actor has become entrapped of a different kind of evil than his agents. What sort of bad is greater than this?

There are abundant examples of mind control, and listing the others all would be out of this book's scope. A dramatic example from Hollywood reveals that though well hidden, dark psychological procedures are common. A collective in California named NXIXM in which the chief forced and exploited people to make up for him emotionally, have sex with them, and even branding itself was named mind control. As this research would later discuss, intentional actions may often be branded as mind manipulation after the fact by people who are compelled to separate themselves from contentious activities. What is obvious is that the elements of Machiavellianism and Machiavellianism were involved. These 2 individuals of the dark triad are significant in the analysis of mind control, and helping men and women target individuals like this is an essential part of this field.

Chapter 3: Manipulation and persuasion basics

Dark Psychology and Manipulation

The images of men such as Jeffrey Dahmer or Ted bunny come to mind when some people think dark psychology or its practitioners, but the shocking idea of this black art is that the ability to engage in it lies in us all. Dark psychology followers maybe your bosses, your important others, members of your families, or even your acquaintances. And this point is not about the actions of particular narcissists with a propensity to do harm. A fundamental theory in dark psychology is that individuals at the community level may be inspired by no cause whatsoever to act with destructive force.

From a historical viewpoint, we have seen the dimension of

dark psychology. We have seen how modern communities of the past taped human beings' dark tendencies, and how more modern nations brushed these traits under the rug or transformed them into skeletons in the wardrobe that could pop out when they were least wanted or expected. Indeed, we argued in the first chapter that such a hypocritical approach to dark psychology is likely one of the main reasons why males and females tend to be prey to their strategies. When we claim that human beings are nice but only evil people like Ted Bundy do negative stuff, it opens you up to be prey to an ex-lover who likes to manipulate you to end your life or fellow workers who turn the whole office against you just because they can.

You need to realize that everyone may be a manipulator to protect against exploitation. It can be called the most fundamental type of dark psychology, however, loaded and maligned the word deception can be. Some manipulation books begin with an attempt to sterilize the word, persuading the listener that manipulation is mere "persuasion" as everyone participates in it. While it may be true that anyone wants to engage in manipulation, it is not completely correct that manipulation is normally something that everyone does, basic or harmless. As you will see, or perhaps already understand, the manipulator can do great harm.

The first phase in learning to know about coercion is recognizing that a variety of behavior may be protected by this word. In addition, the difference between coercion or persuasion is at least in part a theoretical problem. In the next part, persuasion will be addressed more but it is commonly regarded as the power to persuade others. Manipulation relates to the methods of manipulating certain people's actions and emotions. Therefore, the distinction among manipulation or persuasion is really a concept which generally views persuasion as benevolent and usually beneficial or manipulation as devious and potentially harmful.

3.1 Psychological Manipulation

The word psychological manipulation is often used to relate to the act of manipulating the thoughts and actions of another person by psychological techniques which others may find mysterious. In reality, the most method includes some sort of psychological tactic, although that strategy is merely positively or negatively reinforcement. Just a conditioning strategy requires manipulating the other individual's neuronal network since it ultimately includes imprinting a trait into a mechanism of incentive and punishment. This structure of rewards and sanctions establishes a relationship within the brain of the individual during a normal act and the consequent positive or negative outcome.

If we embrace that all manipulation is physiological, since it involves trying to access the capacity of human beings to identify stimuli from outside oneself and create a connection between things, then we are rendered with the scenario of failing to differentiate the bad manipulation from maybe not so bad ones. An often-applied classified scheme is to split coercion between ethical coercion and immoral manipulation. This section acknowledges the reality of deception: that while we sometimes equate coercion with malicious intent, there are individuals who exploit in order to help us, rather than with any hidden purpose lies deep down within.

Most people will read this and get some concept of what ethics means. Ethics is the reading of beliefs about wrong and right and since at least traditional times, people have been researching and composing about ethics. In manipulation, ethics provides an additional distinction because it affects what

Dark Psychology and Manipulation

the inspiration for manipulation is. If manipulation is conducted for the reason of doing anything positive with either the consequent act and the purpose for the encouragement falling within appropriate standards of good actions in the social structure then that is taken as ethical manipulation. If motivation is to harm others, or if an act outcome in harm even when there is no specific motivation for it then this might be termed immoral manipulation.

Immoral manipulation is indeed a weapon in dark psychological art practicer's arsenal. It is a weapon that is truly a toolbox full of its own firearms. As the reader will recognize at this moment, an evil deed need not be undertaken with an intention that is necessarily evil. And by this we don't mean the purpose that is obvious to all concerned people, we mean just every aim, including implicit ones. As we have seen, living creatures have the ability to behave in a violent, cruel, or destructive manner without any inspiration, and this shows human beings' ability to tap into a sinister energy well.

If you are studying this even though you are involved in protecting against coercion then you need to be secured from immoral exploitation. Manipulation was defined, and it is essential to note that this term shows a variety of activities used to control other people's actions or beliefs. It is necessary to emphasize this dimension of attitudes, as while the acts that are affected can be the most obvious indication of a manipulation impact, the manipulator also approaches the person's emotions that they try to control as they are the performers that contribute to behavior.

Recognizing manipulation throughout this manner makes it possible for the reader to admire that persuasion could be harmful as the result of this tactic can be influenced by beliefs. Yet persuasion is just one technique in the deceptive arsenal. Below we mention some of the activities under the framework of coercion that a manipulator may indulge in:

- One-trial behavior
- Reinforcement
- Seduction
- Rationalization
- Punishment
- Bandwagon effect

Some individuals have fairly amorphous, deceptive thoughts. They perceive it as a technique or strategy some individuals use to force others to give them what they need. Though, manipulation is not without shape. Manipulation can be viewed as a series of strategies rather than only one and both of them may be employed in a drastic manner to manipulate others. Punishment allows for a basic kind of exploitation. While punishment intersects with constructive reinforcement, it is a strategy typically used for incentive intervention when punishment doesn't generally have a purpose to promote a behavior.

A manipulator, for example, can "punish" you to render you mentally vulnerable, demotivated, or because they are happy to do so. It may be challenging for someone to relate or understand, but it is not necessary for a manipulator or narcissist to have a goal in giving their victim punishment. Their aim might be to degrade you to such a condition as to make you easy to be vulnerable to their violence, or they might act against you only because they can. While one may think of sanction as having a specific purpose in the sense of manipulation, sentencing may be a part of a broader continuum of manipulative habits which together serve the purpose of leaving you destabilized and dependent.

A further significant method of coercion is reinforcing. Reinforcement connects actions to a consequence, so if you do anything the manipulator likes, they can either reward you or punish you instead. The first form, positive encouragement, is intended to validate or promote action by connecting it to something in your head that is good. This positive outcome or recompense may be anything: food, income, age, care. The manipulator might have interpreted you correctly enough to evaluate what you value in their manipulation plan so that they can use it. Indeed, manipulators depend on data you give people

Dark Psychology and Manipulation

so among the most valuable defense tools is to keep that stuff about yourself because others need not know for themselves.

Bad reinforcement often ties actions to an outcome, although the effect is bad in this situation. A manipulator may use any retribution to discourage your behavior. In some countries it is common for factory managers to condemn their employees by cutting employee working hours, paying workers late, or stalking them for talking about employment conditions. The purpose of manipulative negative behavior in this example is to dissuade complaints, limit individual thoughts and actions, and create fear.

If reinforcement is negative or positive, the goal will be the same: to put you deeper under the manipulator 's control. Manipulators are going to behave in a predatory way so any leniency you offer them is simply encouraging them to continue their manipulative tactics. For example, once the manipulator finds their methods succeeding, they would be likely to go on with this procedure. This may be that they have a hidden purpose for you that they intend to achieve, or that they are manipulative or psychopathic and seek to impose suffering or mental illness on you.

3.2 Why human beings manipulate others

This naturally leads to an important component of manipulation that needs to be addressed. The question of why

Dark Psychology and Manipulation

people exploit others has been focused on but in the sense of dark psychology, there is a special dimension of this issue. Manipulation doesn't necessarily need to be unethical, as we have seen. For ethical reasons, manipulators may engage in their actions, generally with an urge to affect others in what they interpret in a positive manner. The query of whether it is ever positive to influence others to do what you need them to do would be outside the range of this project. This will be up upon you to make a decision whether someone else's desires supersede your own urge or necessity for the agency, even if they're well-intentioned.

Yet a prevalent concept of coercion is this belief that the manipulator needs you to do whatever they want you to do. And someone who manipulates you for ethical purposes requires you to act in a way compatible with your own beliefs. The theory of motivation is significant in dark psychology, as it represents the psychological principles of purposeful and destructive behavior. The issue with manipulation really is either the manipulator behaves out of narcissism, out from the power to dominate you, or out of broader, compulsive reasons.

Even putting aside situations where the manipulator wishes to impact you because they recognize some ultimate benefit for themselves, the primary objective of manipulation is still in control. Either you or the manipulator is able to take action that has a purpose and that represents free faith. The manipulator wants to utilize their free will to have your act in the way they choose. Even if their intentions appear benign or optimistic, they still have the goal of controlling because they look at their own needs and wants is paramount to their own.

Thus, what a manipulator truly wants is control. Even if you are engaging with your dog in a negative or positive reinforcement scheme, the aim is still to handle the dog's actions. You don't want the puppy to run onto the bed so that you can beat him. You're pleased as the dog finds the thing you've tossed and you're going to praise him. Using manipulation, you control your dog's actions and so does the manipulator try to dominate someone else using the tools available to them.

3.3 Standard traits of a Manipulator

The characteristics of an unethically behaving manipulator will coincide with features associated with the personality traits of the dark triad. The dark triad of Machiavellianism, narcissism, and psychopathy symbolizes types of personality falling into a dangerous spectrum. These are people who participate in the wanton destruction and harm of people irrespective of the consequences. These people would be implanted with personality disorders such as a narcissistic character disorder, personality disorders, or a psychiatrist's borderline personality disorder.

Some features of manipulators include:

Dark Psychology and Manipulation

- Disregard for other people's feelings, wishes or concerns
- Consider that their own desires or emotions are paramount to those of others
- Unconcerned about endangering others, including people with whom they may be in close relations.
- Profound love or hate emotions
- Difficulty managing impulses
- Able to insinuate yourself with others because of strong social communication skills
- Able to keep secrets or to conceal their intentions or motivations
- Superficial or Shallow
- Extremely perceptive
- Easily annoyed by a propensity to behave purely dependent on their feelings
- Unconcerned about others' safety or their lives

A manipulator may hold any or all of those traits. A manipulator could also be capable of creating an assault weapon depending on what is required at the moment. Remember that, like a narcissist, a manipulator makes a firm decision of who you are so that they learn how to handle you. These people are greatly perceptive, and this will become apparent if you pay awareness to the things they say. They can say stuff you've never informed you, which may make you think they've stalked you or investigated you in any way.

A manipulator 's characteristics seem to include a list of negative or bad qualities, although it is necessary to remember that manipulators may possess strong interpersonal skills, in relation to being generally smart. Because of the huge skill set possessed by manipulators, they may even respond to brainwashing to get what they want. Brainwashing can require removing your mind 's thoughts, behaviors, or motivations and substituting them with each other.

Brainwashing may be the consequence of hypnosis but it is often the result of effective manipulation use. Since human beings are inherently so impressionable, a manipulator may easily brainwash you through offering you an idea by persistence, affirmation, or any of the other coercive techniques previously described. That is called brainwashing since the manipulator was capable of taking their own thought or intention and bring it into the head. The power of recommendation should never be misjudged since it can be the most powerful tool that leads to brainwashing and you might be completely unaware that it is being used toward you.

Persuasion is the power to affect others and can be considered as being merging with manipulation or a more benign category of manipulation. In general, persuasion is thought of as guiding somebody in a specific direction or persuading them to get a belief or to engage in an act that is advantageous to themselves. In brief, persuasion is more positively perceived than manipulation even though there is a narrow line between the two.

Find the door-knocking salesman. They look friendly, have an engaging, compassionate attitude, and usually seem to be involved in doing you any good. The positive they're trying to do is to persuade you to repair your roof at home, even if your roof is just 5 years old. They note you've got some stripes on your roof and they're telling you these show you've got water harm. Under the shingles, water collects and the last item you need to do is pause until a severe storm hits and your house gets flooded. For tests may be an agent can avoid so you can pick up the new roof.

That person wants you to help, right? Okay, maybe not. That person is trying to convince you to buy a new roof you really don't need. The streaks that they saw in the ceiling were attributable to the shadows from the big trees with their wide branches that you have on the lawn. Your roof is fairly new so you may need to have an inspection at most, but most probably not a substitution. What the salesperson does is to manipulate your thoughts by proposing a concept of their own for you. Your roof gets broken, so as soon as possible you need another. They tried to convince you.

Dark Psychology and Manipulation

Although the primary objective here is completely mild – to convince someone to buy a new ceiling – persuasion can range widely to relatively benign ideas and behaviors, and those less so. You can convince someone to go for dinner tonight to one restaurant instead of another, or you can try and convince your grandmother to alter her will, identifying you as the sole owner. Persuasion is seen as a step away from manipulation, maybe a move in the good direction, but the impacts of the conditioning it involves can be quite dramatic.

3.4 How to Control People

Men and women who are skilled in the art of persuasion to understand how and when to affect you. Indeed, "people persons" are the best manipulators and persuaders who know how to get along well with someone else because of their interpersonal skills. What it really means is that they have a high level of emotional intelligence, or at least they are highly self-conscious and good at being fed into other people's emotional states. As the reader has already seen, emotional intelligence also requires empathy and using it to guide one 's actions so an emotionally vulnerable or conscious person is not necessarily intelligent emotionally though they may be.

Because manipulators and persuaders are closely aligned with emotional responses, they are excellent in people reading. They will be mindful of the impact their phrases have on you. If they

Dark Psychology and Manipulation

say anything which makes you have a furrowed brow, they're going to make a mental note of it, or if they say something which makes you laugh, they're going to note it too. And since they are highly attuned to other people's emotional and internal states, they can make these evaluations instantly, and even unintentionally. Even the changes in behavior resulting from their consciousness of you may not be fully conscious.

So, we can describe a collection of competencies that are helpful in persuasion. Remember that persuasion can influence others. The behavior and feelings of others in particular are the ones that are usually wanted to be affected. Here are some characteristics which a person skilled in affecting others will have:

- Excellent memory
- Emotional awareness
- Agreeable personality
- Excellent understanding of human nature and normal human behavior
- Great attention to detail
- Intelligent
- Ability to identify with others and to get others to identify with you
- Ability to mask one's own feelings and motivations

Dark Psychology and Manipulation

These kinds of features are essential in persuasion also because the concept in this strategy is for a persuader to trigger the target's thoughts to correspond to their own. What this implies is that the strongest convincing arises as the persuader interacts with the objective and renders the subject more responsive to advise or control. It is organic for human beings to choose to recognize with everyone so if the persuader is able to establish an area of similarity so they're more likely to succeed to impact the other individual.

Establishing this relationship or connection can take the form of trying to make the other individual smile or laugh, helping or being regarded to protect the person in some way, being receptive to the other person's emotional state or issues, and demonstrating that consciousness, and conveying an image of acceptability or benignity. The concept here is that you should be seen by the person to be impacted as someone akin to themselves or herself. When they see you as divergent, then they're less likely to be affected by you since they don't perceive you as someone they can or want to connect with.

Once you've established a relationship with everyone, you can now participate in the initial act of persuading. This argument would include the presentation of a concept with the intention of getting the same concept for the other party. If you're a salesperson, the concept is that you'll get a new roof from the potential client so your purpose is to motivate the individual that they should. Through your phrases and demeanors, you have encouraged them by creating an emotional relationship with them, which now opens them up to be more suggestive to you. By finding out an issue with their roof you seem to have performed them a favor and you are sincerely involved in supporting them.

3.5 How you can prepare certain individuals (and be trained too)

If you adopt the strategies laid out in manipulating people, otherwise you'll be participating in the cycle of training them to be responsive to your power. Conditioning means preparing or acting someone for a further process, in this case, the procedure of persuading or manipulating people into whatever you're doing. Although training can occur in different ways, it simply involves some kind of connection to be made between 2 people to leave the other party open for modification by the other individual.

Training is a mental process that takes place in animal species. An animal may be conditioned so that it is sensitive to or insensitive to pain. An object may be trained to desire conflicts and aggression or maybe a pacifist. Training occurs all the time and is occurring everywhere over us. We are influenced by the programs we display on tv, and by the books we read in school as we grow up, to have those opinions regarding life.

Dark Psychology and Manipulation

Conditioning is a method by which learners understand what is typically think and behave, even after we are becoming adults, training continues.

In persuasion, other convictions may be dependent upon the goal. In this context what this means is that the person has somehow become open to a concept. Conditioning may often result through coercion although we mostly find this form of conditioning to be more painful. An individual can be influenced in coercion by emotional or physical trauma, or by the poorly-thought-out usage of words or acts.

Just as other people can be habituated, so can you also be encouraged by others attempting to affect you. Teaching to be careful about other people's intentions is a great first defense, even if it happens to come with its downsides. Not every person who tries to control you does so because they need to exploit you or convince you to do anything which benefits them. Often, being vigilant of unfamiliar people is a smart idea, because you don't realize what their motives are. You can be more accessible about the thoughts and the true self, recognizing that these are weapons a narcissist will employ against self, over time, when you get to know them better.

Chapter 4: Body language reading strategies and laws of manipulation

As much as we like to think that we are doing a fairly decent job at masking our true emotions, little do we know that our bodies are giving us away from more than we intend. The invisible language of human nature says more of what you're feeling and how you feel more than your voice can ever do because when something you're doing out loud doesn't suit something your nonverbal signals are suggesting, that's when someone who's paying close attention can tell that something special is really happening.

To begin with, if you understand the indication to look for, reading the body language of another person, which is a very delicate business, can be great leverage in your hunt to explore who manipulates you and who is genuine. Understanding the signs of body language can be beneficial if you are the one who attempts to subtly persuade or manipulate another to do what you want them to do as you are totally aware of the signs that are responsible for providing away your real motives.

But decoding body language isn't as easy as we would imagine. One signal might have several various connotations that normally change based on the circumstances and the other elements that may influence the feeling of that person. You might presume, for example, that a guy who has his arms wrapped in front of his chest when talking to you would be either irritated or closed off, so if they were in a place that was especially cold, that might actually cross their arms in an effort to remain warm and that's it. The very best thing you should do in a case like this will be to look out for the implicit signs and see if what they're asking you mentally is in line with what their behavior is doing. If there is a disparity, that is where you ought to begin charging more care.

Body language is also an incredible skill to develop for those who have been intrigued by what someone thinks and feels about it. It will expose a lot of private knowledge, the innermost confidential thoughts that may be going through the mind of an individual they don't want to hear about someone else. The information which no one can detect except you. A little like a secret communication line between just between you and the individual you are watching. It's a complex concept, even more so because, admittedly, we all wanted to read someone else's mind at one time or another. Okay, there's a way to do just this now, so that you're not only interpreting their thoughts either but their whole body.

4.1 Methods to help in the analysis of body language

Language of the body. Pretty simply the body language. The

facial expressions, contrary to what others might believe, are not the only sure sign as to how somebody might feel. The nose, as they claim, is just the tip of an iceberg, so there is far more to discover under the water. When we talk, our entire body is engaged in a process. Every element of your mental and physical state contributes to what's going on, but the sections you're aware of (the words you're thinking about saying) and those you're unaware of (the body language).

There's one thing you have to keep in mind before you start jumping into the 7 methods for analyzing people and reading body language from top to foot. Avoid concentrating too hard to look for signs you're becoming too intense and pragmatic. Remember, just as much as everyone, your body language could really give you away. Keep calm and confident, be normal, and analyze clearly without being too harsh and overthrowing all the signals you get.

Here are the 7 methods you want to use to decode the secret emotional responses that others keep hidden:

Strategy #1 - Appearance. The face of an individual is probably the most visible clue and an instant sign that you would like to pay close attention to that when you encounter them. Will they have a newly shined power suit? Are they capable of making a powerful feeling, dressed in for success? Are they clothed for informal comfort denoting that they feel comfortable and relaxed? Are they seductively dressed on a first

Dark Psychology and Manipulation

date, purposely seeking to attract your interest? Have they an item on them that suggests they may be spiritual? Like maybe a Cross pendant? There is a number that you can draw away from there just from staring at the way they pose.

Strategy #2 - Posture. Is the person you're talking to trustingly hold their head high? Or are their shoulders mildly hunched, suggesting they may feel insecure or unpleasant? Are they walking in such a way as to show their indecisive feeling? Assembled in a packed place, who strut around with their chest bulging out, making it known that they have confidence and maybe a big ego to join that? How about the person who is sitting in the corner trying to fit in so nobody will remember them? Observe if the person leans to you in a conversation or tries to distance himself from you. In general, whether we like them or are relaxed in their presence, we prefer to consciously or unconsciously lean toward the individual and we seek to create some gap when we don't like someone. The best body pose to find is to cross the arms in front of the eyes, but consideration should be given to the toes too. If you note the toes of someone or the peak of their leg pointed to you, that is a sign they are relaxed with you. Besides observing the way, they sit or stand, while you are attempting to decipher body language, hold an eye out for hand positioning. Somebody who has their hands in their pants put around their backs, or in their laps may indicate they're trying to keep something secret.

Strategy #3 - Face. None of it gives away how an individual feels more than their body language, from all the other body parts of the body. The emotions that are etched along all our faces are more potent than we could say. The intense frown which shrinks the forehead. Small, pursed lips. The crinkles across the eyes often following a sincere grin. A mouth clenched. These are all signs that indicate the feelings that may be going through the body of an individual as you examine them, and if there was ever a position where you were searching for mismatched indications and indications, it would be the facial expressions. A verbal "yes" with pursed lips, a tight jaw, and a slight frown between both the brows send a strong signal that this individual is hesitant and unable to answer "yes." A smile that doesn't quite reach the eyes to make it "crinkle" in such a way that only a genuine smile can let you understand that this individual is plastering for good measure on their face with a fake smile when, in fact, they wouldn't smile at all if they can get away.

Strategy #4 - Eyes. How often did you hear the sentence "look me in the eye and give me the reality"? We tended to believe that keeping eye contact becomes more difficult for them when a person is lying. To some extent, there's some truth to that, but skillful liars wanting to intentionally cover up the lies they say will deliberately keep eye contact, but that's also where they appear to slip up, and the most. By trying to compensate by holding on to the physical contact for way too long then they need till it becomes unpleasant because they are lying. On average, an individual will keep eye contact from 7 to 10 seconds for anywhere, normally longer if they listen to the speaker attentively. When an individual looks at you with a look that makes you nervous, particularly if it's followed by hardly any blinking and completely still body poses, that's your sign that something may not be right and this individual could be talking to your face.

Strategy #5 - Tone. Remember the other 38 percent that comes from the use of the tone of voice? That's the number four good way to help you have a read about how to evaluate the person before you. The language and total frequency used throughout a discussion will provide a glimpse into the feelings of an individual. Is the tone calming, low and soothing to use? Speaking to this person makes you feel completely comfortable and relaxed? Or is it short, precise, abrasive as well as clipped, which makes you feel definitely uncomfortable as it gives you the perception that this individual is less than excited to have a discussion with you? The voice and sound intensities we use to convey presentation create vibrations, and a person's tone has a way of impacting the way you feel, even if you may not think twice about it. As the expression of the face, if some say "yes" but followed by a short tone, clipped, you know that "yes" isn't the real answer they wish to send at all.

Strategy #6 - Torso - We were also instructed to stand up straight, to hold our back straight, to stand up erect, and to retain a healthy stance. There is a valid explanation for this therapy. In general, it's not only good for your posture, but it also signals to others that you feel confident and in control. A person who is highly emotional would have difficulty thinking straight, let alone focusing on standing upright. If you analyze somebody who occurs to have a severely saggy body position, followed by other indicators they feel uncomfortable when they are in the presence of others, it is a pretty strong sign that they suffer from low self-esteem. Hunched posture is a classic sign of avoiding attention if someone prefers to.

Strategy #7 - Legs. The way in which a person's legs are placed when they are either sitting upright is key aspects of what they think and feel. Holding them closely crossed (not in a comfortable way) when sitting down, shows the feeling against the other party "locked off." It appears to demonstrate when a person does not feel especially confident, secure, or at ease throughout a conversation. For instance, if a woman wears a skirt that may have transformed out to be somewhat smaller than she expected when she sat down, worrying about a possible dysfunction in the wardrobe will translate into another rest of her facial expressions because that's what her mind is

Dark Psychology and Manipulation

concerned about. The conversation can deteriorate rapidly when its obvious discomfort becomes apparent, and when the other persons present during the discussion misread the cues. People who have dealt with anxiety can unknowingly translate this information in form of leg-shaking or foot-tapping through their feet, which wants to send a very clear and loud message to everybody else across them that they either feel irritated, anxious or both. Since the legs of a human are the biggest limbs we have, it's incredibly tough not to note anytime there is unnecessary activity.

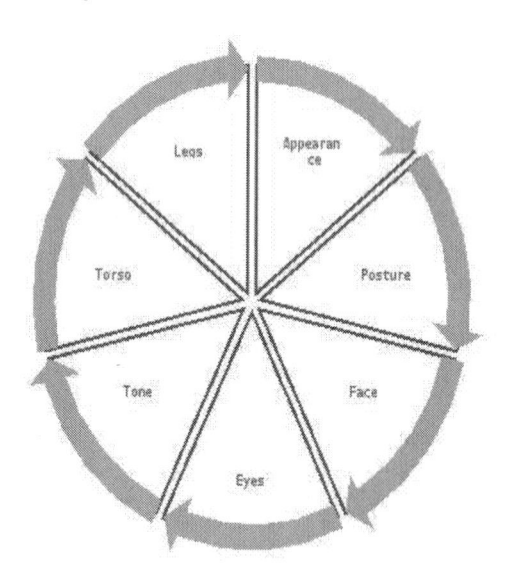

Besides having your eyes to search for all the hints you 're trying to find, there's something else you need to focus on when it comes to interpreting the body language correctly. Its intuition. Even as you are pretending to respond to your head, pay attention to your gut instinct and what it is trying to tell you.

There's more to awareness than just relying on logic alone. Gut instinct and compassion will take you that much further into their story than will let you see what your eyes are. One of the core competencies that those with high emotional intelligence possess is the capacity to interact with others. Sensing the emotional energy generated and determining what is occurring through their instinct. The subtle signs of energy can be a powerful indicator of a person's character. Being around happy, enthusiastic people raises your morale, boosts your overall satisfaction and attitude, whereas being around dishonest and pessimistic persons leaves you feeling tired and exhausted.

The mental energy that is released is sometimes getting little consideration, but it is really among the markers that you might use to get a reading on what the temperament of someone could be. If you've ever been around anyone that always seems to have a black shadow hanging over themselves no matter where they're heading or what they're doing, it may be the indication you need to realize that person is somebody that has a deeply negative outlook, or whether they may be deceptive.

4.2 Certain body language searching indicators

There is a multitude of ways to gauge facial expressions, going beyond the key 7 techniques listed above. Humans have complicated beings with fascinating characteristics and, like a good novel, on every movement of a page, it becomes more fascinating, particularly as more secrets are unwound all along the way you look deeper.

Many markers of facial expressions to watch out for as you want to evaluate someone are:

The Handshake - Nothing like a good, strong, genuine handshake to let you understand when someone feels confident and comfortable. But what if the opposite was the handshake? Hobble, reluctant, and like they can't wait to release their hand when they touch it? Although it doesn't actually have to signify something concrete, a handshake less than a firm may clearly suggest that the individual lacks self-confidence, feels awkward, is non-committal, tentative, or is by definition an introvert. On the other hand, cold and clammy hands could signal the person's feeling scared and upset, as we all appear to sweat a bit when we have those butterflies in our bellies.

The Micro expressions - Strategy number 3 aims the most

Apparent facial expressions occurring during effective communication, there is another element to what scientists call display rules that play a very important role in letting others feel good. Perhaps you're still talking about something. Those really tiny face and body actions are recognized as micro gestures and tend to focus specifically on the areas around the eyes and mouth. Those micro gestures, combined with the majority of the facial movements, will totally refute what you're doing and

Dark Psychology and Manipulation

someone who's willing to interpret nonverbal signals will automatically pick up on it. An individual that believe they're doing a decent job of disguising the anxiety they're experiencing while attempting to reassure the individual they're communicating to, but and the always subtle drawdown of the muscle around the mouth region may let away how insecure they're feeling inside. The scary part about micro signals is that when a person may feel stressed or upset, they don't just happen. They arise when someone lies, too. It's not that quick to conceal a little white lie because your tiny face muscles are letting you away.

Raising Eyebrows - There is just 3 major explanation that will lift somebody's eyebrows. They feel either surprised, frightened, or worried. Try lifting the eyebrows the next moment you're in a comfortable and friendly discussion with a buddy, and see if it's simple to do. At best you could come off looking weird. When someone talks with you and the discussion doesn't involve a subject that will either cause surprise, fear or worry as they raise their eyelashes, keep up your antennas as someone else's could happen under the surface.

The Chin and the Neck - Yeah, sometimes the jaw and neck have their very own hidden language that they're attempting to inform the rest of the population when you're utterly oblivious of it when you make a concerted attempt to reflect on those two places and what they're doing while you're having a talk. I f your

Dark Psychology and Manipulation

chin jiggles out in front of you, others might just get the impression you're either somewhat obstinate or stubborn. And the way you treat other people's neck helps them to realize how you look internally. Shy introverted people who are clearly nervous in a big community of people prefer to tuck their heads under and they're eyes locked on the floor or prevent interaction with the eyes, while others that are relaxed and erect appear to keep their necks strong and straight.

The Arm Cross - We all realize the meaning has a part to play in the arms crossing, so usually, if, for example, you cross your arms during a meeting, the indication you send is that you feel close to what the other party says. Even if they have a smile on their face and they engage in the conversation as pleasantly as they do. How they really believe when their arms are traversed in front of them is that they feel emotionally, mentally, and physically closed to whomever they speak and what they're being told. This gesture is completed so unintentionally most of the time, that it makes this the most exposing indicator of all. So, if Henry Calero and Gerard Nierenberg recorded and over 2,000 negotiations as part of a survey for their novel How to Read an individual Like a novel, not one of those negotiation processes resulted in a deal if one party had their arms or legs crossed and during negotiation.

Excessive Nodding - At the cost of appearing like a garden gnome, the only explanation anyone might over-nod when

Dark Psychology and Manipulation

You're talking to them if they're either worried about what you're thinking of them, or if they're worried you might doubt their capability to keep up with your commands (employees occasionally do this when the boss offers a string of commands and they're trying to entertain them by showing they can keep up with anything they're saying).

Tightly Clenched Jaw - During a discussion, the only way someone's jaw should be firmly clenched was if they were getting anxious. If you realize that the phrases they say may make this sound like they're all right with a concept but their teeth are clasped while they're going to say it, that's the message you really need tells you they're not as ok with the concept as they're contributing you to believe it.

The Feet - Another component of your body that could cause you trouble by sending out contradictory signals. When you swipe your toes, somebody might get the perception that either you're cause illnesses or you're in a rush to bring the talk to a close. Pressing your toes when you are trying to get someone else's attention is a way to get them to recognize you without disturbing a conversation they might have. Toe-tapping is a process to signal when you feel strapped for time without spelling it out immediately because you don't want to sound rude. There's a reason most individuals tap their toes, but this doesn't necessarily mean it's the main means of communication, particularly since either way you'll be perceived as rude when you continually tap, tap, tap on someone else. Imagine the feeling of having someone tap their toes at you.

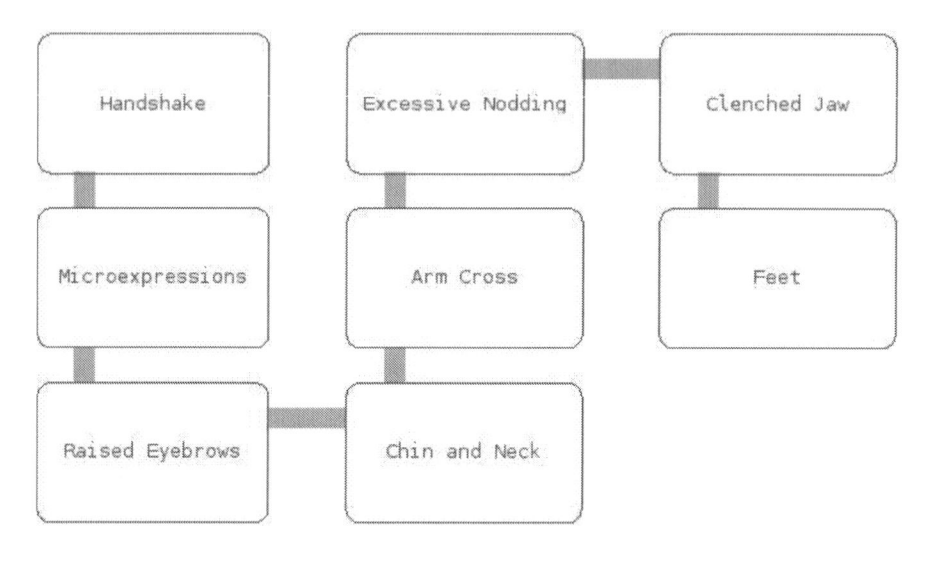

```
┌─────────────────┐   ┌─────────────────┐   ┌─────────────────┐
│                 │   │                 │   │                 │
│   Handshake     │───│ Excessive Nodding│───│  Clenched Jaw   │
│                 │   │                 │   │                 │
└────────┬────────┘   └────────┬────────┘   └────────┬────────┘
         │                     │                     │
┌────────┴────────┐   ┌────────┴────────┐   ┌────────┴────────┐
│                 │   │                 │   │                 │
│ Microexpressions│───│   Arm Cross     │───│      Feet       │
│                 │   │                 │   │                 │
└────────┬────────┘   └────────┬────────┘   └─────────────────┘
         │                     │
┌────────┴────────┐   ┌────────┴────────┐
│                 │   │                 │
│ Raised Eyebrows │───│  Chin and Neck  │
│                 │   │                 │
└─────────────────┘   └─────────────────┘
```

4.3 Manipulation Laws

Manipulators may come in all types and dimensions. There are several aspects that manipulators have now in popular with each other as different since they may be as people, and that's the fact that they're deceptive, sneaky, and dishonest and will revert back to using any strategies if it implies they receive what they're doing at the end of the day. For that matter, they care little or nothing about your emotions or anybody else's, even the folks they love. The only problem that matters is to them, they have their own agenda and get whatever they need.

Dark Psychology and Manipulation

Manipulators respond to one, two, or more tactics to reach their aims, always at the expense of someone else. While the strategies may vary from manipulator to manipulator, there are 13 manipulative laws each manipulator are using at one time or another:

Law #1 - Hide Your Intentions. Lying may be the oldest and most effective manipulative form around. Manipulators often respond to this strategy when trying to avoid responsibility or to twist the truth to their advantage. Some manipulators also admit to lies where there is no particular justification to do so, only living on the joy of causing confusion or knowing that they play with the emotions of someone else. A talented manipulator knows how to operate so subtly on this angle that you don't even realize the lie they are spinning until it's too late. There may be various reasons why a manipulator needs to resort to telling lies. It could be another to take advantage of. To hide their true intentions, so that you do not know what they are up to. Or maybe even to level out the playing field so they can stay a point ahead of you. An employee worried about their job could reach the owner and ask about the possibility of being fired or laid off. In an attempt to conceal what's really going on, the boss might tell the employee there's nothing to worry about when in fact schedules are now being made to start replacing him once he's finished work on the project to which he's been assigned. A colleague who has witnessed the same promotion that you are may withhold potential information in order to be able to put themselves before you.

Law #2 - Attention Seeking. A little excitement in existence makes things exciting but chaos occurs all too much for a manipulator. Why? For what? And they set it up intentionally. Manipulators want to be the center of focus for validating themselves and offering their egos the boost of trust they feel they deserve. A friend at work may have recourse to generating friction among colleague A and colleague B by sharing tales about each other. This guarantees that while colleagues A or B are at odds with one another, they then transform to a manipulator for "comfort," making the manipulator look special afterward. One person may continuously pick a conflict in a partnership to ensure that the other's energy is consistently centered on them and attempting to fix an issue that does not exist.

Law #3 - Behaving Emotionally. Manipulators may be individuals who are extremely emotional, prone to sensational, and even hysterical rantings whenever they want stuff accomplished their way. Overly dramatic, rude, offensive, over-the-top, a manipulator can revert to irrational actions even at the smallest provocation, which is much of the time unacceptable in a social environment. A pair fighting aggressively in the cafeteria when one spouse is acting unreasonably because things are not handled their way resort to this action, thinking that their spouse will feel humiliated sufficiently to cede to their requests allows this an incredibly successful coercion tactic when employed correctly.

Law #4 - Playing Victim. Everybody always feels bad. They really appear to have the world's toughest luck. Any issue you might have, they search a way of making you feel bad for even thinking about that by finding out how "10 times worse" their issue is than yours. Every now and again we all profit from a bit of bad luck; however, the manipulator has learned to use that unfortunate streak skillfully to raise their own "victim" status and to place themselves above all others. A buddy who is continually bringing up all the bad elements of his life when ignoring the problems is going to resort to this cynical technique to get the publicity they seek. Tell them you've got a rough day since you've had a flat tire on the drive to work the next morning and they'll remind you how fortunate you could still have a vehicle to worry about because they're trying to suffer the public transit difficulties. This emotionally exhausting technique is used by manipulators to receive support from people, that is another means of getting publicity and ensuring that all is centered on them.

Law #5 - Taking Credit Where It's Not Due. Manipulators don't hesitate to get you to do all of the legwork, and afterward, swoop in at the last moment to take credit as they did the job of the lion. A common tactic that is often used in a skilled setting, normally in group or team-work projects. Such crafty manipulators are fluttering around delegating tasks, apparently "busy" when they don't really do much at all, however, when it comes to claiming credit, they have really no problem brushing you back and demanding credit for the innovations and the effort you've put into it.

Law #6 - Depend on Me. Manipulators want you, in your life, to feel like you need them. That you just can't live without them. They are the "popular" ones in a social setting to which everybody seems to flock, making you anxious to want to become a part of that community. They might be the partner in a relationship that keeps reminding you "what you would do without me" or "how you would survive without me." They do you favor and assist you out at a moment when you need it the most, going to make you feel deeply in debt to them so that at a later date they can come as well as cash in on those favors. Manipulators generate this delusional idea that in your life you need them, and the more you rely on them, the more they have control over you, which is precisely what they need. They prey on the weeks and make themselves the "indispensable friend" they have created in their lives, basking throughout this special status. The more support you lean on them, the more potential they have to take advantage of your emotions and manipulate you for their own benefit.

Law #7 - Selective Honesty. Have you ever felt so disarmed by how a generous person you know could suddenly turn around and stab you in the back? Or felt so wrong-footed when you realized you only knew half of what was going on? That's because the person who was feeding you with information was a manipulator, and the reason you feel stabbed in the back or wrong-footed is that they only fed you information that they WANTED you to know while purposely withholding the rest. Selective honesty, a powerful manipulative tactic that can be used to disarm an unsuspecting "victim". A tactic that is today very prominent within professional settings especially. Manipulators at work use it all the time to get ahead. If there are five people up for the same promotion at work, the manipulator will try to give themselves the upper hand by withholding important information that they know while simultaneously assuring everyone else that "this is exactly what's going on". They lead you to believe that they are being generous by clueing you in on what's taking place but in reality, they're making sure you're at least two steps behind them every step of the way.

Law #8 - Pretending to Be A "Friend". Don't be deceived by the exceedingly pleasant person you merely met at the office on your first day. They might claim to be your buddy while collecting information regarding you that they could use to everyone's advantage later on. While some individuals may be

Dark Psychology and Manipulation

genuinely friendly, if this individual is a little too pleasant, start raising the red flag by posing very specific or inquiring questions, especially if you've just met them. Inside a professional environment, this technique is popular and if your gut tells you something wrong, it's definitely off. The manipulator may also live inside your own friends' group. They pretend they are your "friend" by being subtly the one in control of the discussion. The discussion will be always what they influence it ought to be, and only when they evaluate this should happen will it happen. This "mate" may also put pressure on you to make decisions by allowing you almost no time to think. Phrases like "if I am truly your friend, you 're going to do this for me" roll out the manipulator 's tongue too quickly and always to their benefit.

Law #9 - Non-Committal. Do you know whoever has a hard time willing to commit to anything in your life? Even after you told them how essential it is and just now you could use their support? The non-committal person is not your mate, they are a manipulator. They find delight in withholding their authorization or support if it means they have a chance to give themselves the advantage to control the situation to their advantage. They just look out for themselves, and will especially deter from contributing to something if it involves taking liability. Being non-committal is a tactic of manipulation which is often used in romantic relations. When a romantic partner is non-committal, it helps to keep the other on their feet and keeps them coming back for even more, thus giving the upper hand to the manipulator. The longer they withhold their dedication, the more you will be willing to bend backward, just to get their approval.

Law #10 - Playing Dumb. Is that friend you really do not know what's going on? Or will they feign ignorance to prevent shouldering additional workload? Playing stupid is a deceitful tactic that is often neglected, but if people pay attention, in a lot of talented settings you will find that obvious. If you were a community project leader at work, should you delegate the extra duty to the one member of the team who "wasn't as confident about anything?" Or assign that additional responsibility to someone else? The worker who was "playing stupid" tries to get away with just doing far less but receiving the same quantity of recognition in the group as everyone else. When a community of friends is in disagreement, could one person who "doesn't realize what's going on" say the truth? Or may they be feigning ignorance, realizing full well that they were solely liable for causing the conflict? In a loving relationship, can your spouse, who "doesn't know what you're talking about," tell the truth about a problem when you interrogate them? Or could they be "acting foolish" to stop getting swept up in a lie? The "innocent party" may not have been so innocent at times, after all.

Dark Psychology and Manipulation

Law #11 - Pointing the Finger at Others. In the first place, a manipulator would always strive to maintain their hands clean, never take accountability, and in the second place by always attempting to point a finger at somebody else because they get off brit-free when a problem arises. Particularly when that issue might endanger their credibility and reveal them besides who they are. You could be trying to deal with a manipulator if you know someone in your relatives, mates, or even with other coworkers who always criticizes the issue on everything and anyone other than themselves. Keep an eye out for anyone who's behavior pattern always involves making someone the scapegoat.

Law #12 - Telling You What You Want to Hear. When you're flattered, it's impossible not to think good and you're more willing to like the person who does all the fashionable more than the others. If there is one person that constantly asks you all the stuff you want to learn in your life, wouldn't you be more likely to pursue them or invest more time around them? It's impossible not to think good about such people but going to tell you all the stuff you would like to listen to is not certainly a better friend's sign. They might be buttering you so that at a later date they can money in on a big favor that you will be "guilty" to help them with "because they were so nice to you."

Law #13 - Controlling Your Decisions. A classic setting is within a loving relationship when there is manipulation in the

Dark Psychology and Manipulation

type of regulating another's decision. While it is completely normal for your partner to base or start changing your decisions, is it because there is a genuine desire within you to make them happy? Or do you do it because you don't want them to risk getting angry? There is a very fine line in one relationship between what constitutes deception. If you find yourself with friends canceling schemes far too often because your partner conveys their disappointment or makes you feel bad, that is manipulation in the play. It's a subtle type of coercion if you keep from wearing clothing that your partner criticizes, or from having a haircut after your partner said "they don't like short hair" They are manipulating the choices without actually making it clear they are. It could start casually enough with a comment or two, with something so negligible like conveying how the clothes you wear don't look better on you and the kind of dress you wear should be something else especially if you find that their things have turned into nothing more than decisions that don't make you happy because they are dictated by somebody who claims to love you.

Dark Psychology and Manipulation

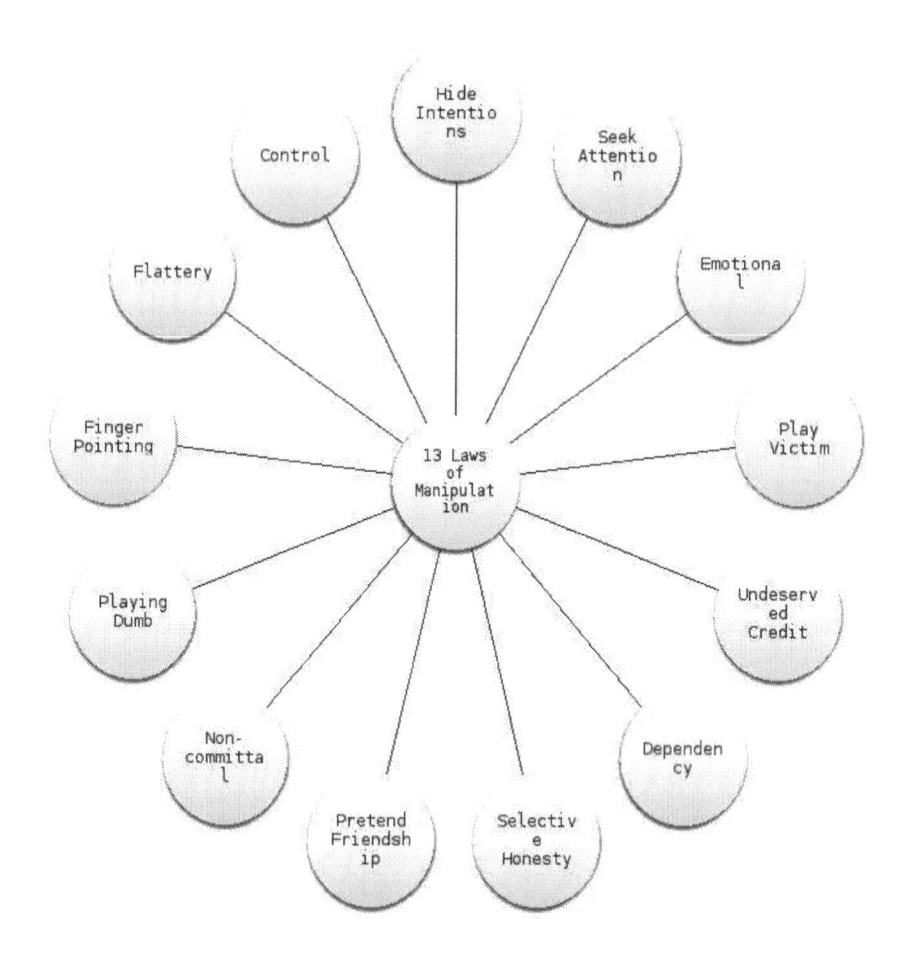

13 Laws of Manipulation diagram with nodes: Hide Intentions, Seek Attention, Emotional, Play Victim, Undeserved Credit, Dependency, Selective Honesty, Pretend Friendship, Non-committal, Playing Dumb, Finger Pointing, Flattery, Control

Chapter 5: Understanding dark triad personalities

There is a concept in the world of psychology which is called the dark triad. The obscure triad is a set of three traits of personality, namely Machiavellianism, narcissism, and psychopathy. This group of three is labeled dark owing to the

Dark Psychology and Manipulation

usual malignant habits correlated with certain characteristics. The dark triad's dramatic opposite is the lighter triad, which is a topic and debate for another book in itself. Although the three traits depicted on the dark triad in their own studies are distinct, it is seen that they also overlap in fact. What this indicates is that with blurred boundaries, a person who increases the success on the dark triad exam will likely have all these traits present. It might be hard to tell, for example, where narcissism stops and where psychopathy begins.

Discussions about the Dark Triad concept were initially begun in 1998 by 3 psychology experts who asserted that Machiavellianism, narcissism, and psychopathology occurred overlappingly in normal samples. Two psychologists by the titles of Williams and Paulus would later invent a name for this group, in 2002: the dark triad.

There have often been discussions and debates about the part played by nature in seeking to comprehend the personality traits of the dark triad. To put it simply, psychologists, behavioral scientists, and researchers were keen to know whether born or bred are Dark Triad persons. Are we born stupid and manipulative, or have we become so as a consequence of the things that we grow up to be exposed to? It has been noted, according to various research done, that a dark triad has an important genetic basis to it. That is, some born with such susceptibility to the dark traits of the triad. However, in terms of heritability, narcissism, or psychopathy rank greater than Machiavellianism. That is when contrasted to a parent that ranks high on the Machiavellian scale, a psychopathic mother or father is more willing to switch the characteristic to their offspring.

The dark triadic characteristics have been seen to also be-represented in top-level management in reports which might not be really friendly to someone who is working. When the elements of the dark triad are unpackaged in the segments below, it becomes evident why this recognition may be so. And besides, very few CEOs, if any, arrived by playing nice to where they are.

5.1 Dark Triad: Narcissism

A narrative is revealed in the Greek myths of a young man named Narcissus. Narcissus was indeed a hunter renowned for his striking, good looks. Narcissus did not have a time of day for them given the adoration he got from his admirers and even forced others to take their own lives to show their devotion. While there are multiple versions of the story of Narcissus, all of them refer to him being extremely self-absorbed, which eventually ended up in him going to die mortality that was retribution for his selfish ways. Thanks to the story of that young man, Sigmund Freud first coined the term narcissism. Freud, aptly titled On Narcissism in his famous 1914 essay.

Narcissism in the simplest terms is the increased and compulsive self-admiration which a person has towards himself and his personal features. A narcissist is always easy to recognize since they quickly offer away their behavior and values. Asking yourself if you have a narcissist in their life? Here is what you should look for:

Narcissists tend to feel good, and always have the ability to be entitled

Normal, good relationships involve a significant amount of giving and taking, whether they relate to work, individual, or business. Narcissists are not subscribing to that logic. They love doing all the collecting while somebody else does all the sharing. They feel owed the things they demand, even if that is not the situation. Narcissists are relentless in one's pursuit to be at the focus of things and always right. A narcissist would never accept accountability in the job over everything that goes horribly wrong inside a squad. Whenever a problem occurs, the narcissist will try to shift the blame from itself and place it on a different party. They consider themselves, after all, to be innocent and unwilling to conduct misconduct. If you're a narcissist dating, they 're going to try and do it all regarding themselves. You have to sleep whatever they say, do the stuff they want, and cling onto your identity to keep them satisfied. They 're going to have no trouble with all the stuff that average people might frown about as they're really doing you a favor in

Dark Psychology and Manipulation

their eyes by dating you. If you find these indications of severe self-centeredness in a person, you'll probably be trying to deal with a narcissist.

Type-A perfectionists are also narcissists

Faults and flaws are a part of life for many. If a party isn't going exactly as planned, most people have no difficulty kicking back and admire it all the same. For narcissists, this is not so. If something isn't perfect for a narcissist then it doesn't count. Narcissists target perfection in all they do even though they believe they are great and thus merit the only perfection. If you're trying to date a narcissist, they're going to ask you for perfection as far as your dress, the way you speak, the kind of mates you keep, the area you live in, or just about anything. It'll be an ever-ending fight you'll most definitely fail. Seeing that greatness is often so difficult to get through in daily life, narcissists frequently feel miserable and irritated.

Narcissists have an unflagging thirst for control

When called upon, it is essential to always be ready to take command. This is a hallmark of great leaders. It helps to have a good sense of influence over different things of your own life. You can't wander around life now and then with no sense of meaning or course, after all. However, for narcissists the desire for power is more visceral — they have to remain in charge regardless can happen. Know their immense desire for perfection? Okay, narcissists believe they ought to be in charge so they can attain this quality. They simply cannot have confidence that other 'lesser beings' will be in control, because they'll mess up everything. A narcissistic friend will want to define what kind of friends you will have, whether or not you should have a job, whether or not your mates can come to your home, and almost every other detail in your life. You may notice that, at the start of a partnership with such a narcissist, you misinterpret this desire for dominance for undying affection and loyalty. However, later on, you'll continue to feel suffocated and mistrusted, and that will signal the start of the end. Narcissists in the workforce are fond of manipulating any part of the job of their workers. A narcissistic manager won't give his juniors any space to maneuver and will do all they can to make sure he's the one calling the shots.

Narcissists don't have sense limits

Your limits are the rules you have developed to decide how your relationships are going to proceed. Inhabitants what is appropriate in your life, and not reasonable. Boundaries are part of the routine to many. Most people, for example, will not accept criticism while they lie down. It's just not appropriate to insult them in this way. Ordinary people are capable of recognizing limits in their daily lives. But on the other hand, the narcissists have no moment for such frivolous things. A psychopath would have no trouble intruding into your private space as they feel they are right to be present. Since they feel such laws should not extend to them, they have a high from violating societal expectations and regulations, because nobody will do something about it because they are equal to anyone else regardless.

How people are controlled by narcissists

Now that you realize how well a narcissist looks, you're possibly curious about what the narcissist is doing to manipulate you in your life. A narcissist's traits mentioned in the previous part seem to be fairly easy to notice. How difficult can it be to remember, after all, that someone is attempting to manipulate you? The response is, it can be quite challenging, particularly when this person conceals their acts as only searching for you. Many narcissists are typically very clever and can fit in their daily life without drawing attention to them. They could also be very creative and talented, and the allure that tries to draw you to them will usually be that. When you're out there going to look for a narcissist-shaped monster, you might not be going to look for that skilled and super artistic friend who's always having a solution to everything. And still, she might be the only narcissist in the life who just thinks about competing for irrespective of who gets injured along the way.

Narcissists are also quite keen liars, in addition to using their previously mentioned characteristics to the best of ability.

Narcissists conduct routine the skill of deception in its various forms in a bid to be the celebrity of every show. Deception is the way the narcissist throws you off reality so they stay in control. In either scenario, they always exist in an altered world where they are good and everyone else is inferior to them. Hence, deceit is just a means for them to draw you through this repetitive story where they are the principal character.

5.2 Dark Triad: Machiavellianism

Niccolò Machiavelli, sometimes referred to as the founder of modern social science, was a Renaissance-era Italian who favored loads of hats. Machiavelli has been amongst others a historian, politician, poet, humanist, author, and diplomat. Machiavelli composed his most popular work, The Prince, in 1513. Machiavelli in this book defined and advocated the usage of unscrupulous methods for obtaining and retaining political influence. The word Machiavellianism arose from this work and its endorsements, that was used to refer to the kind of politicians and tactics Machiavelli mentioned in his book. This word was later coined from psychology researchers to define a psychological characteristic marked by a lack of empathy and a drive to succeed at the detriment of others, be it by deception, coercion, or the flouting of traditional laws of dignity and morality. A person who displays Machiavellianism is, in the simplest form, willing to do almost anything if it meant playing.

Machiavelli is the purpose of why the ending phrase justifies the means that exist.

Most work has been conducted since the introduction of the word Machiavellianism in philosophy to ascertain precisely what determines the people who score highest on a Machiavellianism test, better known as high Machs. High Machs have been found to tend to value power, money, and competition above all else. High Machs put a very cheap cost on things like building a community, family, and even love Among those that score low above the Machiavellianism index, better known as low Machs, the opposite is accurate.

High Machs Characteristics

There are High Machs all around. Through your own job, you either meet one or even work with one. High campus management is powered, and effective sometimes. They have trained tirelessly and wise to get where we are, always walking unapologetically on the toes of others. If you understand somebody who is extremely successful or seems to have been feared by those around you, then you will probably be dealing with the high Mach. So, what precisely differentiates a person who increases the success on the scale of Machiavellianism?

High Machs hate framework

Structure comes with regulations, and Machs has high rules of hatred. Ergo, likewise, high Machs dislike structure. High

Machs would rather have been left alone while they go about creating their own laws. They just hate needing to do it if someone else has said so. Rules make no sense to them and the structure is in jail. Consequently, high Machs thrive in an environment where they are limitless and available to be as inventive as they wish. High Machs generally prefer corporate environments as far as the professions go, while rejecting any career path that ultimately helps others. For example, High Machs makes a very effective salesperson by counting on being ready to tell deceptions to sell products if it receives them a commission. A person who scores low on the scale of Machiavellianism may feel guilty of selling hot air to a customer. Not so with a high Mach. As long as he is awaited with the benefit of a fat commission and bonus, a high Mach will make sure that customers give them their money in exchange for whatever they sell. In other words, for a high Mach, the end would always justify the means.

High Machs are extremely opportunistic

When other citizens get to life enjoying the roses and performing certain clichés that render average people satisfied, high Mach's view life as a competition that they have to compete. They think about life as a big game board where you have to get closer to victory with every pass. Strong Machs, however, are extremely deceitful and will jump for any opportunity they will be able to catch for ahead. On the game board, they have little regard about anyone as they assume that there should only be a single king while others stay on as cannon fodder being used as weapons about dominance and rank attainment.

High Machs have an emotional isolation

High Machs have the unsettling ability to stay emotionally unavailable from any situation they find themselves in. They prevent commitments and often make relationship partners very frustrating. For High Machs, feelings and emotions are simply obstacles that will potentially hinder their objectives. If you're ready to marry a high Mach, when all family time is substituted with work commitments, you might discover yourself very lone. Work must be performed to the high Mach, in order to attain power and wealth. They don't care they are ignoring their family. They just have to do what it takes to do. But this doesn't mean every perfectionist is a high Mach. This is usually the case, however, as often as not.

High Machs are also vulnerable to getting multiple sexual encounters because of their tendency to separate their feelings from circumstances, often with those they are not well-known to. For that, there are two explanations. Oscar Wilde once said: Everything that's really about sex in human life, except sex. Sex is also about Power. No one is better at this than a high Mach who has persuaded yet another invasion to join him in a room. The second explanation for the multiple sexual partners is the emotional detachment capacity, which enables a high Mach to hop from individual to individual without having some sort of connection to someone.

High Machs are short of empathy

Empathy is described as being willing to express someone else's feelings. Looking that high Machs really aren't mentally accustomed to situations and people, it needs to be noted that for being empathic they are not precisely in the best position. This lack of compassion also works to their advantage in that they can quickly harm others without blinking to get ahead. Overall, if you are unwilling to sense anybody's discomfort, you still have no difficulty in the first place giving them the discomfort.

Strong Machs are good coworkers but not true mates

You ought to get a friend who can help you earn the top award while you are playing in a competition or in a discussion. High Machs make really good team members in games, due to their willingness and competitiveness to use any methods to get ahead. The same cannot be said in relation to personal friendships. While a lot of people are going to rush to partner up in a high Mach, not much is going to be willing to start dating them or be great buddies. This is just because they are not making very great mates. A high Mach will put you to the drop of a hat under the bus, even if you're friends for years. High

Machs then again don't really build relationships — they just collect instruments and pawns for later use.

High Machs are often mysterious

High Machs seldomly put their heart and soul on their sleeves because they think they are playing this game. They are hard to find out and are sometimes considered to be aloof. Most people sometimes have no problem mixing with one another and sharing their own bits of information. This is trivial and needless; would a strong Mach consider. They have a hard time, because of their emotional instability, sharing, and bonding with others. Also, since they think that life is a game that needs to be won and played, they are afraid to disclose any information that might lead to a loss. As such, they tend to keep strangers at a distance, rather than allow them in. High Machs often prefer to be feared rather than loved and thus do not have quite enough time for side-holding and other friendship-reserved niceties.

5.3 Dark Triad: Psychopathy

Psychopathy is a feature of temperament marked mainly by a loss of empathy toward others. Psychopaths barely experience empathy for others, and will rarely feel remorse even when other people have been hurt. There are various views about psychopathy, but many of them always seem to agree on the 3 primary features that differentiate a psychopath from any

Dark Psychology and Manipulation

normal individual. These three traits include fearlessness, lack of restraint, and meanness that any other person would consider uncomfortable.

Psychopaths are brave and aggressive and are not reluctant to step into new terrain even though they could be in danger. Although most individuals are usually overwhelmed by these conditions, psychopaths should be coping with such scenarios as if doing their everyday activities. Psychopaths often have a high degree of self-confidence as well as social boldness that allows them to interact with individuals without the shyness or anxiousness that others may have. Often, whenever a gruesome crime has been committed, you could perhaps hear about the nature of the investigation and shudder while going to think to yourself: how can a man live with himself for doing so? It's business as usual for a psychopath to kill someone and then grab a sunny face up at their local restaurant. This is not to say that all psychos have killed somebody. Some psychopaths instead rendered their lack of sympathy and susceptibility to other transgression and crimes.

Psychopaths show impaired regulation of the instinct, so they cannot regulate their impulses. When a regular human gets a desire of any kind, they are sometimes able to bring it under control and speak out of that state themselves. For instance, if you're having to deal with an irritating colleague who just won't be shutting up regarding their forthcoming bridal shower, you'll probably be able to combat the desire to slap them in their face. On the other hand, a psychopath will often be resolve by instinct and will react without giving it a second thought about the cost of everyone's decision. Psychopaths are susceptible to snapping, in a simple way. Even one gets injured as they pop.

Common decency, when dealing with others, demands a certain level of decorum and kindness. This is not something of concern to psychopaths. While the majority of the people are worried about kindness and caring, the nicest person in the room will have no issue being a psychopath. Based on the situation in hand they might be dramatic or execute about it.

In addition to these 3 main paths of similarity in their personality traits, psychopaths tend to have some other distinguishing features:

They represent risk-takers

This is relevant to their fearlessness and boldness. When everyone else is afraid of their protection, psychopaths are not spending two seconds having to worry about security — theirs or anyone else. This characteristic is a benefit when used for the good. On the contrary, taking big risks could be costly, particularly if someone else carries the responsibility of the danger. Therefore, it is no wonder that psychos nurtured in controlled situations continue to become wealthy entrepreneurs and elected officials. And besides, they are normally prone to take the all big risks in politics and business that'll get them forward with.

They are absolutely charming

A psychopath puts on his best suit, wears the best smile on his face, and tells you all you need everything you need hear, and you'll never be able to determine you've heard this from a psychopath. Although psychopaths cannot feel or encounter things in the same method as everybody else, they are wise enough to understand that people will expect specific things to go some way. So, while your deadline may not really fall in love with you after dinner, they know they should act as if they're somehow. Psychopaths are excellent teachers of life in how they can imitate everyday behavior, enabling themselves to live unobserved for the longest amount of time. Do not drop for a psychopath's charm — it's fickle, and it comes with a high price.

Sometimes, they lack long-term goals

There's nothing exciting regarding long-term goals, normally regarding the psychopath. Psychopaths are living for the moment's adrenaline rush and not waiting ten years for an objective to materialize. The perennial pretty boy who failed to grow up and is not committed to a serious relationship could well be a sociopath who simply cannot surmount his hereditary genes.

5.4 The Dark Triad practice

The dark triad test is a gauge of how one score as for the three practices of narcissism, Machiavellianism, or psychopathy, is concerned. The test is sometimes used in various settings, and by law courts and police in particular. The dark triad test is also used by corporations to gage their employees. The primary reason the dark triad method is implemented is to assess the personality characteristics of an entity and likely forecast their actions for the purposes of preventing unsavory behaviors. It was noted that people who score high on the dark triad study are more likely to cause problems and social distress whether it's in the work environment or even in their state of employment. At the same time, these people will also likely have an easy time to attain leadership positions and gain sexual partners.

The dark triad test asks you to address a series of questions on a range of subjects like how you think about others and yourself, how you maintain track of details you could use to harm someone, and your general opinions on existence, death, and social experiences, among others. The dark triad test may be a nice way to gauge how you perform on the dark triad scale, when self-administered. The dark triad test might not be very precise when administered by law courts and police as the respondent may purposely alter their answers to make them look better than it actually is. This is a primary drawback of the triad check in the night. If you're willing to take the dark triad exam, there are some online places where you'll be able to complete a study in minutes. Be careful to take the test results too personally—sometimes the justifications you give are based on the type of day you are having and not on the type of person you are being. In any event, if you recognize yourself as a respectable human being who always respectfully treats others and never harms others, then you shouldn't worry very much about what an experiment says about you. But on the other side, if you seem to always run into disputes and justifications and have to continue to talk oneself out of endangering others, then the justification you have also been waiting for all along might be a high score on the dark triad test.

Dealing with Dark Triad Personalities

They might have not passed a test and gave you the outcomes but in your life, you likely know some dark triad character traits. This is easy to identify.

Chapter 6: Neuro-linguistic Programming

A powerful tool for mind control is neuro-linguistic programming or NLP. NLP strategies are employed in tv and cable news by news anchors and others, by leaders, trainers, and other media personalities, and by people who behave to manipulate you. However, most NLP goals don't know they're under mind stimulation command and is one of the factors that makes this technique so strong. NLP uses different tools to stimulate a hip hop or trance-like nation in individuals who make them endangered to the recommendation. The tools used in the Neuro-linguistic program NLP are a form of hypnosis and many of those methods have been used for years by manipulators as well as others associated in mind manipulation.

6.1 What is NLP?

Neuro-linguistic programming was developed in the 1970s and is a form of mind management. This was a moment where many researchers were dealing with new theories of behavioral and psychology, which you can learn as we dive into history early. There was the flexibility to approaches such as those of NLP because they appeared to use Knowledge and skills that had been collected both as a result of men who had used hypnosis and mind control in the past, and the new areas of social knowledge that were revealed by the hard natural and social sciences.

When we talked about the history of mind control, we talked about men like Rasputin for a minute, who seemed to utilize arts so dark as well as mysterious that it's hard for others to understand how they attempted to do what individuals did. Looking at Rasputin's pictures, his eyes are the one aspect that seems most surprising about the house. He seems to look out of the frame, almost as if he were sharing the space with you. Rasputin's manipulation and control techniques were little known at the time, but it seems we can see aspects of what we'd call NLP mind control in some of his tactics today.

Effective communication is a tool used by NLP mind manipulation practitioners to induce relations in their goal. Even though NLP guides are more focused on the tactics and less about psychology, this form of tactic pumps into a human intention to build an emotional and psychological relationship with everyone. Very strong eye contact in combination with other words, gestures, or other indications can access the other girl up for mental control or even placed them in a trance. Many people these days use NLP strategies to pursue their goals, even if the goal is to offer you stuff for a slim profit margin on their side.

6.2 History of NLP

In the 1970s Richard Bandler or John Grinder, two people from California with expertise in Psychology and linguistics, developed neuro-linguistic programming. The most striking aspect of NLP is that it incorporates research from various subjects and incorporates these with a profound understanding of the human condition and motivations. Those of Fritz Perls, Milton Erickson, and Virginia Satir are the customs most applicable to the NLP.

Milton Erickson is a word that has had great psychological and hypnotic influence. Indeed, different people and very well-known public speakers such as Tony Robbins supposedly used his techniques. Ericksonian methods were used in psychotherapy nowadays, but NLP hypnotists and therapists have also co-opted them as they make the person more perceptive and more likely to be influenced and regulated.

Ericksonian technologies are designed to gain access to the collective unconscious, something NLP achieved in very dramatic ways. In the 1980s and 1990s, the NLP grew in popularity.

6.3 The Techniques of NLP

The NLP techniques are clever, so clever that most people who are inexperienced with NLP will actually be willing to slip under the radar. Neuro-linguistic training methods have been claimed by the likes of the recent US president, Barack Obama, whose remarks are used as instances of permissive speech hypnosis, an NLP strategy. As stated earlier, NLP technologies are extracted from a knowledge of how the mind works, what encourages human behavior, how humans form a relationship with each other, and also how human beings normally interact and act.

In other sections of this guide, we mentioned that a manipulator and narcissist is paying attention to the indications which indicate your psychological response or your aspirations and intentions. Also, an NLP practitioner is paying attention to you, trying to figure out ways to establish the relationship bond, searching for clues on how you think, and exploring opportunities to stimulate a trance. Here is a list of many of the things a person who uses NLP techniques looks for:

- Defines how your brain develops using eye movements

Dark Psychology and Manipulation

- Defines how your brain stores data using eye movements
- Evaluate what feeling of view is prominent in your brain
- Determine what side of the brain has a predominance
- Make a determination on when you lie

Neuro-linguistic coding is an aspect of dark psychology that, in the context of general knowledge, is fairly near the surface, as many individuals use it, but it is still a powerful tool for mind control. Later on, we will see how those inspired to protect oneself can break off their programming.

Physiology Update

Often shaking up the physical environment can be the very thing you need to use the NLP to convince or evaluate someone else. Maybe during the discussion, there is something trying to block your way. You might actually consider moving with both you or the person you are talking to create a much more friendly place. If you feel the discussion isn't going in which you would want, perhaps take a break in the toilet and give a person some moment alone.

If you are heading back from the toilet and things are all the same, say you turn the place up. You might want to go for a journey or move out onto the patio. You don't really have to drive too fast, though. Maybe even changing your body position or the way you're seated is enough to see the other individual reengaged.

Visualization

Visualization is a good way to enhance its goals for some people. There are so many aspects that may seem out of control, but if you just conceptualize what you want, you'd be amazed into how much you can achieve.

Something can start by talking into presence. If you'd like to be moving to L.A. Start dreaming about it, to be an actor. Don't tell people that at some point you just need to do this. In fact, say you're going to go through it, and you're going to be surprised how far you can impact yourself toward those goals.

If you have to, write it down as well. It's more like a self-persuasion tool than the one you would employ on anyone, but it definitely also helps to talk and write about the aspirations and desires that you want to see achieved.

Taking away the capacity to Say No

We touched briefly on this higher but took away another person's ability to say so that is an NLP tactic that you can are used for persuasive communication. Rather than saying, "Would you like to come out tonight for dinner? "Ask somebody," Where will we dine tonight? "You did not offer them the option of saying no to their dinner date. Anyway, they may claim they can't, but normally you decided to take the possibility away.

Dark Psychology and Manipulation

Rather than saying: "Can I get a one? "Tell me, 'How much can I have? "Most people won't even recognize that their capacity to transform you down has been taken away.

Chapter 7: Understanding the concept of brain washing

Brainwashing is maybe one of the most powerful types of social control given that it involves a whole lot of brainwashed and victim involvement. Brainwashing, sometimes known as mind management, thinking manipulation, or manipulative coercion, it isn't a method that can be implemented with success on a one-off level. It needs continuous manipulator feedback up to the stage that they can split the target down to their actual goals. You've heard more probably than not someone presented as indoctrinated. People might have also used the word yourself to relate to anyone who shared views that appeared too bold to be real but clearly is not theirs. Although many people still use this phrase broadly in daily speech, the true scope of this coercion technique is something

that can be grasped after all the details surrounding it have been accepted.

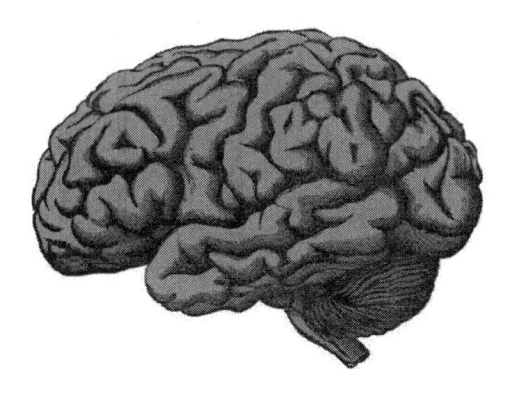

Dark Psychology and Manipulation

First things: often methods of coercion, or methods of social control if you choose, depend on particular techniques to produce expected effects. There is the compliance approach where you are making a topic do anything without truly trying to care about its underlying beliefs and ideas. Then there's the approach to persuasion which tends to make somebody do something by attacking their views or attitudes. A manipulator can seek to convince you, for example, that doing anything would benefit the patient or become more effective. In other terms, they try to persuade you to pursue a particular mentality toward yourself or the future. Finally, an approach is called the method of propaganda or the method of education, if you like. By teaching them the mistake in their past practices and exposing them to new forms and values, this method aims at attracting converts. It's close to going up to somebody and telling them that up to that point everything they've ever trusted in has been a deception, thus letting them realize you're the only carrier of the real truth. The explanation the brainwashing is really effective and hard to reverse is that it incorporates these three methods. To persuade someone who has been influencing that you are not brainwashed is also virtually difficult.

Brainwashing is a routine thing, in the real world. So far as brainwashing is concerned the government is an especially malicious suspect. Media groups have been responsible for disseminating data through their own discretion, since ancient

Dark Psychology and Manipulation

times. The media agrees on the tone to establish around the board for specific social, political, and economic issues. TV programs, TV stars, marketing teams, and trendy modeling magazines have described time and time again which ideals of attractiveness are appropriate and which ones aren't really. As a result, a large section of society is left with the feeling of not being wonderful or worthy enough if the media have said so.

So far as brainwashing is concerned, the lawmakers and faith figures are two very major culprits. Many elected officials are self-serving and will do anything in the political world to get ahead. We perfected the technique of brainwashing crowds of citizens to fall behind them, and the most brainwashed followers we get, the most likely they are to succeed. Brainwashed followers also aren't asking their leaders for much responsibility. It is by brainwashing that a certain lot of elected figures have succeeded in mobilizing their supporters to commit heinous offenses that should not be undertaken by a rational individual with reasonable thought and morality.

On the other side, political figures who brainwash their adherents are eager to associate themselves with individuals that can be manipulated quickly and who trust in the same values as the members themselves. Think of it — if you were yourself a self-serving faux-religious figure, you might like to see a submissive audience that did what it was said. The final thing you would want is an outspoken large crowd who question every single sermon you give. That is something that has been noted by many controversial religious leaders, much to the disadvantage of their supporters. Maybe several of the best examples of the impact of brainwashing on religious environments are the numerous mass suicides that have happened while congregants under the guidance of their faith representatives try to aim towards the afterlife.

One indication of this is the collective suicide of faith community Heaven's Gate adherents. Heaven's Gate group, designed by Marshall Applewhite, believed their deaths will also help them get onto a spaceship that might take people to the other world. A guy who considered himself to be the embodiment of God on Earth carried this conviction about by months or years of brainwashing. Throughout comparison to the Door of Heaven, there were several such incidences where thousands of individuals were convinced to end their lives regardless of one religious conviction or another. Even when congregants are not persuaded to commit suicide, some faith authorities may brainwash their supporters in other, often harmful ways.

Maybe one of the concerns that spring to the brain when you learn of these incidents in past is this: how could a human be so trusting and gullible to the degree that they are so blindly pursuing him? The response is straightforward: Brainwashing removes you of your personality and unquestionably requires you to adhere to another's will. In reality, tearing down the persona of your target and bringing them into doubt everything they have ever learned about them is the first phase in brainwash.

7.1 Ten Steps of Brainwashing

As noted earlier, brainwashing isn't an experience of one day. Sometimes, it requires months of effort to absolutely brainwash a human. It is no surprise then why certain members of cults would take years to create a follow-up before actually making their place in the community, although infamously. Although they can intersect from moment to moment, brainwashing phrases are mostly separate and can be generally divided into three levels. The first stage involves all the methods the abuser takes to tear down their prey; the second phase requires convincing the prey that there is a possibility of redemption; and lastly, the 3rd stage involves guiding the survivor to heaven, or at most their own idea of redemption.

First Stage: Breaking the Target

Step 1: Identity Assaulting

To break down a predator's target they may be the first target that makes the victim what they are: their ego or identity. Each human being has in his mind an idea of himself which is what they claim to be. This is the way they define themselves. Multiple identities are possible. You could be a mother and a career woman. You may be a smart businessman and an uncle. You may be a hard-fought student at the class. You just might be a Christian. You can choose between endless identities. That identity is your solution to the declaration tell me about yourself a little bit.

Take a moment, and believe about your personal identity. What are you / who?

Suppose one day you wake up and someone advised you that you're not really what you believe you are. How do you manage to hear that? If this was discussed in passing, you should possibly shrug it off and go on with your career. Or maybe you'd worry about it for a few hours or minutes, and maybe get frustrated for a bit, then push on. Now imagine someone comes to your home every minute of the day to remind you that you're not the guy you believe you are. How'd that help you feel? If it lasted through months or even weeks, then by the end of it all you will actually be out of your head. You will be startled and left to question where to draw the distinction between fiction and fact.

If you'd thought about yourself as a great writer before, you'd start to doubt it. If you thought you were your children's biological father, you may start questioning him. If you've grown up thinking you 're a real catholic, hearing daily contradictory reports would make you start thinking you might not be.

The first phase in the brainwashing cycle is when the entire dirty work starts taking hold. An individual who has planted the ugly seed of doubt in them is endangered to manipulation. We want to think the best of ourselves, as human beings. In addition, we like having other people believe in us the best. Yes, there are individuals who may not care about someone else's validation and approval. That's admirable and we should all be working towards that. But at the last of the day, the guy who goes to bed thinking he is the worst of the bad periods of sleep more restlessly. Having high self-esteem and a strong sense of self, of course, saves you from the predators willing to attack you, but that's a subject for another section.

The result of the first phase of brainwashing is a completely-blown identity issue which the predator could really prey on for the second step's purposes.

Step 2: Guilt manipulation

Guilt, as it's been called, maybe a negative emotion it is also a quite strong feeling. Guilt can start making you, as a person, promise things outside of your scope. Guilt will make you sit awake for hours wondering if you're such a bad human being because you're really not. The human creatures around us are continually harnessing the strength of culpability.

This is how the second phase of brainwashing tends to work: a brainwasher has indeed convinced its victim that they're not really what they've always assumed to be. Hence, the survivor is

Dark Psychology and Manipulation

in a state of uncertainty because they try to address for themselves the issue of identification. Such that, if they aren't a decent guy, why are they then? The predator glides in at this point and begins to take them for the entire sorrow trip of their lives. When you're uncertain who you really are, it can be really tempting to accept every falsehood you 're getting fed up with about you. A brainwasher would also make a statement convincing their perpetrator that they are basically a nasty friend, irrespective of the context this adverb is being used.

A brainwasher, for example, might try to persuade a teenage mom that they're a bad person or a bad mom because they've agreed to immunize their kids or chose the glass to the breast. An abuser may use every chance to warn the survivor that they are failing in a specific sector or in other aspects of their life and that responding to and embracing what the offender has to say is the only path to salvation. In their assault on the offender, the predator is ruthless because the ultimate goal is to split the victim gets to the fact where they are powerless and entirely free from their accurate identity and self-image.

Steps 3 and 4: Personality-betrayal and breaking point

Even citizens themselves are intensely loyal. They 're going to protect themselves and their behavior, and struggle to hear their words. Particularly the individuals who are afraid of speaking up for anyone also will speak up for themselves. A person having been brainwashed is the total opposite. Brainwashed people have no trouble rejecting themselves and anything else connected to them despite being continuously bombarded by signals about being the reverse about what they once considered themselves to be. Which involve their family, associates, value framework, and all other relationships they might have that link them to the old identification which has been 'evaluated' by the brainwasher and found 'seriously missing.'

There are several reasons why a person who has been brainwashed can easily find himself in this step and cannot fight back. For beginners, they've already moved through the first 2 phases and come out in doubt and guilt, feeling drowning and disoriented. But frequently they don't have the strength to strike off. Keep in mind that there is sometimes a risk of serious harm if conformance is not accomplished, so the goal may be too scared to contradict all the replies that the predator receives from them. At the same time, there is a way for culprits to want to compensate for their evil deeds. For some individuals, especially those broken down by brainwashing, making up consists of splitting ties with everything related to their 'sinful' past.

Sadly, what often occurs is that the offender is often decided to leave in a much worse place after their mates, relative, and belief system have been disowned. They've felt the shame and guilt before they widen. They are, after all, a liar today, and the reality that they may not remain true to their family is ample evidence that they are as evil an individual as the abuser had thought. It is really easy to watch that brainwashing is psychological warfare aimed at tearing a person to get to the fact where they are incapable of thinking in a coherent way. It's all-exhausting and consuming, and victims often struggle to get out of their predators' jaws, especially if they do it with the other phases of the brainwashing method.

Second Stage: Dangling a Salvation Carrot

Step 5: The Olive Branch

After the first 3 stages of brainwashing mentioned above, a survivor of brainwashing sometimes feels so bad about themselves because they try to save themself at whatever expense. The survivor is also in bad emotional health and has a weak self-image. Those who have forgotten their longtime sense of belonging and will clutch up on any straws offered to feel something again. At this stage, a victim becomes expected to experience a nervous collapse, and that is the signal for the attacker to leap in and deliver redemption.

The manipulator would also offer an olive branch after tearing down their objective for a long period of time so that the goal will slip into the pit of thinking there is any hope at the last of a tunnel. An olive branch at this point could be something from a sweet word to a gift, or perhaps even some type of personal

Dark Psychology and Manipulation

affection. This olive branch helps to demonstrate the goal that when they're on the right side of the manipulator, there is certain leniency to gain. A manipulator is above all a 'normal guy' who wishes them the best. That is at least what they have learned since the start of brainwashing.

Step 6: Being forced to confess

Take into account: You have been confined for an amount of time to intense mental abuse by an individual. You have wasted your sense of belonging and feel confused and indignant. You 're facing a psychotic collapse or you've already experienced one and can't make every part of your life head or tails. Since leaving the social network you have existed in solitary isolation and can't think of the last moment you had such a decent meal. Then, one day, this individual comes up at your door carrying a steaming coffee pot and freshly prepared muffins. They just say they want to chat. You are inviting them to your building. You just can't believe it. It's the only love you've been receiving in the longest period of time. What do you believe your former abuser will be reacting to this unusual kindness?

You'll experience a sense of sovereign debt more often than not. Human beings enjoy being kind enough to reciprocate that compassion. Whenever somebody does something good for you, then in exchange, it is natural and wants to do anything better. For a brainwashed human, the desire to pay back is much greater as they believe they still have to compensate for anything they are incorrect about. The brainwashed side, therefore, will be more than willing to offer away some type of kindness. This goodness would always come in the shape of a lie, in their troubled minds. The perpetrator would usually give the alternative of an apology as a means to get paid back.

Step 7: Guilt channeling

A brainwashed survivor is frequently filled by so much crushing remorse that they still have no scope for any other feeling after weeks or months of becoming told they're mistaken on anything. The goal has been swamped by so much abuser psychological torment they don't really realize what we feel most bad for. The victim simply knows he's guilty of anything. In this misunderstanding, the manipulator glides in and persuades them that guilt is due to all the bad people they've believed in before. The predator, in other words, streams the guilt into the system of belief. The victim now begins to associate their beliefs with the guilt and the responsibility of having to deal with the guilt. By fact, the abuser wants to help their prey continue to equate all the negative emotions of their history and at the same time letting them think that if they select different values, there is a possibility to be rescued and to feel stronger.

Step 8: Guilt Relief

The victim is beginning to feel a little relieved at this point to recognize that he's just not deeply bad; perhaps, it is his perceptions that are wrong. He can be correct again, by detaching himself from his beliefs. He sheds his remorse by relinquishing anything and everything related to his prejudices, even those nearest to him. He admits the mistakes of his previous ways and is able to embark on the current set of values that the brainwasher provides.

Third Stage: Reconstruction of a Brainwashed Self

Step 9: Harmony and Progress

At this stage in the process of brainwashing the target is keen to redeem itself and look very good in the brainwashed 's eyes. Even so, they will start rebuilding a new identity based on the manipulator 's offered belief system. After passing through the torture and suffering of the early phases of brainwashing, an offender is assured that only pain and guilt will come from their old system of belief. They are glad to be rid of the former life and replaced with a new self that is their safe place from all their suffering past and present.

Step 10: Rebirth and Final confession

The survivor also experiences a sense of satisfaction upon embracing the current moral structure to be finished for their history and all of the resulting pain. Like the stereotypical last rope on a sinking ship, they must stick to their new identities as this is the only happiness they have experienced in a long period. At this stage, the brainwasher succeeded in obtaining a conversion, and might even be conducting a ritual to invite the latest conversion into the holy inner circle. At this stage, it is typical for the majority of offenders to be totally separated from their families. They're going to get it in their heads that they're better individuals today and don't have to deal with their previous negative stuff. A brainwashed family member who has moved through these 10 steps is typically nearly impossible to convince that they've been brainwashed. The harm caused here is so enormous that a think-over is an uphill journey. Medical support can be tried to rescue a brainwashed loved one but it is rarely a promise of success.

The ten stages of brainwashing are attributed to studies by Richard Jay Lifton, a United States psychologist, and innovator of the reform of thought. Lifton questioned prisoners of war and read on the social effects of their encounters.

7.2 What makes people brainwashing susceptible?

Which causes one person more susceptible to brainwashing than another? Do you ever question that certain individuals appear to be more quickly drawn into extremist cults than others? There're conditions for this.

There're certain individuals who have a vague sense of belonging for one cause or another. An individual is not born with an individuality; self-identity is anything that evolves over

Dark Psychology and Manipulation

time as a kid grows into adulthood via puberty and. Self-identity is formed by a person's experiences, the activities they experience, and also the decisions they make. If an individual cannot convincingly define who they are, they run a greater fear of harm prey to brainwashing. It is because, in the first place, they have no name to defend themselves. A clear, stable sense of national identity makes it more challenging for a brainwasher to pin you down. For e.g., if you genuinely believe that you're just a solid, optimistic, intelligent, and loving individual who is a Christian and a successful sister and mother, telling you otherwise is almost difficult for someone else. But a depressed youth who believes he is a failure can quickly accept the lies he is being served by the brainwasher. He still has an incredibly weak view of himself, after all, and is most definitely seeking away and out his self-imposed mental

cage.

The disappearance of a support network is another factor that makes a person more impervious to brainwashing. The crucial function played by a group of loyal family and friends who unite behind you in times of distress can never be overrated. Sadly, the support network is lacking for certain citizens. In the lack of a large group of people searching after you, an attacker could swoop in and rob you of the community you are so eager to see. Brainwashers realize the value of a help system; thus, they would go to considerable lengths to separate their victims from the people they care for. It's true there's power in numbers, and that kind of intensity is just what a brainwashing operator doesn't want to be their goal.

Some individuals do not seem to hold the skills needed to effectively move through life. As an infant, you focus entirely on your parents or family to help you survive, at minimum to the best possible degree of their capacity. When you get older, you ought to go out to the best of ability to make the most of your life. If you're on this path to self-actualization, certain abilities come in handy. These abilities involve learning how to do decision-making, how and when to generate income so that you can at least provide for your journey through the simple requirements, taking care of the self correctly, keeping a healthy outlook, and also creating nice, productive ties. Most individuals make it through maturity without the requisite coping skills, often by no fault of their own. We appeal to us for help as this occurs. The first individual who always seems to know the way would be preceded by a guy who doesn't know their way in life. Think of it this way: you wouldn't matter who put on the life belt if you died in the shallow end of the pool; you will accept it and be thankful to the person forever. This kind of debt and rescue feeling is what some indoctrinated people are experiencing when they eventually get the 'life jacket.' What they don't know is that what looks like a life vest is currently a trap to maintain them hovering in false waters.

Dark Psychology and Manipulation

The type of family establishment to which one is exposed may also end up making one more susceptible to brainwashing. That can be asserted in 2 directions. First, a neglected child will often tend to lean toward the first person who shows attention in them. They are after all used to getting crumbs and, so to speak, would do anything for a proper meal. Secondly, when an infant grows up in a household that is excentric in its values and attitudes then an infant is at a strong risk of brainwashing. After all, they grew up witnessing things beyond the norm — what is another one thing?

Individuals working in dangerous economic situations also run a high risk of brainwashing. Perhaps a person who can hardly afford a food a day is not in the strongest state of mind to choose well for himself. Added to that, the commitment of a better life can be used to attract them into a brainwasher's choice belief system. For example, certain radical organizations were known to attract young people from socially deprived communities, with the prospect of cash incentives and attention. To a young adult who is accustomed to being socially insignificant and sometimes even such a compensation is beyond all the disinformation, however unknowingly, that they may be exposed to.

7.3 Shield yourselves from brainwashers

Predators who try to manipulate your brain walk the same paths you do, and therefore even stay at your house. While some brainwashing attempts may be obvious and easy to identify, others are subtler. As such, the process can be sucked in while unsure. The essential thing is to stay alert to any type of violence and manipulation but always second-guess whatever you hear. In brief, go about life with the requisite sprinkle of salt in order to taste all the knowledge that you exchange. In addition to having a good healthy quantity of skepticism, there're many other ways you should support yourself.

Be aware of your weaknesses

Often note that the mind is vulnerable to make errors with the way it handles information, however wise you can consider yourself to be. Occasionally, your mind may get messy and make you susceptible to external forces controlling you. Also, try to check out by the people that matter throughout your life that is particularly vulnerable based on how their brain works. For e.g., the aged and a very young are prime targets for brainwashing due to the inexperience-induced naivete and out of contact with conventional brainwashing schemes.

Beware of spun tales

A person can dress up reality to the extent it turns into a blatant lie. This is especially culpable to the government. There's a wise person who said the news is when a guy bites a pet and not a man bites a dog. In an attempt to show the man biting the dog, media outlets are every time aiming to make what they report sensational. A media corporation might perform a short poll of ten people living in Michigan and then announce it as a study of Midwest American men. It's not a representative study but this way it brings a bigger blow. Also, be mindful of the dimension of speculation and ask for references to be quoted, if possible, on any argument you came across in media.

Don't trust the hype

Have you ever found that many products that attract the most attention are overhyped? Many advertising gurus have perfected the art of dismissing their services and products as best in town when they are not, in fact. Before you think that all the hype generated about an individual or item takes a period to take into account why that entity demands so much advertising if it is as good as it claims to be. There is no need to reveal a thing of importance because citizens would obviously rush to it.

The environment today is increasingly invested in propaganda, especially because the knowledge, false or otherwise has become very much simpler to disseminate. A person only has to compose an essay or make a video that can 'go viral.' Before you realize it, there's an adult on the other side of the planet that thinks that a certain entity or company is the answer to all of their problems.

Look out for group thought

Groupthink is, in the simplest form, the unfortunate tendency of an otherwise smart person to achieve stupid mistakes just for the sake of agreement. Groupthink is a keyhole for people who don't like to stand out in the audience or be the voice of dissent. Brainwashers are especially pleased with the presence of group thinking because they don't like their objectives to query them most often. Groupthink is why hundreds of supporters of a controversial religious leader are going to make choices that do not appear to anyone else natural. Anytime you find oneself in a house with everyone where you need to make a decision, don't be scared to be a voice of sanity that the room needs so desperately. You might just save yourself from becoming brainwashed, and a few others.

Choose temporality over patterns

Which phone are you on? What happened with your last phone — has it outlived its value, or had you purchased it because you thought you needed to update? Do you buy stuff when you need or just because you feel forced to get it? Based on how you answered such queries, you may start to see a pattern of your choices: maybe you're the sensible kind who buys for convenience or the fashion junkie who wants to grab any new iteration of the iPhone as it's launched. There's really nothing bad with buying the lightest new design of anything, but if you've been fooled into thinking you have to have the latest of all you have a large issue on your hands.

Through always preferring uniqueness over patterns, you will shield yourself against further fall down the hill. Most improvements are often not even enhancements. A supplier may say that everything is fresh and better because they have simply modified the packaging. A manufacturer like that will only prey on your urge for shiny new shapes. The manufacturer cannot be blamed — that's how individuals remain in business. Only make sure you don't slip for their tricks.

Beware of the gut feeling

Whether you're going to term it experience or hunch, your gut instinct is something you can remember when you go through your regular life.

By trying to listen to that grumbling internal monologue that many loves to ignore, many individuals have saved themselves up an entire lot of pain and trouble. Before your conscious brain does, your conscious brain can quickly take on the danger. Listen to your gut instinct if anyone is offering you a concept that doesn't sound good. Your conscious brain has already grabbed signals that are not sitting right and having to send you red flags for the preservation of your own.

Chapter 8: The art of deception and persuasion

Merriam-Webster explores persuasion as a capability to influence while persuading is further described as moving to a faith, position, or plan of action by reasoning, entreaty, or expostulation. To seduce someone to do anything is to convince anyone to do something in lesser terms. A persuasion is a form of art that anyone wishing to get individuals to do anything must master. It's an awesome resource to have, particularly if you're continually supported by friends who every now and again need a bit of prodding.

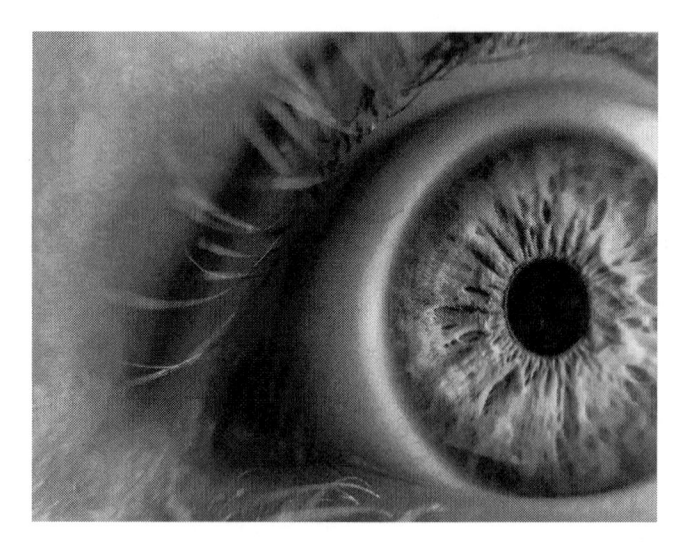

On the other hand, deception is explained as the act of triggering somebody to believe that something which is false or invalid is actually valid and true. Deception is a form of self-manipulation and also an instrument by which you can achieve your goals of persuasion. So far as persuasion goes, this is probably where stuff gets blurry. Debates have been going on for the longest time about the fine distinction between coercion and convincing. There are facilities that are absolutely convinced of the vindictiveness of persuasion, whereas others think that persuasion is a completely harmless way for people to get what they want. The manipulation theme in itself is a blurred line for many people. Morality is relative thinking; it depends on the metrics which different cultures and societies put in place. The problem of whether deception is wrong or right is one that must be personally resolved.

That being said, certain technical differences exist among persuasion and manipulation. Manipulation has a straightforward self-interest whilst persuasion can be undertaken for a whole community's greater good. Take the issue of an activist who is persuading farmers to plant trees for the environmental good. Until they get the numbers they might need to push and prod to make the tree-planting workout a victory. Some people may see this as manipulation, but in the end, the result of their attempts benefits the whole community.

Persuasion sometimes provides a strong and logical justification regarding a specific situation, while deception also requires a distortion of evidence aimed at distorting a person's view of truth. At the last of the day, manipulation and persuasion often accomplish the same thing, which is to persuade them to do something you need them to do. The big distinction is how the party leaders choose to do it: there are the all games on the table technique, which really is persuasion, and the technique of manipulation of the hidden cards.

8.1 The Principles of Persuasion

To order to learn the practice of persuasion, you need to be mindful of the fundamental principles which will allow you to leverage your power. Human beings are an oversensitive lot; one false decision and you're going to take down all ability to persuade people to join your team. You need to make strategic decisions that are guided by the fundamental concepts that are needed. Consistency, reciprocity, social evidence, liking, scarcity, and authority are the six dimensions of persuasion.

Reciprocity Principle

Reciprocity just does to others as you'd have them do to you. Reciprocity calls for courtesy and generosity as you go regarding your everyday interactions. It's a positive idea to display compassion to someone that helps you feel comfortable about the relationship. More than that, the method of accumulating chips so you can cash back later is to do well. If you've been nice and kind to someone else, you have a better chance that they will be kind and nice to you.

If you are trying to impress a human, you must act towards them in a respectable manner. Speak a word of kindness, give them a massive favor, or even purchase them a gift. They would be more accommodating later when you try to persuade them to do something. Overall, you have proved yourself to be a caring human being who worries about him.

The Consistency principle

Consistency of persuasion operates this way: once you have induced them to adhere to smaller ones, individuals are more inclined to stick to greater projects or favors. Which is, once you want someone to raise a puddle for you, you might get someone to dive seas for you. A few experiments have been done to support this hypothesis. For example, in one study, a team of researchers kept asking some property owners to make up a hideous Drive Safely signboard from their front garden. So, few homeowners announced yes. The investigator then took a further method to the study: first, they got homeowners to comply with the small dedication to going to put up a Drive comfortably greeting card in their home's front windows. Ten days later they appeared with the order for a billboard. This time, given its lack of visual appeal, many homeowners wanted to open up the billboard. The explanation for it is that owners consciously or unconsciously feel obligated to follow up with their previous reaction.

The strategy of foot-in-the-door enforcement is premised on accuracy. It includes having others to commit to a bigger demand by first utilizing smaller requests to check the waters. If you want to cleverly execute this method, your target will need to be conditioned to be compatible with their reactions to your proposal. Of starters, because you want your people to work the late shift, you may try to convince them to decide to work the late shift — or vice versa based on whatever shift in your company is the least desired one.

The Liking Principle

If a person wants you, they're more likely to encounter your demands, no matter what that might be. A person who is undesirable and who is, therefore, unlikeable can learn far more often than a person who is well-liked. But how is it that you get people to like you? The key to being accepted is a mixture of three primary factors according to scientists. First of all, citizens want the ones close to them. You will reach a compromise with them in order for you to look close to the individual you are trying to convince. For starters, many foreigners also learned that studying and understanding the local language is the easiest way to become more relatable. The other thing you need to be aware of is flattery when making yourself more relatable. If you are using it well, Flattery will open many gates for you. People like those paying compliments to them. If you want to ask somebody to do something for you, begin by giving them a sincere compliment first. Only because this is called flattery doesn't imply you ought to be effusive about it. Too extreme in your praise will actually be detrimental to your need to be actually enjoyed. At last, be the type of individual that is usually pleasant and cooperative in achieving mutual goals, and you will be one small step to being pleasant. If you're constantly jumping on the toes of someone to achieve what you want, you'll have very little mates, so that won't support the cause when you try to impress anyone in the future. Also, being friendly and helpful doesn't mean becoming a doormat. Occasionally, it simply means putting some little effort into helping a person reach a goal that is important to them. For example, if a friend struggles with a due study, try to assist out with the mailing and printing phase. It's not a lot of effort, but you're going to move from an uninvolved, unwritten colleague to a caring and compassionate colleague. You will cash this chip later if you wish.

The authority principle

As opposed to a total newbie, an individual who is an authoritative figure in a specific field would have a simpler way to influence others. If you want to persuade most people to do something specific, you need to build your validity by trying to make yourself seem like you just have expert knowledge in whatever field you play. This concept is the main reason why professionals in their field display their diplomas. Think about

Dark Psychology and Manipulation

it — when, for example, you walk into a therapist's office, you will probably deliberately lookout for the sort of qualifications they have tried to hang on their walls. If your psychiatrist has a whole lot of qualifications displayed in this way, you will probably feel a feeling of comfort in their knowledge and experience. As such, you'll easily welcome and implement any suggestions they have for you. Essentially the therapist has tried to change you without really saying a word.

It's a fact that if you're the only one speaking about it your authority won't be taken very seriously. As such, you have to make sure, so to speak, that you recruit everyone else to beat the drum beats on your behalf. Subtle ways exist to do this. You can identify a field in the office that you are enthusiastic about, and become that field 's office guru. This may be Microsoft office or Reporting for some people. The guy known as the Excel mentor office will have a much easier time getting information out of people as they already believe he knows what he's talking about. He has also demonstrated to be relatable and helpful by solving all of their problems with Excel, and his colleagues would want to charge him back in some way. You don't need to learn Excel to start making your mark around the world. There are many other fields in which

you can excel and show yourself as a figure of authority.

The Scarcity principle

The laws of supply and demand are clear and transparent in economics: when supply is small, and the price is high, prices increase. To translate this, the value of scarcity builds. But if you're a business person who wants to persuade people to purchase your service or product, it helps to draw attention to the fact that the item is on a deal for just a limited time. Furthermore, let your consumers know that if they do not obtain this product on time, they will lose significantly. If the advertisement campaign is delivered in this manner, more customers would be racing to reach the time limit on your offer.

It is necessary to become a scarce commodity yourself in the businesses and personal relation universe. If you're not there for someone anytime they need you, you'll easily lose your worth. If you wish to maintain the aura of secrecy and power over you, you will master the art of remaining unreliable and unavailable. When you finally appear, your phrase will be revered further than a person's word that constantly appears and speaks out of all relevance and value.

The Consensus principle

People search for those that are close to them in daily experiences for hints as to what to do or do. An individual who is a strong influencer knows that buying into their concept is all it requires is one individual and the whole crowd does. There are different directions you can use the compromise theory to your advantage. For e.g., in an office environment, you might get a group of workers to commit to a cause and advocate that encourages their peers to do so. Such coworkers are much more probably to be persuaded of the noble cause if their superiors have said so.

If you've ever purchased everything from eBay, you might have seen that it includes a section showing the other products purchased by consumers who purchased the product you just bought. Why do you believe that's so, and how does that segment affect you as a purchaser? Most often, you'll probably recommend purchasing those other products because they were bought by these clients who clearly have similar interests and requirements to yours. Originally you might have not planned to buy the extra items, but it's just the reality that it was done by others will make you think you also need to. That is in effect the concept of consensus.

8.2 Persuasion Ideas for Daily Use

If you are trying to look to influence people, simply understanding the methods persuasion isn't enough. You also need to grasp the simple and effective ways you can use those principles in everyday life.

Dark Psychology and Manipulation

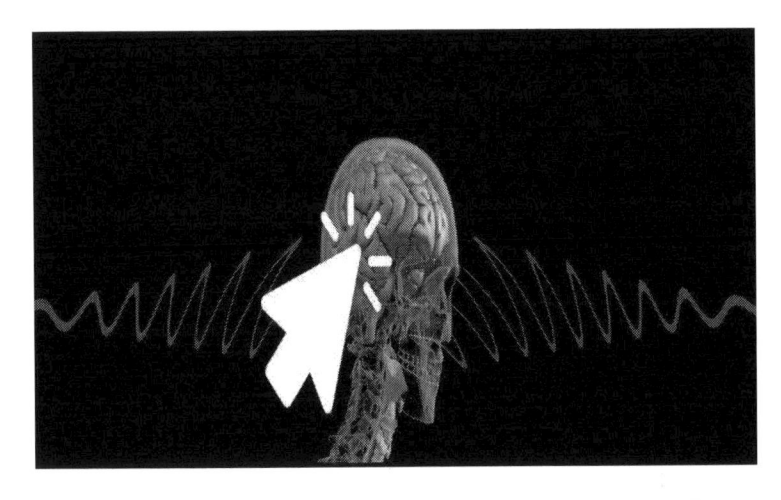

If you're a persuasive individual, you'll get a much simpler moment in life and your qualitative research will often be achieved without needing to climb through hoops. A few of the strategies to be more convincing can be quickly applied whereas some would take a bit of training.

Tip #1: Appear confident

Confidence will not apply to us all, obviously. Some individuals seem to be confident more easily while others are struggling quite a bit. Even if you're not automatically optimistic, you need to ensure that you still look assured to others. If you're insecure about how you look at a particular topic or your skills, nobody else wants to understand that. Do not provide a platform for your feelings to shine on. Instead, pretend it before you have it.

In this world, there are individuals who don't know a number of stuff and yet have handled to get dozens of people to encourage them and their concepts. Rationale? They represent the epitome of trust. They sneak into the rooms as if they were their own. They speak confidently even if they're unsure what they're going to talk about. Trust means you understand what you're thinking about. People encourage experts who understand what they're thinking about to trust themselves.

Tip #2: Be careful in your approach

Even when they enable themselves to be convinced to do something, many people tend to believe that doing it was their concept in the first case. No one appears to think that they have allowed a certain idea to be tossed down their necks. You have to be dramatic in your strategy to a persuasion for success. Think about starting with such an anecdotal story rather than incorporating a certain topic in full-on. If you are trying to convince others to buy through an investing, begin by explaining what you and your buddies went on a cruise last week after getting your Investment X payoff. Don't even attempt to offer them the investment. Conversely, get the other individual who thinks about how they might have passed for the cruise too if they had invested in the asset class. In brief, incentivize people with your tentation without it being too obvious.

Tip #3: Be flexible with your methods

The persuasive techniques aren't fixed in motion. Different

Dark Psychology and Manipulation

individuals react to different stuff. The same individual will also adapt to various methodologies differently depending on the occasion and time. You need to know when to shift positions as appropriate. Occasionally you will have to work with the liking principle and some other times you would have to base your technique on the authority principle. Reading social signals will enable you to determine what methods to use.

Tip #4: Timing is all it takes

If you want to reassure someone to purchase a home, if you draw them when they're purchasing for houses, you'll get more success. Most items keep that true. If you want their crush to go from crush to fiancé, if you speak to them while they are looking for love, you would have a simpler way. You also have to master the art of realizing when the moment is perfect, to expert the method of persuasion. If not, you'll make the mistake of assaulting people to come to terms with things they're not interested in. No one likes a person who constantly plagues them into doing kinds of Stuff, especially in the strangest times.

Tip #5: It's a bonus to be interesting

Many convincing individuals don't get bored. No one pays a lot of attention to boring people. To converse with dull people is not pleasant. They're not engaging and definitely, they're not enjoyable. If you'd like to win convincingly, you have to be an attractive person. The great news is there are lots of interesting ways to be. You just have to identify and amplify anything

Dark Psychology and Manipulation

unique regarding yourself for the world is seeing. It could be a talent or a hobby you're very good at. Maybe it's even your good sense of humor or the way you look. Maybe you'd also like to express your special perspective with your viewers. Whatever you're opting for, make sure it helps people recognize you long after the discussion is over.

Tip #6: Listen more than you speak

You may assume that being convincing implies talking a lot, but that could not be any further from the facts. You have to train oneself to be a great listener to be influencing people. Skills in listening serve various functions. First, as far as people talk and you listen, that means you're gathering important information which you can use for your benefit. Second, guys like a great communicator. Why? For what? Because people just love to talk about themselves. Hold your mouth closed and your mind open and you'll be well on the way to raising the quotient of likeability. If you don't believe this is critical when it comes to affecting others, please refer to the liking principle as mentioned earlier.

8.3 Types of Deception and How to Get stronger at them?

Deception occurs in two forms, which are all designed to throw away a subject from the truth. We described deceit at the start of this section as the act of forcing someone to think something which is not real or accurate. In this segment, we're going to discuss the various ways you can trick others, how to get good at these techniques, and how to defend yourself from deceit in your daily life.

Lies

Lies are the most commonly used type of illusion. During chit chat, meetings, relationships, transactions, whenever you want to get out of an unusual position, and in almost any sort of discourse or circumstance, they are used daily. A lie is an

assertion that is very literally the opposite of reality. An example of a fib would be convincing your employer that your grandma is dead and you can earn sympathy leave because your grandma is still alive and you really want a week off. Lies are simple to discern — you just have to identify and say the comparison with the facts.

Dark Psychology and Manipulation

Equivocations

An error refers to the use of a specific phrase or word to change a sentence's meaning to knowingly move the directed message. Equivocations are seldom used in daily conversation, though some smart people may find a way to incorporate them through their network of illusion. Equivocations are wordplay, in nature. They come under the wider definition of fallacy, described as flawed logic, which is meant to make a statement seem stronger than it really is.

Examples of misconceptions include:

Dating my boyfriend poses a total headache. Aspirin may cause headaches to go away, maybe I'll just take an aspirin to get my boyfriend off.

I have the right to freedom of expression. So, it is right for me to just tell what's on my mind.

Equivocations are also a perfect source of amusing stories you 're ready to share at every moment. For instance:

Two cannibals were chewing a clown and one switched to the other, asking, "Does this flavor funny to you?"

However, in all honesty, errors are not the main problem when it becomes to deceit. At best, errors will carry you some joy in the life-span; at worse, you would actually wind up frustrated, but just for a few minutes until you find out what is going on.

Dark Psychology and Manipulation

Concealments

When you start engaging in concealment, for deceit purposes, you omit the information. It is a favored method of deceit, particularly because when you're captured it's simple to get off the hook. You can just explain oneself by saying you have forgotten to reveal that particular fact. Occasional disguises are often referred to as omission lying. For e.g., let 's assume you intend on buying a home. You meet a successful realtor and for your unique requirements, you reach out to them. The realtor has a few units that meet your criteria, and you'll arrange a visit to the site. On the day of, you 're pleased with this one specific building, ideally placed near your office, and large enough to fit you and your pets. You want to make the offer on it, but you only need to answer one question: Why did the last proprietor give up a unit?

After spending some time in the department for three years, your realtor informs you that the former tenants opted to

relocate on to greener pastures. The realtor, however, efficiently glosses over the fact the requirement for greener pastures was made necessary by the reality that property values decline in the area in which you want to buy your house. By removing this crucial fact your realtor will persuade you to purchase the house. They weren't telling an outright lie-they just refused to tell the truth. That is the idea behind camouflage.

Exaggerations/Overstatements

Exaggeration is an expansion of the facts. Some people don't like telling the truth in its simple form, because it sounds boring. Instead, they'll sensationalize it to the point where it's hard to recognize. An overstatement or exaggeration looks like this: your mate is putting their money into a small investment that gives them $100 per week in returns. Instead of your colleague reporting on their returns accurately, he goes around showing everyone he's making bucket heaps of cash out of his investment. Relying on the economy in which you live, $100 may be several coffees and a nice meal, or a quarter of a month's rent, but it's hardly the summer-paying, prepared-to-retire fortune your buddy wants to make it look like. Yes, he's making a living, but yes, he's stretching the truth as well ... Maybe to make you jealous.

Understatements

Understatements are the exact result of exaggerations. Understatements are often referred to as the avoidance of reality, which includes downplaying a fact because it doesn't sound as horrible as it is. Understatements are sometimes used by individuals who deny things or those who need to rationalize a decision they have made otherwise irrational. In a confrontation with or about their victims, abusers may also underplay the truth so they can shed some accountability for their abuse.

Dark Psychology and Manipulation

For example, let's say a couple who've been allowed to marry for ten years agree on having the husband run the household 's finances together. Confident in the market sense and financial acumen of his father, the confident father is faithfully adding to their savings kitty and making the husband do all the saving. Sadly, the husband is making a few bad investments which will wipe out all their cash, leaving the others with nothing but paychecks for a few months. Sensing something is wrong, the wife needs an update where the man says things are not good. The husband has technically told the truth: things are not good indeed. What he did isn't saying exactly how bad things are, either. If he were frank, he should have said conditions are bad and are on the verge of financial distress. In this case, there has been a manipulation by the type of understatement and the husband gets to stop sleeping

on the sofa for at least another night till the piling expenses blow his cover.

Dark Psychology and Manipulation

Now that you understand the different forms of deceit you have to ask if you might learn the art of deceit. For example, it is necessary to remember that deceit, as far as morals and ethics go, isn't necessarily a good thing. You don't really want to base all of your actions and friendships on deceit, because then you'd be having taken away from people around you while yourself. Genuine partnerships focused on integrity and sincerity have a great chance to stand the passage of time. That said, it is also important to recognize that life in black and white will not always turn out. In between, there are sometimes other colors that call for us all to be creative. You would have to use trickery once in a while to get where you'd like to be. You'll understand to be very cautious about how you purchase your deception in such instances.

Your body language is one thing you need to be cautious about. You may have in your mind the most extensive lie outlined and send it precisely as you had performed in front of the mirror, and still fail in deception. Why? Of what? Since you give away your facial expressions. There are other signs from the body which can offer away a liar. These include failure to manage contact with the eye, to fidget, and even to stutter. Several individuals were supposed to rub their nose if they were lying. Watch out by this tell-tale symbol of lying, and

make sure that you steer clear of it as you spin your big tales.

Dark Psychology and Manipulation

The 2nd thing you have to be cautious about is the explanation for the deception when you're truthful. Deception is just worth the hassle if you have what you desire, or if you just need to go anywhere. Besides that, deception is nothing more than a waste of time for everyone. If you get into the custom of lying for the sake of, everyone will think of you as a narcissistic sociopath that can never be respected. This would destroy whatever reputation you might have built up so you won't be willing to exploit or control others anymore.

Never intermingle your stories. That is the surest way to be captured. When you plan to trick somebody, make sure you've set out the entire tale in case you've had to address some inquiring queries. You don't want to get caught up in an unconfirmed rumor which has more holes than the net of a fisherman. Perhaps most amateur liars get wrapped up in their world of lies since they cannot recall what they were saying about whom and when. If you need a journal to keep hold of your misinformation, please do so. It could just focus on saving you the humiliation of being trapped in lies.

Chapter 9: The Truth of Hypnosis

If you think of the word hypnosis what is the first question that comes to mind? The solution for many people is this: a Hollywood movie with an overly performed scene together with a hypnotherapist and his mysterious revolving watch. Around the hypnotist is a poor person who is about to be decided to send to some location in their mind they have still yet to visit in more than twenty years. The fact is, the hypnosis is less effective in the modern world. Hypnosis is, in the simplest form, a type of manipulation involving reducing a person's awareness of their outer surroundings and increasing their internal attention. We react more favorably to advise while a person is under hypnosis since their rational thought is damaged. That is why the film will show a subject unquestionably responding to a hypnotist 's commands.

Hypnosis has some psychology to it, so it includes knowing

how the human mind functions. The human brain is built in such a manner that experiences are contained in the conscious mind that governs rational thought, and the subconscious mind. The rational mind is what advises you that it is risky and foolish to cross a busy street without looking; whilst the subconscious brain is likely to warn you that weight loss is impossible as the images of the last time you attempted losing weight are held in it. Hypnosis tends to work by altering and replacing the subconscious required you get about certain things with stronger and more useful thoughts.

9.1 The Misconceptions about Hypnosis and Manipulation Burst

It seems almost difficult to believe the use of hypnosis in our daily lives, but the simple fact of the situation is that it is so. You might not have had any twirling watches in your face, and during your waking hours your eyes may be constantly open, and you are most certainly hypnotized when you go about your everyday life. How could it be?

When is the last moment you read a book that really made you lose sight of what was going on around you? You were effectively hypnotized when you were in the condition of being completely immersed in your work. They assess potential are you weren't even distantly aware of people standing near you and living their lives. Really quiet, you were riding somewhere on a train, along with the main character's actions and thoughts. That is real-life hypnosis. No hypnotizers, no continues to watch your subconscious brain take a journey to an alternative universe.

Self-induced hypnosis is often normal in children who often fall into this trance many times a day at least. That's why, when they watch their special cartoon series with no reaction, you'll call your boy. They don't want to ignore you. They actually cannot understand you because they have blocked out the aware mind and the universe because they live in another realm where they are completely blocked to the subconscious. Throughout their shows, musicians and performers requiring concentrated attention to succeed brilliantly in their sport or craft quite frequently fall into hypnotic trances. Many will mention this trance as being 'in the zone.' What sometimes happens is that the mind of the artist is so concentrated on what they are doing, that during this period nothing else matters. Writers often get in the groove when it comes to the writing process. When this occurs, you may notice the writer being transported into the universe they've created their words with. Reluctant or unable to abandon this planet, the writer can produce thousands of words a day when, due to writer's block, they have historically been unable to venture past a few hundred lines.

Some individuals and groups have experienced suitable methods of utilizing hypnotherapy to their advantage when it

Dark Psychology and Manipulation

comes to mind control and manipulation. Making a long speech and conducting a lengthy and almost never-ending lecture, for example, all have the purpose of bringing the listener into a trance-like area. That may be due to boredom or fatigue, or a mixture of both. If an individual is in this condition, they are more friendly and willing to sign up for anything you sell. This is something that has been mastered by many cult leaders and would understand why many cultural meetings are sometimes long and dreary. A cult meeting has rarely ended in a few mins. If you arrive at the conclusion a meeting in 15 minutes, the minds of the attendees will still be strong and doubting. But when you go on about for hours, they start unknowingly falling out of control and will not be as resistant to your advice as they would be in the first 15 minutes.

Another tactic used to accomplish hypnosis is to present contradicting knowledge as if it were not contradictory but completely logical. What do you mean by that? As previously mentioned in this chapter there is a critical reasoning area of the brain. By helping you filter vital details, this region of a brain is just what keeps you safe and out of danger. If this area of a brain is swamped with conflicting data without adequate time being given to handle it, it closes down. When your rational reasoning has been disregarded, you are apt to follow any ideas offered to you even if they may not be agreed by a normal-minded individual in harmony with their mind's reasonable pieces.

9.2 How to Hypnotize Someone Without Them Knowing

You can use hypnosis in everyday life to obtain what you want from people without them beginning to suspect what you are up to. One positive thing about hypnotherapy as a manipulation tool is that it's subtle and leaves no evidence behind it. Except lying where you could find yourself caught in your lies, hypnosis does not leave any traces behind. No one is going to walk up with you and start accusing you of hypnotizing them. Even in the worst-case situation, you can just be convicted of getting away from it.

The Jake, they'll claim, he's got away with the girls.

What they don't know is that you've developed the habit of hypnotizing ladies doing just as you're saying.

The first process to effectively hypnotize a person is to establish a connection with that person. You can very rarely hypnotize a random person to whom you express no connection at all. It's fairly simple to establish a link with a human. You only need to observe and react correctly to your facial expressions and theirs, and their body language as well. The entire point of creating a bond is to make sure the other individual is accessible to you and can react favorably to your overt stimulation of the mind, better known as hypnosis. Make use of some of the following suggestions to hypnotize them after being certain of the presence of any connection for both you and your subject:

Tip #1: Turn them away from familiar

Humans love patterns. They are simple, straightforward, and soothing to understand. Patterns are a significant component of the comfort zone and do not require any logical thought. What patterns did you set in your life, and how do they assist you? Patterns simplify life for many. Let's consider a simple method that can be interrupted with a person's intent to hypnotize. let's say you and your fiancé have a method of saying goodbye before work every morning, which involves a kiss on a cheek and a quick hug. You feel particularly philanthropic one morning and decide to start replacing your pattern with a tight, residual hug and a full kiss on the lips. The mind of your spouse will be thrown into chaos because that's not what mentality is used to. You'll have a short opening for a hypnotic order in the five seconds of uncertainty that will ensue in your spouse's head.

Now you can make lasagna?

Your spouse does respond instantly, of course.

They should have sat back on every other day and remembered the labor involved in creating lasagna, and would hopefully have proposed an option. On the day you toss them off your sequence, they'll say yes without too much thinking, because you've essentially shortened their conscious mind.

Tip #2: Use the Zeigarnik-effect

The Zeigarnik effect in psychology is the principle that consumers are more inclined to recognize unfinished tasks than the ones that have been finished. Think about all this: if you're planning to do your laundry, you 're likely to have that thought persisting in your brain until you actually wash and put away all your dirty clothes. You will no matter how much experience you have any interest in memorizing everything to do with laundry soon after you have completed your laundry duties. The Zeigarnik impact was named after a Russian psychologist, who had been inspired by her professor to investigate the phenomenon. The teacher, one Kurt Lewin, made the point that the orders which were still unpaid could be remembered more precisely by a waiter.

In certain cases, Zeigarnik's influence is seen in daily life. In particular, soap operas and tv-show are eager to leave their listeners wanting more by ensuring each series ends with such a cliffhanger. When an episode runs out anticlimactically, your brain will store this as an incomplete task in your short-term memory. That's why you keep returning to your favorite soap opera because your brain knows you to complete what you begin. As far as the incompleteness lingers in your brain somehow, your mind will be attracted to it.

Try sharing an entertaining tale with breaks in between throughout which you send them hypnotic orders to hypnotize anyone using the Zeigarnik method. This may sound something like this:

YOU WON'T BELIEVE WHAT HAPPENED WHEN I WANTED TO GO CAMPING WITH MY FRIENDS LAST WEEKEND. WE WALKED UP THIS VERY DESOLATE PATH WHEN ALL OF A SURPRISE, WE HEARD THESE ODD SOUNDS COMING FROM THE WOODS [COULD YOU KINDLY CLOSED THE DOOR FOR ME]. THEY SOUND LIKE A CROSS BETWEEN A BEAR AND A COYOTE AND THEY GREW LOUDER AND LOUDER THE FARTHER WE WENT UP THE ROAD. OF COURSE, WE 'RE GETTING VERY WORRIED AT THIS POINT BUT WE KNEW THERE WAS NO GOING BACK. THERE WERE FOUR OF US, SO WE WERE ABLE TO BATTLE EVERYTHING THAT IT WAS ...

YOU MAY ASK YOUR DIALOGUE COMPANION TO DO FAIRLY MUCH WHATEVER YOU LIKE, WITHOUT MUCH RESISTANCE, THROUGHOUT THIS STORYTELLING. THAT'S BECAUSE THEIR BRAIN IS CENTERED ON THE STORY YOU 'RE TELLING, AND THEIR NERVOUS SYSTEM IS ANXIOUS TO FINISH. THEY 'RE YOUR PLASTIC TO WORK WITH WHILE THEY'RE IN THAT TRANCE-LIKE STATE.

Tip #3: Stay contentious

Ambiguity keeps a guess on your audience. If you want to stick on people's minds who you connect with even after the interaction is finished, you have to find a compromise between being unforgettable and staying vague. Ambiguity continues to keep the mind-blowing: What did he mean exactly and he explained this or that? You are in the power of another person as far as their minds ask. It confuses the conscious mind with vagueness and ambiguity. There are aspects that the human mind cannot perceive and one of them is the nature of uncertainty.

Ambiguity in the world of relationship and dating can serve a vital role in persuading others to go somewhere with you and date you. Many involve personal will agree that a bit of a mystery will serve a long way to keep life interesting. What doesn't explain most is why. The possible explanation of why secret is so interesting is that as far as a person's conscious mind has not properly confirmed and understood you would always stay in their minds. By always making sure you remain vague and enigmatic regarding one or two things, you will hypnotize your friend or girlfriend into doing what you need them to do.

Tip #4: Negative words impact more

The mental state is often believed not to be able to hear negative ones. Any negatives transmitted to a subconsciousness are then perceived as optimistic. Of starters, if you were to say, someone, when I'm away, doesn't go creeping into my space, the person is probably to translate that subconsciously as, when I'm away, go and pee into my house. This is likely the reason why so many irritated parents of children appear to be doing the complete reverse of what they are advised not to do.

Even so, if you are trying to convince others to do things without being too straightforward about it, you may use derogatory language to hypnotize their conscious mind. Rather than telling his friend:

Aid me to load up for my forthcoming move please stopover.

Please consider:

You don't have to come out to help me pack.

Throughout their day, the subconscious brain of your friend would inform her she wants to help you prep your step, and that's how your comment was understood by the mind. Of course, whether or not your friend is actually coming over is a matter of how much price she puts on your friendship.

Tip #5: **Good Keywords**

Have you noticed how many selling copies or ads have this precise language that lets you picture all the opportunities provided by a given product or service? When it came to hypnotizing men, through phrases carry a specific appeal. For eg, if you ask a child to visualize anything, you 're already taking them into a trance state, where they're turning to their mind and emotions. They become more suggestible while they're in this condition, and would definitely do what you're telling them to do. If you don't believe this, look up any advertisement for travel destinations and have a listen. You'll probably have thought of reserving your next holiday to that destination at the end of it.

As long as something is imagined by the subconscious mind, then that particular thing gets programmed. This helps to explain why certain people are afraid of the dark — they've envisioned the shadows to involve bad things, and the fear remains clear and valid as long as that creativity is active. It also shows why people are scared of horror films. Think of it-there's nothing frightening about horror films. They're just a bunch of average people acting out fictional scenarios, so why are you so scared? Since your imagination has dreamed that something is true, that's why.

9.3 Keeping Yourself safe Against Hypnosis

The daily self-hypnosis in the context of a fascinating book or video is welcome every time. Once in a while, it helps to avoid the harsh daily reality. But what might not be so easy is the hypnosis brought about by other outlets that you don't feel that good with. How do you defend against the hypnotherapy that happens in your everyday life? For example, it's necessary to realize that you may not actually be able to remove all the hypnotherapy that is involved in your existence. Combating will be too much of a fight. This being said, as far as hypnosis goes, there are many fights that you should fight.

One of the things that help you guard against hypnosis is to continue living by principle. A person who lives by principle doesn't really mean being stuck or relentless when you're supposed to be flexible. It just implies deciding what you're going to embrace, and what you'd rather forgo, rather than just moving with the tide. If you're the kind of person in the address of being easy going with the flow, you might find that you've strayed too far from the secure store. Manipulators who use hypnosis to prey on others know how to counter those who are not securely anchored to something unwavering. If you're the kind of person who, having been told to assume how simpler your life would be with brand X rushes to unquestionably buy Product X, you'll find yourself in your life from a whole lot of clutter. Having one or two values on other facets of your life lets you make more rational choices and are not affected by certain people's behavior or phrases.

There's a smart guy who once claimed you'll find it when you go hunting for it. The explanation they hypnotize too many individuals in their everyday life is that they don't really search for hypnosis because they can't even detect it. As soon as you are mindful of the reality that there is hypnosis, you should be able to spot it from a mile away and be actively protecting themselves against it. You'll note it when your mate attempts to get you to commit on something you wouldn't usually agree with and you'll remember it when your sly boss wants to get you a favor. Being aware of the existence of people who are attempting their level best to take benefit of you is going to go a long way to protecting oneself from mind control.

The freedom will that is conferred on any human person living in the modern world is a wonderful thing about life. A free-will ensures you can pick what you want in your existence, and what you don't want through the doors. There are various channels in today's world that are used to impact you. TV, videos, movies, the phone, books, newspapers, radio shows, songs ... the list is infinite. You are able to pick what you want in your life, and you can be confident that several of these networks are designed to place you in the same frame of mind that is beneficial to channel operators. In short, you'll be able to decide what's filtered from your life. Choose wisely

9.4 What about Hypnotherapy?

Hypnosis is often used as a type of therapy for specific conditions. When used in this way, hypnosis is called hypnotherapy. Hypnosis is simply minded management where the individual in influence has granted a licensed practitioner their permission for the same. Like most alternate solution methods of therapy, the effectiveness of hypnotherapy has divergent views. The fact that the study on the same subject is very limited does not do the argument for hypnosis any nice.

Hypnosis as a method of therapy is used to help people overcome unhealthy behaviors and poor eating patterns, as well as alcohol recovery, eating disorders, and even depression. Hypnosis can also be used in pregnancy where pregnant mothers are advised to hypnotize themselves so that they can mentally prepare themselves for almost pain-free childbirth. This is called hypnobirthing which entails basically training the inner self for pain-free labor.

Chapter 10: How to defend yourself against dark psychology

The fact of the matter, whatever you might also want to assume in the best of all, is that as long as deception goes, we are all lying ducks. In this country, people leave their homes with just the lowest of intentions. My motives are to harm us and to get the best out of us without offering something back.

Dark Psychology and Manipulation

The dark psychological knowledge explained in this guide is not designed to be used to hurt people to others. Rather, the principal goal is to assist you realize manipulation for what it is in its different forms and to turn the chairs to safeguard yourself when necessary. If you can deceive a manipulator until they get you the best, that's a win for you as well as the

rest of mankind.

10.1 Factors which make you more manipulative

Besides knowing how to identify a predator, it also helps to understand what makes a person more vulnerable to psychological attacks. Simply put, there are sitting ducks that are closer to the line of fire than others.

Dark Psychology and Manipulation

You are Wise.

You're obviously mistaken about this one because you've always believed smarter people are more difficult to outwit, right? Yet here's the thing: Intelligent people want to use reasoning to support their controlling procedure. Logic becomes more deceptive. Therefore, when you circle them with reasoned reasoning, smart people are much more likely to get manipulated. Less smart folks are difficult to support with logic and in the face of evidence and scientific explanations tend to become more stubborn. It's no wonder that many people scammed by manipulators and Ponzi schemes occur to be individuals who are extremely intelligent and you wouldn't expect to be fooled easily. The explanation that is always the case is that scammers know how to manipulate evidence and figures to cater to this type of people. People that are less educated can be quickly ignored if they

don't recognize something that looks like hullabaloo.

You are confident and you like to believe the good about everyone

Believe it or not, this world is full of bad people. Every morning, there are people leaving their homes with the intent to harm others. There are individuals who don't mind inflicting heartburn and turmoil on others. While you may be sitting in your home worried about mega-rich corporations stealing from the poor, there's a conference room full of big corporate shots about to grab from the very needy you're concerned about. Simplest terms, not everyone shares your empathy and your conscience. People have different wired-ups. Individuals on a dark triad are connected even more than you might ever have imagined. It's noble to just want to think the best of them when you make contact with a new person but it's wise to expect a surprise, not in an a-so-great way. Keeping people's expectations to a minimal level is a great method to protect yourself from anyone who is trying to have a piece of you.

You also ask for external approval

A person who is actively striving validation to others is similar to a sheep walking in a lion's den when it reaches to manipulation. It's only a matter of seconds before the sheep from the face of the planet is completely annihilated. Manipulators are very capable of noticing and exploiting loopholes to their advantage. A large, glaring exemption for just a manipulator is a socially isolated or insecure individual who at whatever cost wants to have some companionship.

Everybody is likely to feel alone every now and then. We are social beings and we can often feel dejected and unloved in the lack of company. Should not search for public affirmation to the extent that you are rendering yourself a recognition sitting duck. It's Cool for everyone to like you, even if they don't like you, it's fine too. Nice enough to like yourself. When you've put on the body armor of acceptance and self-love, you start making it a little more difficult for predators to crawl through your defensive lines. That's not to say any manipulated person doesn't love themself enough. Nonetheless, you should only defend yourself in intimate affairs, because you have already accepted yourself emotionally before going out to the wild.

You've gotten isolated from friends or family

You have likely heard the same story before — a senior citizens person living alone meets on the Internet with a charming young man. This online get-together rapidly becomes a romantic relationship. The young man is doing all the right words a couple of months down the track, and seeing money transferred into their account every week. A year down the track, the older lady or guy has spent all their investments in retirement is recovering from the realization that their belief in online love was a pure con. Whereas the victim is wallowing in humiliation and wiping out finances, you must only want to know how the con pulled off a scam that's so easy and straightforward it's laughable. You wonder how can a person become so gullible? It is really simple. One person is easier to fool than many are to fool.

One guy who genuinely had some insight in him expressed it this way: occasionally you might fool half the people and some of the individuals all the time, but all the time you can't fool all the people. That's a reality hunter know — it's far safer to kill the solitary antelope when it wanders through the savannah, isolated and vulnerable from all the world's hazards. When you are protected by relatives and caring friends, you have a shield around you that holds the monsters out. And if you're convinced you're in love and your wife is the greatest thing that had happened to you, there'll be the one person in your group whose rational reasoning hasn't been compromised by a fresh partnership excitement. One person is going to be your shield from exploitation. It's no wonder that many individuals who exploit their relationships and assault them want to hold them apart from their families. Those abusers and manipulators know that their whole gig will be up if another group comes into the mix.

You are extremely emotional

Strong emotions. It is a blessing to be able to feel pleasure,

laughter, disappointment, passion, sorrow, and any emotion in human life. This blessing was offered out in spades for certain men. You are extremely susceptible to coercion if you're the type of person who moves across life experiencing stuff rather than think things. Manipulators will falsify feelings as they tell and do anything you have to listen to. They don't really have to make any sense — they only have to express the things you are looking for, so you're being offered. Now, if you're extremely emotional, you can't do a whole number of stuffs to modify yourself. That way you are born and you can just learn to cope by being so extremely emotional. Of this said, we should always ensure you

Dark Psychology and Manipulation

are mindful of your feelings, and they don't necessarily determine the choices for you.

You don't put up yourself

You don't need to go away to school and learn all the ways people try to exploit you. The positive thing about spending life in this country today is that technology is easily accessible at the disposal. You just have to be ready to learn. A whole number of people are getting manipulated because they don't realize the techniques that manipulators use. If you don't know which manipulators have something known as the technique of mirroring, you might think you and your schedule simply have great chemistry when that's absolutely not the case. A great thing regarding manipulators is that they already have most of their methods in the novels all you'll have to do is grab a book and get to read. This way, you can prevent any predator in his paths before he comes too close to cause any harm to you.

The free flow of details in the same breath ensures that you should still look up somebody so you can verify their identity before they have a chance to snatch something from themselves. Those days are gone when a private detective used to be retained to run a background search on someone. In today's world, somebody on the Internet can run a background check and have the outcomes ready within mins. This could be either a paid search warrant or a simple cursory review of their social media accounts. Luckily, today, virtually the entire planet is on social media, so a lot of us want to overshare.

You should follow basic techniques to defend yourself

Whether you take into account yourself extremely vulnerable or impervious to manipulation, it helps to always be safe than sorry. Fortunately, you can keep the psychopaths, narcissists, and high Machs in your life at a safe distance. How will that be?

In our offices, in corporate dealings, in our intimate relations and also in our family's psychopaths are active. You can't just avoid a psychopath sometimes by nature of the relationship between you two. Of starters, ignoring or preventing your psychopathic employer would not be practical, since you have to do your work, get compensated, and develop your future, or just pay your expenses. If the manager is a psychopath, then sometimes you have to work with him. For e.g., you would have to work out a way to hold your connections to a minimum. But if you've ever chosen not to deal with a sociopath, pick up it and run. For example, if you begin to get to understand a new individual with the willingness of dating them and begin to realize certain tendencies that complement the psychopathic criteria, run and don't look back. You don't have to stick around anything or somebody that isn't great for you.

Do not fall for the trap of thinking that you are able to turn a sociopath, psychopath, or narcissist into a better person. This is not only not your work, but it's practically impossible too. For

Dark Psychology and Manipulation

example, the elements that render people dark and dishonest are so profoundly rooted in their minds that they literally cannot be eliminated and substituted at will with candy and spice. Second, the transition is a personal decision a human creates. A person who changes is doing so because they really want change and not due to someone else has asked people to. Last and not least, if you're working with a psychopath so you believe you should improve them, you're fighting a fight toward evolution so genetics in nature. Why do you suppose he'll win?

Pay more attention to the acts than to phrases. Predators are really effective at their writing, and their most important weapons are language. Instead of concentrating on what a person has to say, consider what they are doing. Have they kept the pledge they made to you of doing something specific? Should they handle everyone and make things sound as well as they wish? An easy way to test whether a person's acts suit their language is to use something called the threes law.

Here's how it tends to work: if a person appears to be telling a lie or promising not to keep on one event, you may be trying to deal with a mere misinterpretation. If this occurs a second time, a significant error is likely to occur which involves addressing. If there's a third case, however, then you're definitely working with a liar. Lies also reflect the first indication of coercive behavior. If this repeated phenomenon can be found in your partnership or experience, then you realize you have a problem on your side. How you want to cope with this scenario could make a difference between liberating yourself from a manipulator's jaws and chaos, or holding on for the most frustrating journey of your life.

Let the psychopath succeed wherever possible but not at your cost. The personalities who enjoy winning are also competitive and would go to considerable lengths to make sure they beat their rivals all around. If you ever consider yourself placed on a negotiation table with a psychopath, always go with the option that assures a victory for you all. This is an effective way to ensure you don't spend all of your energy having to attack off a sociopath who is aiming to finish you off.

When interacting with customers, whether they are saints or sinners, listen always to some of what their gut has to admit. Experts who have sought to understand gut instinct claim it's the body's response to a threat in intraspecies. That makes a lot of sense as you think how bad you often feel with someone you don't know just to find out later that this person wasn't a nice guy. Do not encourage your gut feeling to go unheeded because it works so hard to keep you from making mistakes. Psychopaths in many instances assume characters such as boss, mentor, overseer, guardian, church leader, or even caregiver. While those roles are noble indeed, your gut may be yelling that the leader of the church is not as reliable as he might like to

Dark Psychology and Manipulation

make you think. If that is the case, the gut feeling is still granted priority. What your intuition suggests is a safer idea than what you believe you do.

Should not allow yourself to be dragged into the games played by sociopaths, psychopaths, narcissists, and other dark characters. Yeah, you've read these books and felt especially positive about the dark triad characters that you care of. You believe in the subconscious mind that you must have what it takes to defeat on a sociopath and victory. What you don't know is that although you've just read the novel, a psychopath has been training on his victims all his life. Should not pull yourself into the manipulations. Entertaining the Psychopath is not your work. When trying to deal with a psychopath your top one job is to defend yourself from their tricks.

Chapter 11: Tips to guard yourself against mind control

There are tips you can use to protect yourself (and break free) from mind control. There are various mental control strategies but NLP, mind manipulation is a common example that has been used in the public eye by someone from self-help geniuses and coaches to elected officials and other important figures. These kinds of mind manipulation have been previously described, but the use of language to stimulate a trance-like country, even ambiguous language. You could even gain freedom from the control of NLP's mind and you can safeguard yourself. Below are a few clues.

Tip 1. Alert your eyes and unpredictably move them about

Eye contact is really a very potent way of establishing a way to establish an emotional bond with someone. To some extent, even animals participate in this. A good way to misrepresent some of your control is to move your eyeballs around in such a way as to be unpredictable. This stops them from the use of eye contact as a power inducer, which can, therefore, trip them up which renders them nervous.

Tip 2. Be cautious of using unspecified language

Learning the strategies of mind control is interesting because

Dark Psychology and Manipulation

many of them are so basic. Vague terminology has been proven successful in manipulating certain people's emotions and intentions. Public speeches that use ambiguous language, in particular, may cause a kind of community trance. Any kind of language you hear from a prospective narcissist or manipulator is not specific to must be a red flag.

Tip 3. Pay close attention

Anyone that employs mind control methods would be strongly tuned to any loss of focus on your side and it could be a signal for them to seek any mind control. Being mindful of the sorts of stuff you're asked when you don't appear to be paying notice, or just paying more consideration in the coming time.

Tip 4. Hold on allowing others to touch you

We talked about handling in terms of coercion so that still happens here. In this case, touching isn't really intended to impact you but perhaps to put you in a trance. A further touch afterward is enough to get you from a trance or keep you back in if you're out there already. It can be as simple to break free from mind manipulation as not to allow others to reach you.

Tip 5. Be careful about those who talk without really mentioning something

Much of what renders hypnosis so disturbing that the techniques utilized by hypnotists to trigger a coma in the audience remain. There are some terms or forms of words that may trigger this condition and it is necessary to consider individuals who talk in ways that look like nonsense to you. The concept isn't that the statements are false at all, and that those who seem to have been saying anything but that when collected together, the words have small significance. Talk of the traditional democratic dialogue.

Tip 6. Be wary about what others might really say

Speech is the method that hypnotists utilize to handle you, so you have to be careful about what they say and what the phrases signify to break free. Someone qualified in NLP can make a point, but terms that may be interpreted differently might be put in there. Those may be recommendations concealed in another group. Be mindful of the ways NLP professionals recommend stuff to you.

Tip 7. Leave situations in which you feel you are being led into a decision

Sometimes when the best step to free oneself from mental control is to get away from a situation. Practitioners are sufficiently skilled to be able to regulate you through recommendations and other strategies whilst you are completely clueless. If you feel yourself being driven into action or judgment, then it might be a smart option to just stop. This is like shutting the door to the Jehovah's Testimony, but sometimes that's what you'll do.

Dark Psychology and Manipulation

Tip 8. Let the individual instincts direct you

Your instinct about people is often correct, particularly when it comes to actions you encounter that seem odd. This is more like the picture in the vector where Neo perceives the very same cat multiple times and his captain tells him this is an indication that something has changed by the agents. If you see or experience anything that sounds unusual to you or appears odd to you, that is definitely so.

Tip 9. Be wary of vocabulary that encourages you to indulge in behavior

You may believe manipulators or narcissist would indulge in terminology that would command you to do something or that, but that's not how programming in the neuro-language function. They use soothing, restrictive language to lead you into a trance. Instructions aren't effective permissive vocabulary is so looking for this.

Tip 10. Don't allow other people to copy your body language

Part of what's alarming about mind manipulation is that it appears to work because people are sensitive to mind power. In reality, you can't really label it ignorant because many people really don't realize what's going on. Anyone who copies the body language may be an indication that they are interested in mind

Dark Psychology and Manipulation

control and one step in stopping this habit is being instinctively mindful of that and detecting risk.

Chapter 12: Misconceptions and myths about dark psychology

There are various subjects that are appropriate for discussion over dinner. Dark psychology is no such thing. The last thing you need to request during Thanksgiving is how Uncle Joe scores in terms of their orientation towards Machiavellianism. Due to the malevolence underlying dark psychology, there are generally very few open discussions about the topic.

Let's take, for starters, the mysterious triad examination. Planning to take this? If so, do you intend to share your results with someone else? The high opportunities are that if you replied yes to the first query, you'll likely reply no to the second question. Many human beings want to think that they are good people. What's more, they want to speak about other citizens as positive individuals.

Dark Psychology and Manipulation

Putting the dark triad test on a show does not really fulfill that function for anyone to see. Therefore, because of all this hush-hush around dark psychology, there's a whole array of misunderstandings and misconceptions regarding the personality characteristics that are main reservoirs for dark psychology. This section examines those myths and misunderstandings while shedding light on the same thing.

Myth #1: Sociopaths and psychopaths are one and the same thing

Truth: Sociopathy and psychopathy are two types of antisocial disorders

In daily discourse, the word psychopath and sociopath " are used interchangeably. Nevertheless, the two characteristics vary greatly from each other. Such two personality traits, though, also have certain parallels. Experts see sociopathy as less of severe illness than psychopathy. The figure below summarizes some of the traits distinguishing a psychopath from a sociopath.

Myth #2: Psychopaths are made and not born

Truth: Psychopaths are born that way

Psychopathy is a really complicated disorder of personality, within these psychopaths are born more often than not. A psychopath comes out of the womb that is wired differently from most. As a consequence, they differ from the tangent of what's usual and sometimes catch themselves in roles that should not automatically be in any other 'average' human. Research study really has shown that the function of the psychopath's brains is different when compared to other people's brains that have no recorded mental illnesses. So, whenever a psychopath is born what happens?

The psychopath will be one of several things according to the sort of environment in which the psychopath grows up. If the child who shows evidence of sociopathy grows up in a supportive environment, he will probably become a much influential political leader or business. When the child progresses up in a violent or stressful setting, it is possible they may become serial offenders or murderers. Across professions like law enforcement and administration, psychopaths that are nurtured in an atmosphere somewhere in the previous two settings wind up in places of control.

Myth #3: Sociopaths are born

Truth: Sociopaths are mostly a product of their surroundings

As a product of the world in which they are raised, sociopaths are more common than not. It often begins with a genetic or biological sociopathy disposition, which is then exacerbated by the sort of nutrition they receive. For example, a child growing up in a society where nobody seems to start caring for him will likely be carrying the same lack of compassion in his later life. If they got older with adults that had no sense of honor and completely lack a moral conscience, the result would have greatly impaired their conscience.

Myth #4: Women can't be psychopaths

Truth: Female psychopaths are recorded in some cases

More often than not, you'll instantly think of a male nature when you learn about the word psychopath. Besides this, Hollywood has made every effort to portray psychopaths on a murder spree as ax-wielding males. It is important to note however that psychopath may also be female. However, unlike their male colleagues, female psychopaths have less chance of being physically violent or aggressive. Instead, they use their masculinity and femininity to exploit people. Also, female psychopaths are likely to have a great number of sex partners.

Myth #5: Murder becomes an addiction for psychopaths.

Truth: Thrill-seekers are psychopaths.

Murder is also one of the ways psychopaths satiate their eagerness for anticipation. When certain people talk about psychopaths, they immediately think about left, right, and middle murders. Even so, while it is possible that a murderer is more likely than not to be a psychopath, it is often clear that psychopaths do not care much about attempting murder than the majority of the populace. Numerous psychopaths get into their lives in search of pleasures and never really cause violent harm to anyone. Yes, as they hop from one sex partner to another and chuck a few people under the bus to climb up, they could perhaps break a few hearts, but that's as far although most of them are going. If you are looking in your life for a psychopath, you probably won't find one if you're only searching for violent acts and murderous intent.

Myth #6: There is a possible cure for psychiatric disease.

Truth: It has no cure because it's a personality disorder

If psychopathy has become a psychiatric disorder, recovery services would be available. Conversely, psychopathy is a mental condition, and this implies that there is no cure that might turn sociopaths into normal people, feelings, and empathy. Because they don't really think anything is incorrect with them either, even if it existed psychopaths wouldn't be involved in treatment. For situations where psychopaths are induced to undergo treatment for the intention of mending broken marriages, it is not unusual to see them attempting to trick the psychiatrist into believing the counseling is successful or has already succeeded. Remember, these members are incredibly manipulative and able to use whatever means are necessary to get oneself out of tough circumstances. A psychopath will have no issue squandering a loved one's time in therapy because of their bold fearlessness and lack of empathy if only to end up making it feels like they are making an attempt.

Myth #7: You can change a dark triad person by loving them correctly.

Truth: Many individuals who score high on the dark triad test remain that way for the rest of their lives.

Love is a curious phenomenon because it lets people think they are worthy of the unthinkable, particularly though the reality is presented before the naked eye. If you're in a friendship with an individual scoring strongly on a dark triad check, your relationship's first few months are likely to be good. Manipulative individuals have a way to love-bombs you into having faith they 're a perfect match you've been preparing for.

Sadly, this is generally just a begin to attract you into a connection that is nothing more than mirrors and smoke. If you've developed yourself in this kind of friendship, the true colors of the manipulator brought to fruition. In many cases, with the hope things will alter, you will discover a happy marriage partner trying to stick around. That love is going to be enough to change things.

Sadly, even that never occurs. The reality that psychopathy is largely hereditary indicates, for example, that beating is extremely challenging. The psychopath will, at best, just direct their lack of empathy into pursuing objectives that are not harmful to civilization as a whole. As far as narcissism and Machiavellianism are concerned, these sometimes stem from profound psychological trauma, which may need a great lot of arsenal. As a defensive strategy, often individuals would gravitate toward narcissism and Machiavellianism. Every effort to bring them out of this would only come off as an assault culminating in them initiating their own defense. Intervention in the context of love may, thus, be completely problematic. Also, it is necessary to recognize that affection and other facetious emotional responses are not exactly the cup of tea for a dark triad person. They do not even know what it is about. Even so, should you discover yourself in a bond with another person exhibiting the dark triad's characteristics, you may want to re-evaluate whether it is what you actually want.

Myth #8: People who score highly on the dark triad are more attractive.

Truth: That has been proved to be false.

Why is it that people always gravitate toward this world's narcissists and psychopaths? Is it because the persons of the dark triad are more appealing than the rest of the others? In a study to satisfy if dark triad characters look better, medical researchers took to study several topics that had high dark triad ratings. The outcomes of this study proposed that the reason these subjects seemed desirable was just due to they dressed up and physically presented themselves in a way that was evenly put together. Those topics did not come as attractive as before when dressed in boring clothes. As such, it is perhaps fair to say that what allows psychopaths or narcissists to look more desirable than they actually are is the commitment and energy that goes into being ready and the trust afterward.

Myth #9: Psychopaths change when they have children.

Truth: Psychopaths cannot have empathic or loving feelings except for their own children.

Psychopaths begin their own families and they generally have a very difficult time loving and caring for their children when that happens. Unlike ordinary parents not on the dark triad level, psychopaths have difficulty in differencing their children as independent things. Rather, they see them as devices or parts to themselves that are open for use whenever they wish. Psychopaths are much more likely to see their kids as trophies that help them appear good than as adolescents, impressive individuals looking for somebody to direct them through their lives. As such, a normal psychopath will drag their children to excel in something they are not interested in, even though it is at the expense of the well-being and mental health of the children. For e.g., if they think their kid being an excellent swimmer or competitor would boost their social status in the neighborhood, they could forcibly enroll their kids in swimming lessons. Needless to add, parents of psychopaths are really challenging to convince because they are accustomed to succeeding themselves and do not comprehend that their offspring are not able and do whatever it requires to get to the edge.

Myth #10: You are either on the dark triad or not

Truth: The dark triad is a process where some score high and others score low

We all have inherent characteristics of narcissism, psychopathy, and Machiavellianism. The main distinction is that certain characteristics are magnified in certain individuals to the extent that they sometimes become harmful to the individuals around them. For example, take narcissism. Everyone has a way of thinking about themselves. You like to think great things about yourself more likely than not. You want to say you're good looking, creative, and quick to please. For a narcissist, the degree to which their whole world revolves around this self-image is taken out of context. It is not sufficient for them to think about this stuff about themselves

— they also want everybody else to think that they are perfect and holy and that all things are good.

On the other side, psychopathy too is a continuum. Everyone's got their position on this continuum. Think about it this way: did you ever do something that wasn't so nice and nevertheless didn't feel guilty? Have you ever acted in such a way as to suggest you 're not exactly empathic toward anyone? If you answered "yes" to any of these queries, then at least once in the life you displayed psychopathic traits. That doesn't mean you'll carry on murdering anyone later in your career. It just implies that anytime the psychopath steps out of you there are moments and some times where you might be able to stop yourself only in time. The way you've been raised affects whether you're able to stop unleashing your psychopath in full.

Myth #11: Your leader is a psychopath

Truth: Your boss could be a psychopath, or not

It is true that in politics, business, and other sectors, many sociopaths who may not become violent offenders continue to become extremely successful. Yet this is not enough reason to accuse your supervisor of becoming a psychopath. Few people are simply motivated and requesting because the necessity for success is what they know, and understand. In every event, with their employers, not the whole group of folks have sleepwalked and brunches. A supervisor-employee connection is expected to bring a certain dynamic. Your hard-talking, a ruthless manager can be such a different person if they don't carry their supervisor cap. Don't go and think everybody in positions of authority is really a sociopath or a psychopath. That way it isn't always working.

Myth #12: Your ex is just a psycho

Truth: A friendship came to an end on a bad note. It would not turn all of you into a psycho.

A lot of people tend to refer to the exes as psychos. A friendship concludes every once and a while on a positive note that both sides move together to become best mates for the rest of its life. Unfortunately, most relationships don't play this way. Many romances end with crying and accusations, and the calling of names. Evaluate the indications explained in this book before you contact your ex a psychopath and find out if your ex's conduct matches any of those. Of course, once you're through with the partnership, that shouldn't matter, but it may help you from falling into some pit of dating somebody who shows the same symptoms. If you are already engaged with somebody displaying some of the indicators listed here, you may want to suggest abandoning them to your own protection. This is necessary to note that the method of losing a psychotic or narcissist varies from that of losing a regular individual and does not view the departure of their own entity as an affront.

Dark Psychology and Manipulation

There are many services accessible to those trying to exit marriages that are coercive and dishonest. With a quick web search, you will locate certain tools.

Chapter 13: Some frequently asked questions about dark psychology

1. What is dark psychology?

Dark psychology refers to the techniques of persuasion, manipulation, hypnosis, and mind regulation which manipulators and others practice and learn. The term is of current interest, highlighting attention in a spectrum of procedures that had been at work for many years but had not previously been grouped and studied as a particular field. Although dark psychology lies from the outside realm of an academic psychology experiment, it is defined as a field of psychological disorders and is based on aspects of the individual theory of psychology as encouraged by Alfred Adler in the 20th century.

Dark psychology is researched by both those who are interested in practicing it to their advantage and by men and women who are effective in learning others how to protect themselves from the acts of manipulators, narcissists, and others who use these tactics. Dark psychology encompasses a broad array of behaviors that can be done deliberately to cause harm or indicate a deep motivation to act in a darkly destructive manner. For some men and women, this element of dark psychology is difficult to understand or relate to, but it represents a crucial aspect of a sector that explains some people's behavior.

2. Was dark psychology a method just practiced by narcissists?

An essential idea within the philosophy of dark psychology is that every human being is suspected of performing actions of violence. Many men and women may believe they are good and unable to behave in ways that would be defined as evil, but research on human actions by research groups in dark psychology and many others have made clear the ability of humans to behave in a willfully cruel or destructive manner. The assessment that living things are able to behave in this manner is not anything discovered by psychiatrists and psychologists, but it is an assessment that has been made for decades.

Indeed, much of the literature of 18th-century French thinkers concentrated on the question of humanity's intrinsic goodness or badness out of a humanistic drive to help understand the world's youth. Such thinkers arrived at the assumption that Man was always deliberately willing to act with considerable brutality. It is necessary to remember that all of these individuals nowadays will not be characterized as narcissists, demanding that they view the nature of human violence from a specific viewpoint. Although animal behavior specialists may (and have) asserted that mammals normally behave in an

Dark Psychology and Manipulation

egotistical or cruel manner the variety of behaviors shown in dark psychology encompasses what is observed in other animals, contributing to a concept that some relate to as dark singularity.

3. What is the term dark singularity?

Human beings have been found to be able to enter a deep well of malignant or malevolent actions and some interpret this as reflecting what is perceived as a dark singularity. That's distinct from the dark triad proposed by some as the characteristics in a dark triad represent conscious behaviors that can be described by classical key theories. What dark singularity symbolizes is a deep well of "evil" which can be accessed by human beings on an individual or group basis. A significant feature of dark singularity is that, unlike, for example, manipulative behavior which is usually deliberate, it might not be completely aware.

It can be rewarding for many to realize what this dark singularity truly relates to since it is not a concept typically found in academic or conversational studies. It may be claimed that Christianity has followed this definition through the creation of immoral deeds that are the product of a ghost, an evil force, or Satan's influence or provocation. Therefore, dark singularity reflects this kind of cruel, purposeless inspiration even without an external agent like Satan to condemn the action. Instead, the cause would be a profound component of human creatures which can be obtained as a component of dark psychological practice by a manipulator.

4. Why do manipulators and others participate in the art of dark psychology?

In psychology the issue of what inspires us is significant. The psychology schools can be differentiated by a motivator they focus on as important to human behavior. Sigmund Freud psychoanalysis emphasizes on sexual desire as an integral part of human activity, whereas behavioral psychology views humans as being motivated by purposeful and personal desires.

A significant theme in contemporary solutions to the dark psychology is a notion that both implicit motives and purposeful intentions will inspire human beings, Any dark psychology instructors believe that human creatures are intentionally driven but that they are able to interact in what is often considered a dark singularity, with it being a form of an action directed at hurting someone for personal benefit or for no cause whatsoever.

5. Is there a difference between persuasion and manipulation?

Manipulation is a term for loading. Because of a willingness to disinfect the term manipulation for book publishing purposes, research, and other justifications, some have tried to promote a range of dimensions a variety of activities that most people

Dark Psychology and Manipulation

would not consider so bad. Because many people have bad associations with a word manipulation, some interpretations have broadened the term to also include behaviors that most would consider rather than manipulation to be persuasion.

The differentiation between persuasion and manipulation was in fact always somewhat blurred. Persuasion falls within the scope of behavior patterns that would be regarded as manipulation, thus making this first term responsive to the needs of a type of behavior patterns that would be considered technically manipulation. In their daily lives, often men and women participate in convincing, whether in a work setting or with members of their families at home. Through inspiring viewers to consider coercion primarily in terms of persuasion, authors on this subject will encourage readers to address the concept of utilizing deception in their everyday lives primarily freely.

The truth is that coercion is a form of deception which can be seen as the first move towards activities synonymous with narcissism, Machiavellianism which sociopathy, and this so-called dark triad. The aim here is not to scare the reader away (as other people do) from utilizing persuasion in their everyday lives, but to make them understand that human actions exist on a continuum and that the range that involves persuasion often involves mind control and much fewer savory stuff. By recognizing this, the viewer understands dark psychology not as

Dark Psychology and Manipulation

a secondary collection of practices utilized by a select community of psychopathic narcissists but as a toolkit upon which all human beings may benefit. You are better prepared to protect yourself against others who would use anything as basic as bribery to unlock the path to anything much worse by knowing this.

6. How do obscure psychological art practitioners know what I am thinking to manipulate me?

Human beings use verbal as well as non-verbal contact to move on knowledge to others. It's important to listen to the things we say because of the signals they convey to others, but we also have to believe about the nonverbal signals we send that may convey our emotional state to others, especially our fears, anxieties, envy or selfishness.

Skillful manipulators are able to predict who is simple prey depending on the signs they are transmitting that express their emotional condition.

But you don't need to disclose information to a skilled narcissist or manipulator using communication to deceive them. A talented manipulator understands the issues well. They realize that people want acceptance, they want to belong and they seek to create interpersonal relations with everyone. A deceiver will depend on your urge for approval to influence your behavior and to belong to the group. There are tools in the toolkit to manipulate which allow a manipulator to make you think like them or want you to do it. They may be so nice at their strategies that you don't realize a plan you're motivated to follow comes from them, not from your own mind.

7. What is the place of dark psychology in established psychological schools of thought?

Within psychology, dark psychology is not considered a formal field. All of this implies that dark psychology, like abstract psychology, pathological psychology, or psychoanalysis, is not usually studied in the university environment. In reality, dark psychology is a radical topic, partially due to the propensity of existing schools of thinking and certain religions to have a skewed attitude to certain facets of human actions that are apparent to others yet fundamentally unsavory.

We should also make the point that human beings act in hateful, antisocial, destructive, or cruel ways. People sometimes engage in those behavior patterns with no advantage to themself. In abnormal psychiatry and abnormal psychology, the research of these kinds of actions and the people engaging in them is undertaken, but the method of mind control to this topic is rather dissimilar. Dark psychology related to perceived from established psychological schools of thought to explain behavioral patterns without any of the mirrors and smoke or hypocrisy associated with certain psychological theories.

8. Does self-awareness mean that I can accept dark psychology and assert my dark side?

Self-awareness is a concept sometimes used in the area of emotional intelligence to define a form of emotional capacity that is deemed beneficial and promoted. Emotional intelligence is a form of intelligence that focuses on recognizing one's own emotions and other people's emotions and using emotional awareness as a guide to actions. Empathy is a major component of emotional intelligence, too.

Self-awareness is the component of the EI dealing with being conscious of and correctly identifying and recognizing one's own feelings. The argument could be made that women and men must claim the emotional responses and the related behaviors as part of self-awareness that comprises how they experience and are inspired to act. In other words, the thinking of some people may increase them to assume that behaviors dropping under the flag of dark psychology are not to be disheartened because they embody an awareness, however dark, of our own motivations.

While the purpose of this specific point is not to assert one path or the other as to whether these kinds of attitudes should be given in, the desire to protect oneself from dark psychology presumes that there is an acknowledgment that these types of behaviors can (at least) be very harmful to one another. In fact, self-awareness by itself does not contribute to communication skills. Self-awareness is thought to operate in concert with other aspects of EI such as self-regulation and empathy in order to create somebody whose interactions follow a certain pattern with others.

Someone who acts solely with self-awareness will be compelled to behave narcissistically and even sociopathic ally because their own would be the only feelings or intentions that mattered. An emotionally intelligent person is as much aware of other people's emotions and motivations as they are of their own and considers these emotions and motivations just as important in guiding attitude as their own. Therefore, although we can strip away a recommendation as to whether one person or another should participate in dark psychological practice, we would then state that behavior with self-awareness itself does not represent the true EI and that individuals who behave in this manner may be considered as having a personality disorder in psychiatry.

9. Do obscure psychological practices now become more common or have they always been an influential aspect of human behaviors?

A comprehensive analysis of human nature made it very apparent that the types of habits that we find to be falling into dark psychology nowadays might have been present for as long as there were humans. These behavioral types are the kinds of things we see from representatives of a dark triad of narcissistic, psychopathy, and Machiavellianism. These behaviors patterns include those that can-do harm, such as mind-control, manipulation, hypnosis, and many more. Cleary, as testamentary data suggests, such habits been around many years.

The question is therefore whether these behaviors patterns are becoming more frequent today than they used to be. There is reason to assume that these behaviors patterns are becoming increasingly common nowadays, and the increasing tendency of these kinds of actions can be ascribed to different social, economic, and educational factors. As noted in the reply to a prior question, misguided ideas regarding self-awareness as well as individuality can cause people to perceive more narcissistically than would previously have been acceptable. In many cases, this is not intentional but an outcome of mistaken individuality as well as free will ideas.

Indeed, though uniqueness is a quality from which a civilization's wellspring may wellspring, it can be stated that human creatures are by nature not individualistic. We also developed to act in a collective manner and to be imprinted by other people's thoughts and actions like ourselves. What is actually accomplished by mistaken beliefs about self-awareness and individuality is to cause people to perceive narcissistically even though they act on the basis of self-interest and "self-

Dark Psychology and Manipulation

awareness" motivations, rather than behaving empathically and taking into account other people's thoughts and concerns.

10. What is the dark triad?

In psychology, the dark triad represents three traits of personality that are considered to have "dark" or malevolent motivations. Psychopathy, Narcissism, and Machiavellianism are the personality traits associated with the dark triad. This term is often used in psychological science as well as in clinical psychology, criminal science, and management as a way to highlight types of behaviors that may be extremely harmful or tough to deal with.

From the perspective of dark psychology, the dark triad denotes types of personality that may be especially able to act in a harmful or harmful manner, but some make an argument that all human beings have the ability to behave with "dark singularity," as it's often called. What the dark triad does isolate individuals that are perceived as particularly troublesome, though its truth would have been that all men and women in their personality have elements of these individuals. And for those curious what Machiavellianism entails, it applies to persons who exploit and cheat without concern to others, the ideology that derives its name from the Machiavellian concept that certain people are entitled to behave regardless of consideration for the rules and other's rights.

11. How do I understand if someone manipulates me?

There are also indicators you could use to assist you to decide whether you are being tampered with. If you find you're acting in ways you don't understand, it doesn't benefit you, or it seems to come from someone else, then you're being manipulated. It's normal to search for guidance from someone we care for. However, it's normal for us to try to be agreeable to someone, which may lead us to answer "yeah" when we really should learn. A manipulator acknowledges human behavior and recognizes how to employ certain human nature elements toward their victims.

12. How do I realize when I'm the mind control victim?

Mind management is in fact a successful strategy since a number of people do not realize they are a target of it. Recent converts to dark psychological processes can also be less adept at the arts of mesmerism, hypnosis, and mental control than those that are more studied, so people who are targets are often aware that they are victims, but the victim is usually ignorant to them in true, deep mind control. As stated in the response to the question regarding coercion, if you are conscious that you are behaving in a way that appears odd, unlike you, or in which you don't understand the motive, you can learn that you are the target of mind control.

Dark Psychology and Manipulation

A difficulty here is to determine whether you are acting in a way that is suggestive of dark singularity which does not originate from someone else or whether you are actually acting out of mind manipulation. Realize that individuals may be manipulated to act in a damaging or narcissistic manner, or may behave in this manner of their own will.

Some individuals choose to take the support of those who may be capable of breaking them out of the control of mind, and this may be a hypnotist or someone who understands imprinting and control of the mind.

13. Why can I liberate myself from mind control?

Some people themselves are able to break free from NLP's mind control. Once a patient knows they are the sufferer of mind control, they can sometimes slowly release the manipulator's hold by examining the processes the manipulator controls them. A skillful manipulator, for example, may suggest behavior and emotions with you in a way that leads you to believe the thoughts started with yourself. An individual involved in mind manipulation may go one step further. They might have manipulated you so that you could behave in a way that would benefit or suit them. If this is the case, it might not be enough to be mindful of the mind restraint to break away.

In such cases, people could choose to go to the next hypnotherapist, spiritualist, or somebody else involved in dark psychology. This course of action has risks to it. Therefore,

Dark Psychology and Manipulation

human beings have a propensity to behave in a collective fashion if you announce to someone that you were the target of a psychological assault, there would be a propensity for the individual you mentioned this to support the assault, particularly if you are an unknown to them. Therefore, caution must be exercised in exposing that you are a perpetrator of mind control and enlisting someone to assist you. Even though it can be hard to break full of mind control through your own, some women and men can do it by educating their minds in different ways. This can include chanting, meditation, or other divine activity which releases negativity or encourages mental detachment.

14. **In the past, are the wonderful legendary monsters invented merely ways of explaining unsavory aspects of human behaviors?**

Some might claim that the ghosts, fallen angels, and spirits that form the myth of certain cultures and some sects are just an attempt to justify away certain facets of human actions that were hard to understand or were not good. The truth of the matter would be that humans can do evil things to each other. For have a taste into this, what one has to do is crack a history book, and history books often tend to brush over things that don't represent human beings in a good light.

Human beings were known to willfully assassinate, commit genocide, initiate witch trials, participate in actions of hysteria, or start behaving in other methods that are damaging to others and sometimes have no objective. Maybe the authors of holy teachings and myth inventors created the evil spirits and monsters to cover up those people who treated people in a monstrous manner. Will humans put on a mask? Yeah sure, and they dress one because it may be too was unable to look at the image underneath.

15. Do I risk becoming a Dark Behavioral Practitioner?

All runs the risk of becoming a student of the dark psychological techniques, whether as a target of coercion or mental domination, whether they unwittingly reach into the well of black singularity that all living things are aware of, or whether they chose to participate in a way that results in damage to others. Within this book, this question really gets to whether someone can be a practitioner of these kinds of behaviors because of another person's influence and the reply to that query is yes.

A manipulator, mac, Machiavellian, or psychopathic person may lead others to behave in a manner that is destructive by imprinting or mental control, or by other skill sets such as suggestion. The difference between advice and mind control is unclear because suggestion may be regarded as a tool that can be used to influence the thinking or behavior of another individual. If you risk being forced to indulge in behaviors that run contrary to your beliefs and characters then there are precautions you may take to shield yourself from future mind control or just the simplest recommendation types.

One such trick is pretty easy. Learn to be skeptical. This doesn't mean that you'd be paranoid, interpreting every individual around you while a possible threat with sinister models toward you, however when you notice that you are curious after interacting with someone with an uncommon thought or behavior. If someone tells something, for instance, they pointed to you asking why they were being that. A manipulator can recommend you just using their words to dislike or attack another person. If a narcissist makes use of this kind of trick to guide you in a dark psychological ordinance, stop and ask, "Why was I have to do with to do that? Whence came to that idea?"

Of course, a fearsome aspect of mind control is that women and men are often unable to stop sinister behaviors. As much as certain people can consider it difficult to accept this is a basic fact. As creatures, we are guilty of selfish behavior, and as humans, we are guilty of being malicious and inhuman for no cause whatsoever. Yeah, indeed, you are at danger of acting in a way compatible with the dark psychological arts, so if there is morality, then the defenses are possibly better than those of other individuals.

16. Should I engage in dark psychological practices?

Dark Psychology and Manipulation

To many people, the decision of whether or not to take part in practices involving the intentional harm of others is not so straightforward one. As we tried to touch on in the response to a previous question, the question really comes down to the kind of person you are. It must be acknowledged that certain people can read this book just because they are willing to follow the dark psychology path. But others are starting to read because they've been exposed and want to protect themselves to narcissists and other evil criminals.

An individual who is concerned with protecting himself from manipulation or mental control must not engage themselves in these kinds of behaviors because some might consider this to be giving other people permission to cure them the very same way. Also, if you're concerned about psychopathic or psychopathic acts toward you, it's probably because you realize how hazardous they can be, and you're repulsed by these acts. Ultimately, it's up to you to determine whether to conduct, but it's crucial to note that certain societies believe in the eternal spirit they consider karma, and by your behavior, you can open the door to the return of harmful energies.

17. Does dark psychology represent a range of behaviors that distinguishes human beings from other animals?

Most animals have an instinct for hunting, the unfortunate ability to detect and attack prey with ferocity. Humans are

Dark Psychology and Manipulation

comparable to other animals in this regard, as we also have that instinct. In reality, humans are at the top of the shift in food and our prey options are wide and multiple. Yet two characteristics of human actions tend to mark humans out of the animal world as something distinct from other animals. Human beings seem to have a good tendency to prey on their own species, and even kill members. More specifically, human beings are considered to kill without any intent or excuse whatsoever. To know the predator, the essential idea is to recognize that they are boosted by anything, normally a drive to take food, territory, or survival. Human beings have shown time after time also that they participate in violent acts that are truly remorseless: of which the predator has no clear benefit. It is believed that humans are now the only organisms in the human-animal which kill without cause. The word dark singularity was invented to characterize this human propensity to be compelled to destroy without a specific aim or purpose. This dark singularity symbolizes a malevolent well of work psychology that can potentially be harnessed by all human beings, representing the ability of all living creatures to act willfully evil.

Conclusion:

Dark psychology is a set of activities trying to influence and control others to the manipulator's advantage. The techniques of this art lie on a spectrum and include beginner drugs such as persuasion from dark psychology all the way up to mind control. Dark psychology may be learned by those who wish to use it to get what they want, and by those who are inspired to protect themselves from influence.

The method of dark psychology to human behavior may be more Adlerian in core concept, but as encouraged by Freud, with whom Adler spent some formative time, there is room for the psychoanalytical approach to human motivation. Therefore, dark psychology considers human action as purposive, suggesting it has an objective or intent, rather than being simply driven by psychological factors such as libido.

But the idea of dark psychology acknowledges that human beings can behave darkly without purposeful force. This field approaches human behavior in a way that is more straightforward and may be less hypocritical than is often seen in academic psychology, in this fashion. Dark psychology recognizes that, for no reason at all, human beings can behave in a manner that is harmful, destructive, antisocial, or cruel. Psychology's propensity to play around discovering that people

Dark Psychology and Manipulation

will act in this way is part of what makes dark psychology an interesting area of research.

Most people study the topic for defensive purposes. Defending yourself from these dark powers requires knowledge of how, and what motivates, persuaders and manipulators work. Since persuasion may have both positive and negative motives, even those who are not involved in implementing dark psychological strategies will profit from practicing convincing skills.

Neuro-linguistic programming/ NLP is truly an equally prominent field with dark psychology. For more than 40 years it has been studied and used by newscasters, media personalities, politicians, and others. This mind control technique is so powerful that, in a matter of minutes, the uninitiated could go from the available will to conditioned. Therefore, learning how to defend against NLP is essential in arming men and women against dark psychology for protection. So armed, free from the nation of fear and anxiety that the manipulator is trying to erect around you.

References:

boissolm, F. The True Story of Brainwashing and How It Shaped America. Retrieved, from https://www.smithsonianmag.com/history/true-story-brainwashing-and-how-it-shaped-america-180963400/

.Retrieved, from https://www.booktopia.com.au/how-to-analyze-people-daniel-spade/book/9781072375319.html

Brainwashing Techniques You Encounter Every Day (and How to Avoid Them)., from https://lifehacker.com/brainwashing-techniques-you-encounter-every-day-and-ho-5886571

Dark Triad - an overview | ScienceDirect Topics. from https://www.sciencedirect.com/topics/psychology/dark-triad

Help, G., Professionals, F., Listed, G., Help, G., Professionals, F., & Therapist, F. et al. Neuro–Linguistic Programming. Retrieved, from https://www.goodtherapy.org/learn-about-therapy/types/neuro-linguistic-programming#:~:text=Neuro%2Dlinguistic%20programming%20(NLP)%20is%20a%20psychological%20approach%20that,through%20experience%20to%20specific%20outcomes.

Roberts, M The Difference Between Persuasion and Manipulation - Michael W. Roberts. Retrieved, from https://michaelwroberts.com/content/persuasion-manipulation/

The Ethics of Manipulation (Stanford Encyclopedia of Philosophy). (2020). Retrieved 10 June 2020, from https://plato.stanford.edu/entries/ethics-manipulation/

Trust, Persuasion and Manipulation. (2020). Retrieved 10 June 2020, from https://www.psychologytoday.com/us/blog/webs-influence/201309/trust-persuasion-and-manipulation

Understanding the Dark Triad: Managing "Dark" Personality Traits. (2020). Retrieved 10 June 2020, from https://www.mindtools.com/pages/article/understanding-dark-triad.htm

Printed by Amazon Italia Logistica S.r.l.
Torrazza Piemonte (TO), Italy